WU

Also by Jonathan Clements

The First Emperor of China

Confucius: A Biography

Pirate King: Coxinga and the Fall of the Ming Dynasty
(published in paperback as *Coxinga and the Fall of the Ming
Dynasty*)

Mao

The Moon in the Pines

A Brief History of the Vikings

*The Dorama Encyclopedia: A Guide to Japanese Television Drama
since 1953* (with Motoko Tamamuro)

*The Anime Encyclopedia: A Guide to Japanese Animation since
1917* (with Helen McCarthy)

The Little Book of Chinese Proverbs

WU

THE CHINESE EMPRESS WHO SCHEMED, SEDUCED, AND MURDERED HER WAY TO BECOME A LIVING GOD

JONATHAN CLEMENTS

SUTTON PUBLISHING

First published in the United Kingdom in 2007 by
Sutton Publishing Limited · Phoenix Mill
Thrupp · Stroud · Gloucestershire · GL5 2BU

British Library Cataloguing in Publication Data
A catalogue record for this book is available from the British Library.

Hardback ISBN 978-0-7509-3961-4
Paperback ISBN 978-0-7509-3962-1

Maps by Bow Watkinson.

Typeset in 11/14.5pt Sabon.
Typesetting and origination by
Sutton Publishing Limited.
Printed and bound in England by
J.H. Haynes & Co. Ltd, Sparkford.

For Chelsey

Contents

	List of Illustrations	ix
	Acknowledgements	xi
	Family Tree of the Tang Dynasty	xiii
	Family Tree of the Wu Family	xiv
	Introduction: Flowers in the Winter	1
One	The Gate of the Dark Warrior	13
Two	The Favour of Rain and Mist	28
Three	The Family Matter	39
Four	The Treacherous Fox	59
Five	The Supreme Sacrifice	71
Six	The Poison Chalice	86
Seven	The Hen at Daybreak	103
Eight	The Hall of Illumination	120
Nine	The Brilliant Void	138
Ten	The Sage Mother of Mankind	151
Eleven	The Office of the Crane	166
Twelve	The Palace of Dawn	180
	Appendix I: Other Fictions of Wu	188
	Appendix II: Notes on Names	197
	Appendix III: Chronology	202
	Notes	212
	Bibliography	229
	Index	234

List of Illustrations

Between pages 112 and 113

1. Wu in later life
2. A detail of an image of Wu, published *c.* 1690
3. The 'Nipple Hills'
4. Wu's tomb
5. The blank memorial tablet at Wu's tomb
6. The Constellation hot spring bath
7. Taizong's beloved horse Tan Fist
8. A statue of a minister from the grave site of Taizong
9. A building in the Famen temple
10. The grave mound of Taizong
11. Palace ladies in flowing robes
12. A hunting party, Tang dynasty
13. Giant warrior standing guard over the Spirit Road to Wu's tomb
14. Tang dynasty dragon dish
15. Detail of a dish image of a phoenix
16. An envoy from 'Hrom'
17. The statues of Gaozong's foreign allies
18. The pilgrim monk Tripitaka
19. The Scripture Pagoda
20. The Laughing Buddha
21. The vault and corridor leading to the tomb of Prince Yide
22. One of the first cinematic versions of Wu's story. *(Copyright unknown)*
23. A 1960 movie version of Wu. *(© 2006 Celestial Pictures Ltd)*

List of Illustrations

Maps

	page
Empress Wu's mausoleum	2
China in the seventh century	12
The invasion of Korea	31

Acknowledgements

My grateful acknowledgement goes to Routledge for permission to reprint a passage from the *Real Tripitaka and Other Pieces*, by Arthur Waley; also to the Board of Trustees of the Leland Stanford Jr University (Stanford University Press), for permission to reprint three poems from Chang and Saussy's *Women Writers of Traditional China*; to the Curtis Brown Group Limited for permission to reprint two passages from Lin Yutang's *Lady Wu*; and to Snow Lion Press for permission to reprint a passage from Jeffrey Hopkins's *Buddhist Advice for Living & Liberation: Nagarjuna's Precious Garland*. Cambridge University Press acknowledges that my use of material from C.P. Fitzgerald's *Son of Heaven* falls within the bounds of fair dealing, for which I am also grateful. Images of Wu's newly created characters were taken from the website of Dylan W.H. Sung, and appear here with his consent. Every effort has been made to trace copyright holders. Any omissions should be notified to the publishers for correction in any subsequent edition.

The origin of this book lies with Jaqueline Mitchell at Sutton Publishing, who, desirous of a break from pirates, philosophers and emperors, prevailed upon me to write something about a woman. I warned her that a faithful study of Empress Wu would at times be so obscene as to be impossible to read out on the radio or excerpt in newspapers. She thought that sounded jolly exciting, and is hopefully not regretting it now. She did not even complain when I delivered this manuscript six weeks late in order to incorporate new findings, although she did commission a sorcerer to put a curse on me.

The heart of a serpent and the nature of the wolf are best preserved in medieval despots and in contemporary literary agents, notably Chelsey Fox at Fox and Howard. Herself once nearly the subject of a pornographic novel, she takes a small percentage of my earnings, and the entirety of my admiration for the pitiless and cruel way in which she crushes her enemies. She has been my agent for ten years, and my dedication of this book to her is long overdue.

Motoko Tamamuro ploughed through several Japanese texts on my behalf, in order to mark out areas of possible new enquiry. Writing this book involved substantial original research, for which my travelling companion Andrew Deacon aided with hotels, haggles with hawkers and many restaurant insights. He also remained permanently on hand to answer queries on subjects ranging from Chinese chessmen to table manners and, even as I type these words, his Messenger icon is nudging at the corner of my screen and asking when he can see the manuscript. My mother, Penny Clements, knows only two phrases in Chinese. One is disgusting and cannot be repeated here. The other is a run-down of the horses of the Taizong Emperor, the English versions of whose names relied heavily on her understanding of equestrian terminology.

My photographer, Kati Mäki-Kuutti, ran her pristine new camera through a gauntlet of grit and damp from underground tombs to chilly mountaintops, and all the hot, dusty places in between. The camera has never quite recovered, but Miss Mäki-Kuutti's willingness to become Mrs Clements seems undaunted. Others who have patiently lent an ear, advice or assistance include Naomi Benson, Victoria Carvey, Yvette Cowles, Jim Crawley, Mary Critchley, Jane Entrican, Kimberly Guerre, Georgina Harris, Gwyneth Jones, Martin Latham, Adam Newell, Ellis Tinios, Hilary Walford, Bow Watkinson, Jeremy Yates-Round and the rest of the crew at Sutton, as well as a surprisingly large number of women at parties, dinners and weddings over the last year, who have ceased to shock me with their enthusiastic words of support for a historical figure they regard as a much-maligned member of the sisterhood. I am also grateful to the library staff at London's School of Oriental and African Studies, who persisted in providing a stellar service despite facing persecutions of their own. In that regard, I also thank Ken Livingstone and many unnamed staff and students at SOAS,

Acknowledgements

whose protests in 2005 persuaded administrators to revoke unwise staff purges. The spirit of Judge Dee lives on.

And finally, my driver, Mr Ran, aka Mr Slowly, risked life and limb to drive me to the tomb of the Taizong Emperor, a place so remote and desolate that he was obliged to turn his pristine taxi into an off-road vehicle on several occasions. But he probably saved my life by making sure I had the right shoes to climb Huashan, and didn't complain when my desire to see Empress Wu's tomb first hand made him very late for dinner.

The Early Tang Dynasty

(heavily simplified)

Gaozu
Emperor
566–635

Zhangsun Chengwei
(Wei dynasty nobility)

Taizong Emperor = Empress Wende   Zhangsun Wuji
599–649   600–635   c. 599–659

Gaozong   Prince Cheng-qian   Princess   Others
WU ZHAO = Emperor   'The Turk'   Gaoyang
THE EMPRESS WU   628–683   619–644
625–705

Prince Li Hong   Princess Anding   Prince Xian*   Zhongzong   Ruizong   Taiping
653–675   d. 654   654–684   Emperor   Emperor   (Princess of Peace)
                                                      656–710   662–716   664–713
                                     Prince of Bin   m. Empress Wei
                                     672–741

Prince Chongfu   Prince Yide   Princess   Princess Anle   Prince Chongmao   (two elder   Xuanzong
681–711   682–701   Yongtai   684–710   695–713   sons)   Emperor
                               683–701   685–762

                                                                                             → Tang Dynasty
                                                                                             (lasts until 907)

* Believed to be Helan's son by Gaozong

The Wu Family
(including causes of death)

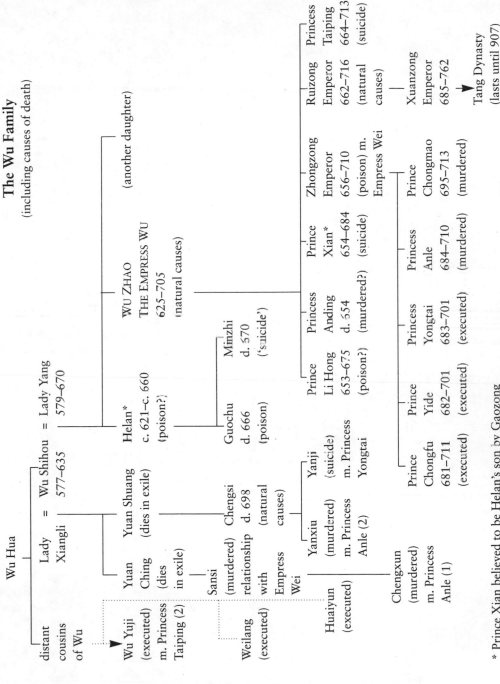

* Prince Xian believed to be Helan's son by Gaozong

Introduction: Flowers in the Winter

When the Empress Wu died in AD 705, she was laid to rest with her late second husband, the Gaozong Emperor. Their joint tomb is the only one in Chinese history to contain two imperial sovereigns. Although the walls and buildings that formed part of the necropolis are long gone, the tomb itself lies undisturbed, 50 miles to the north-west of the modern city of Xi'an.

Folklore about Empress Wu permeates the very geography of the region. The first sight that greets the visitor is not the tomb itself, but the twin hills that bracket its entrance, each topped by a jutting watchtower. Local legend claims the mounds reminded Gaozong of the breasts of the woman he risked his empire to marry – Chinese maps of the period had south at the top, which would have given the site the appearance of a welcoming female torso, its arms outstretched.

Between the two hills, the visitor finds the long Spirit Road, a wide paved path that stretches for a mile towards the tomb itself, flanked by statues of giant sword-wielding guardians, horses and two incongruous ostriches. These latter creatures, based on real-life gifts from allies in Afghanistan, are indicative of another feature of Empress Wu's life and times, her empire's increased contact with foreign powers.[1]

Wu's tomb is set into a mountain, with a climb to the summit so long and arduous that local modern traders run a brisk business in horse- and camel-rides along its winding forest path. At the base of the peak stand several ranks of statues, each modelled on foreign ambassadors who had come to the Tang court to attend on Wu and her husband. Wu's era saw China enjoying far-reaching diplomatic relations, host to Persian princes, Jewish merchants, Indian and

1

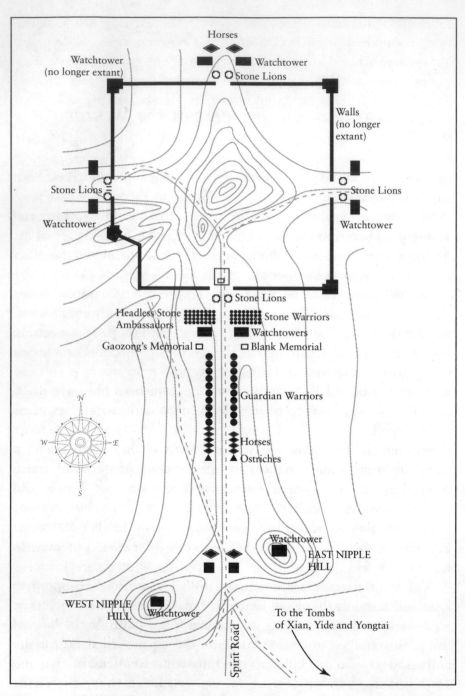

Empress Wu's mausoleum.

Tibetan missionaries. Far to the west, the last inheritors of the Roman empire sent ambassadors from Constantinople, while much of Japanese art and architecture rests heavily on contacts made with China's Tang dynasty. Empress Wu presided over a golden age, as the wife of two emperors, the mother of two more, and, for more than a decade, the recognised ruler herself, the only woman in Chinese history to reign in her own name. Upon her death, the first edict of her successor lionised her for her 'real intelligence, perfect virtue and deep wisdom . . . enduring a life of toil for the sake of the imperial throne'.[2]

And yet there are signs at Wu's tomb of the scandals that have made her so notorious. Two great memorial stones sit at the entrance, one for each of the imperial inhabitants. Since Gaozong predeceased her, Wu herself wrote the words of his epitaph, proclaiming his great deeds and noble character. Her own memorial looms on the other side of the Spirit Road, an imposing slab decorated with carved dragons. Here was the place where Wu expected her own descendants to inscribe their tributes to her, a living god, ruler of all under heaven, the only woman ever to be recognised as such.

Instead, Empress Wu's surviving children left her memorial chillingly blank – the only known occurrence in 2,000 years of Chinese imperial history. According to the polite spin doctoring of court records, this was because mere words could not do this wonderful lady justice. Between the lines, one senses other, more sinister, motives, bitterness and hatred from the family she dominated and deposed.[3]

Close by is the tomb of her son and one-time heir Prince Xian, who was banished to a distant province and later forced to commit suicide. So, too, is that of her beautiful granddaughter Princess Yongtai, its memorial tablet falsely claiming that the 17-year-old girl had died in childbirth, when in fact she was executed in the whirl of accusations and plots that accompanied Wu's final years. Yongtai had committed an unmentionable crime with her teenage half-brother, who was also killed. Neither tomb was built until after the death of Empress Wu, as if her successors decided to lay her errant grandchildren to rest in her sight out of sheer spite.

The centuries have taken their toll, as they would at any site, but there is a sense of malice about the ruins around Wu's tomb. The statues of the foreign ambassadors are inexplicably headless, smashed up by unknown vandals. Memorial stones all over the area have been defaced by treasure-seekers, hoping to increase the value of their rubbings of the texts by destroying the originals. There is a sense, with Empress Wu and her family, of some terrible curse that afflicts all in their presence with tragedy. In her own lifetime, the Empress was haunted by so many ghosts that she spent many years out of the capital where she had committed her most infamous atrocity. When archaeologists excavated the tomb of Princess Yongtai in the 1960s, they discovered that the Tang ruling family's tragedy even extended beyond the grave. Diggers uncovered the remains of a grave robber *inside* the tomb, murdered by his associates as they quarrelled over their hoard.

The life of Empress Wu presents considerable trouble for the historian. It is difficult enough to separate truth from fiction in medieval biographies; all the more so when the subject herself pursued a deliberate policy of disinformation. Almost all sources for early Tang dynasty court history are official documents, subject to many hidden agendas – one must constantly read between the lines, and the lies. The documents pertaining to Wu's own reign were compiled relatively soon after her death, by a nephew with a reputation for editorial meddling, who was subsequently murdered in a palace coup. His version of events was later rewritten under the authority of Wu's grandson, whose own mother had supposedly been a victim of one of Wu's purges. Consequently, the Tang dynasty boasts two dynastic records, the *Old Book of Tang* (*Jiu Tang Shu*) and the *New Book of Tang* (*Xin Tang Shu*), which sometimes do not agree on the motives and behaviour of major figures.[4]

As a young woman, Wu was a pawn in someone else's power game, a honey trap set for a wayward monarch that backfired spectacularly. Both she and her sponsors told outrageous lies in order to cover up her first major scandal – what amounted, at least on paper, to an incestuous affair with her own stepson. In later life, when it was more beneficial for her to boast of her associations with

4

two previous emperors, she tacitly admitted that some of her early protestations were based on false evidence. Her supporters presented her in the best possible light, turning a blind eye to her indiscretions; her enemies mixed reasonable criticism of her actions with falsified claims in order to make her seem like a demon. This propaganda from both sides has continued for centuries.

This much we know. She was beautiful, at least by the standards of the day. Admission to the ranks of palace concubines was equivalent to winning a beauty contest of the most gorgeous women in the medieval world. It is true that Wu's family had good connections, and likely that a cousin may have helped smooth her path to the palace, but, even so, she was unlikely to have been plain. Statues and portraiture of the Tang dynasty favour large round faces and generous proportions; Tang men liked their women stout and well fed, and in later life the Empress Wu sported a double chin. In her youth, she had a charisma and an allure sufficient to cause a prince to break the law. She was also vain – Wu knew she was beautiful and enjoyed looking at herself as much as anyone else. Throughout her life, she enjoyed the sight of her own reflection, particularly while in the act of sexual intercourse.[5]

She was smart. Little trustworthy information survives about her early years – one of the sole surviving anecdotes is a pompous and arch tale of youthful naivety. But by the time she was in her thirties, this formerly doomed concubine had somehow seized the reins of power. If her detractors are to be believed, she used her second husband's incapacitation through illness to rule the empire in his name – an accusation that carries within it the seeds of further scandal. For, although Wu is ridiculed and pilloried in the histories for some of her own behaviour in old age, if she truly were the power behind the throne in the 660s, as her enemies claim, then she should also be held partly responsible for one of the pinnacles of Tang culture.

She was ruthless. Her formative years were spent as a servant and possible bedmate for an uncompromising ruler, who was himself responsible for the deaths of his two elder brothers and the abdication of his own father. Her first husband, Taizong, was a man of grandiose ambition, ready to ride roughshod over Confucian tradition, taking the credit for many of his own father's achievements. Perhaps he saw something in her of himself, perhaps she learned her strategies from him; either way, she entered the prime of her life ready to do literally anything in the pursuit of her goals. The records of Wu's own dynastic scribes report tortures visited upon her enemies in the palace, leading to her characterisation as 'the treacherous fox', and a long series of curses and counter-curses. Her enemies claim that she strangled her own newborn daughter, ready to pin the blame on a palace rival. Her defenders scoff at such a story, but must admit the alternative, that this was a woman who was able to take the tragic cot death of her child and turn it to her own insidious advantage.

She was strong. Despite prohibitions about women in positions of power, she was able to become the ruler of the world's most powerful civilisation. Although her enemies accused her of promoting cronies and persecuting just ministers, the evidence from her reign shows quite the opposite – administration largely fell out of the hands of hereditary officers, often to individuals who had passed egalitarian examinations.

She was, by the standards of her day, sexually liberated. She was only one of many concubines of her husband, but somehow made her way up through the ranks. One of the strangest slurs against her is that she would perform a sexual act that no other woman would attempt, thus endearing her to her second husband and ensuring his cooperation in her ventures. Nobody would have thought twice about a male emperor having more than one sexual partner (indeed, it was considered mandatory for his health for him to have multiple concubines), but Wu was the subject of a series of allegations concerning her relationships with monks, ministers and advisers, not just in middle age, but into her eighties.

Somewhere amid these many faces of Empress Wu is the real figure, but the evidence is so corrupted by age and propaganda that the historian can do little more than steer it past the reader. Her life and times remain controversial for the changes they witnessed, and indeed encouraged. The foreign religion of Buddhism enjoyed a new resurgence during Wu's era, presenting a strong challenge to Chinese orthodoxy. Wu twisted Buddhism to her own ends, using it to challenge China's state religion, Confucianism, and China's local tradition, Daoism. In particular, she used it to fight the insistence of Confucians that no woman could, or should, be permitted to rule the empire.

From ancient times, Chinese political theory had feared the unofficial, uncontrollable influence that women of the harem might exert upon rulers. A folktale, thousands of years old, is a variant of the 'Cry Wolf' fable, in which a Chinese ruler orders the sounding of an alarm to impress his concubine, thereby ensuring that nobody pays heed when a real invasion occurs.

China's greatest sage, the famous Confucius, once resigned his position in government over the influence of women, suspecting that a group of newly arrived dancing girls were enemy agents, charged with poisoning his ruler's mind against him. As he left, he quoted an ancient song:

> A woman's tongue
> Can cost a man his post
> A woman's words
> Can cost a man his head.[6]

This attitude made its way into the *Book of History*, an educationally motivated chronicle of ancient Chinese monarchs, attributed to Confucius. Even if the words were not his own, the selection was purportedly his, with each tale emphasising matters he thought of importance. One of its passages is a warning against putting women in positions of authority: 'The hen does not announce the daybreak, the crowing of a hen in the morning indicates the subversion of the family.'[7]

Confucianism highlighted a natural order of things, a conservative patriarchy in which children obeyed parents, wives obeyed husbands, the young obeyed the old, and subjects obeyed rulers. If everything went according to such order, the world would be a harmonious place and the universe would prosper. But Wu lived

7

during an era in which women enjoyed increasing power. Centuries of unrest had been ended by the accession of the short-lived Sui dynasty, a military aristocracy with strong ties to non-Chinese peoples. When the Sui were overthrown by their Tang cousins in a brief and bloody civil war, many of the old aristocracy were bought off with new government positions or ties to the imperial family. Monosyllabic Chinese surnames were joined in imperial records by names of foreign origin like Zhangsun, as the disinherited Sui aristocracy exerted its influence through female family members – sons might be powerless, but daughters could be married to Tang aristocrats.

Scandalously, women refused to remain hidden from sight. One Tang emperor complained that too many were adopting foreign customs, wearing trousers and riding horses, wearing perilously short veils or neglecting them altogether like the freer, more independent women of the Turkic tribes. Poets sang of blue-eyed girls in the taverns of Chang'an, and magistrates introduced financial penalties to discourage interracial marriages, in a time when China's foreign relations included not just trade and diplomacy, but migration and settlement.

Wu was the living embodiment of a tension in Chinese identity, born of the mixture of southern and eastern agrarian peoples with the nomadic tribes of the north and west. In Chinese tradition, women were supposed to be sedentary and obedient, an assumption challenged by the relatively free position they enjoyed under the influence of northern rulers. Women of the northern dynasties were regarded as pushy: 'it was the custom of women to handle all family affairs, to demand justice and straighten out legal disputes, to make calls and curry favour with the powerful. They filled the streets with their carriages . . . begged official posts for their sons and made complaints about injustices done to their husbands.'[8]

Such behaviour sat uneasily with Chinese tradition, which had long held that a woman's place was in quiet seclusion. Confucius was not the only authority to argue that women should be kept out of politics – in fact his warnings have often been used to blame women for problems in many later dynasties. The mother of China's

First Emperor was ridiculed for her scandalous behaviour, and supposedly turned on her own son, hoping to replace him with one of the children she had given birth to in secret with her lover. Empress Lü, the matriarch of the Han dynasty, was also held up as an example of the disasters a woman could bring to a dynasty – she acted as regent for her weak-willed son, and, on her death, her own family tried to seize the throne from its rightful rulers. In more recent times, it was said that the doom of the Qing dynasty lay in the womenfolk of one particular Manchurian clan, whose last scion, the Empress Dowager Cixi, would preside over the fall of the Chinese empire.

Wu, however, surpasses them all, not only in her achievements, but also in the hatred she has drawn from historical commentators, and the awe she has inspired in authors of fiction. In the sixteenth century, she became the subject of a pornographic novel, *The Lord of Perfect Satisfaction*, which detailed her twilight years, including her love for a well-endowed youth whom she would supposedly call 'Daddy' in the throes of passion. Conversely, the nineteenth-century novel *Flowers in the Mirror* presented her as an unlikely icon of feminist revolution – a drunken despot who wilfully commands the flowers of the earth to bloom in midwinter. The heavenly flower spirits are so terrified by Wu that they obey, leading to their own banishment from heaven and their subsequent involvement in the earthly revolt against her, destroying her army's bastions of Wine, Wrath, Sex and Wealth.[9]

In the twentieth century, her revolutionary actions against the old order, regardless of her methods or motivations, led to her rehabilitation among Communist thinkers. Scholars praised her stand on women's liberation, her refusal to yield to the ruling class and her promotion of an egalitarian examination system. Such praise from Communists immediately provoked a backlash from Republican Chinese, one of whom dubbed her the fourth worst mass murderer in history, beaten only by Joseph Stalin, Mao Zedong and Genghis Khan.[10]

There was something about the 1950s that created an upswell in interest in Empress Wu. Possibly we should note that, courtesy of television, 1952 saw one of the first worldwide media events – the coronation of a female sovereign in the United Kingdom. Soon afterwards, Charles Patrick Fitzgerald's *The Empress Wu* (1955) was published in Australia, and later revised in Canada in 1968. Reiterating a Victorian fancy that the Tang dynasty was 'China's Elizabethan age'[11] and Wu its not-quite-virgin queen, Fitzgerald's book courted the attentions of a popular readership keen on tales of female royalty. But, beneath the dramatic promises of its blurb, its scholarship remains impeccable, as does its adherence to the letter of the primary sources, which are diligently footnoted. Lin Yutang's *Lady Wu* (1957) was similarly well researched, but devoid of footnotes, and tantalisingly framed as fiction, as if told by Wu's grandson. Lin's book therefore incorporates several *stories* about Wu, which, while they have no better claim on truth than the official chronicles, are nonetheless harder to evaluate.

As the ailing Chairman Mao succumbed to sickness in the 1970s, supporters of his hated spouse Jiang Qing promoted the idea of a loyal and dutiful wife, ruling in her husband's name. Her enemies, of course, raked over the coals of Wu's scandals and transgressions, igniting the debate once more.[12] Since then, Wu has formed a peripheral element in several other books, but the only other major scholarly investigation in English is Richard Guisso's *Wu Tse-T'ien and the Politics of Legitimation in T'ang China* (1978), a detailed analysis of the way Wu and her associates kept their hold on power.

In recent years, the only major new studies of Wu have been in foreign languages – there is a daunting amount of books in Chinese, but also Yasunori Kegasawa's Japanese-language *Sokuten Bukô* (1995). Many modern writers on Wu are more interested in her fictional aspects, be they in other people's work, as in Dora Dien's *Empress Wu Zetian in Fiction and in History: Female Defiance in Confucian China*, or in their own, as seen in numerous novels and dramas listed in this book's first appendix.

In the early twenty-first century, Empress Wu faces a new role. Playing on the fad for women's confessional literature in an oriental setting, she has become something of a medieval Chinese Cinderella, presented in novels and television serials as a little-girl-lost, the chosen bride of royalty, whose Prince Charming seizes her in scandal and then abandons her in spirit even while his body lives, leaving her alone to defend the dynasty from an assault led by her own relatives. Her long life lends itself well to epic television, her era a dreamtime of costume and fashions, her dilemmas often brutally timeless. A recent parallel is perhaps the most astonishing – a 1996 Chinese-language biography of Hillary Clinton bore the subtitle: *Empress Wu in the White House*. Whether one should regard that as a compliment depends on what one believes about Wu.

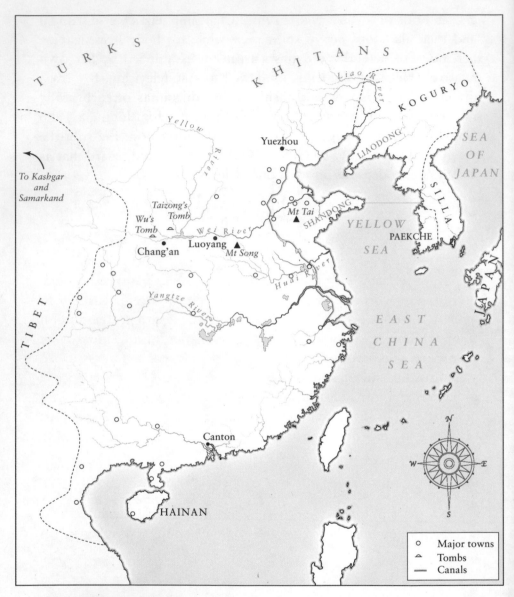

China in the seventh century.

ONE

The Gate of the Dark Warrior

Far away from Wu's tomb, out in the Chinese countryside, along a bumpy, dirt track that threatens to ruin all but the hardiest of modern vehicles, a two-hour drive brings the visitor to the modest tomb of Empress Wu's first husband, Taizong, an emperor of renowned wisdom and uncanny ability, a great soldier, a born administrator and a ruthless politician. For a man who is supposed to have engineered a revolution, a civil war and the foundation of a new imperial dynasty, who installed and eventually deposed his own father and murdered his own brothers, it is remarkably understated.[1]

In consultation with his ministers, Taizong agreed that simplicity was the best policy – there would be no boastful architectural statements for him, but a relatively small temple complex in his

GUO – COUNTRY OR NATION
During her reign, Empress Wu introduced over a dozen new characters to the Chinese language, sometimes for political reasons, sometimes on a whim. In this case, she changed the character for 'nation', keeping the idea of an area demarcated by a box, but filling the box with the symbol for her own surname.

memory. The decision was in keeping with the ancient teachings of Confucius, who had often harangued his disciples on the wastefulness of brash and ostentatious burial sites.

The tomb is like the man it contained. A simple, no-nonsense affair, its most famous decorations are the bas-reliefs of Taizong's favourite horses. Once, these had graced the Gate of the Dark Warrior (*Xuanwu-men*), the north entrance to Taizong's palace and, in his youth, the site of his most notorious deed.

As a young man under the preceding Sui dynasty, Taizong had been the hero who freed his cousin the emperor from captivity at the point of a sword. Later on, he would persuade his own father to rebel against the same ruler, leading to the final collapse of the Sui and the foundation of the Tang.

Still in his late teens at the foundation of the Tang, Taizong had fought bravely in the mopping-up operations that established his father's rule over all China. Stories about his life make him seem far more at home facing down mounted cavalry and enemy archers than dealing with his own family. Even in his later life, there are stories of palace ladies performing 'dances' for him that sound suspiciously like artistic versions of military drill. As a middle son, Taizong had come to understand the dangers of peacetime when he began coughing blood at a family banquet and realised his elder brother had slipped him some poison. Recovering from this attempt on his life, Taizong declared war on his brothers, ambushing them at the Gate of the Dark Warrior, and personally killing one with an arrow before jumping into perilous hand-to-hand combat with another. Taizong's life might have come to an end there, but his trusty lieutenant Weichi Jingde arrived in the nick of time with a lance, and skewered the remaining brother on its point.

In the aftermath of the incident at the Gate of the Dark Warrior, the 27-year-old Taizong 'persuaded' his father to step down, and took his place. His accession ushered in one of the high points of imperial civilisation. This was no remote and out-of-touch ruler. Taizong knew China well because he had personally fought over every inch of it. He set no store by omens and portents, refusing to let ministers filibuster him with talk of *feng shui* and inauspicious days.[2] Instead, he insisted that every arm of his government should have representatives that slept in shifts in an annex of the palace, in order to ensure that a relevant minister would be on call at any time of the day or night, regardless of whether a soothsayer regarded the hour as 'unlucky'. Taizong had refused all talk of moving ceremonies to more fortunate hours and days, insisting that things be done as and when they were most quickly accomplished. Some ministers and subjects regarded his behaviour as a breath of fresh air; others fretted that the Emperor's hubris would reap its just rewards.

This, at least, was the way Taizong ran his government for his first decade in power. As middle age approached, he tired of his heavy-duty administrative regime and tried to take it more easily, particularly hunting and riding. He also began to set greater store by superstition. He gave orders for the images of his generals Qin Qiong and Weichi Jingde, the man who had saved his life, to be pasted on his door to ward off evil spirits – thought to be the first flowering of the 'door god' tradition that survives to modern times.[3] Like the emperors of old, he also made enquiries about immortality treatments and herbal means to prolong his virility. With such wavering resolve in the everyday, he also became susceptible to prophecies and portents, one of which was a legend among the common people. It foretold that the Tang dynasty would be only three generations old before it fell under the control of a female ruler, the War King (*wu wang*). Like much popular folklore, the story seems confused – why would a woman be a 'king'? But, as with all superstitions, the Emperor soon found opportunities to believe it.

For several days, the planet Venus continued to shine long after its usual appearance after dawn, clearly visible during the day. This, too, was taken by some to be an indication of a female power in the ascendant, and the Emperor's Grand Astrologer did nothing to scotch the rumours.

During a drunken banquet at which talk turned to childhood names, the emperor discovered that one of the captains of the palace guard had been called Wu Niang (Girl Five) in childhood. The characters did not match, but they sounded alike, and the coincidence was enough to trouble Taizong, even though it was not particularly rare – even in modern times, Chinese boys sometimes receive girls' names in early childhood, in order to protect them from curses.[4] The offending captain was swiftly sent off to the provinces to assuage the Emperor's suspicions, but the damage was already done. When, confused or perhaps inspired by his experience, the soldier began to seek the attention of local fortune-tellers, the Emperor heard of his consultations and had him executed for sorcerous conspiracy.

Concerned that the danger was still not over, Taizong called his Grand Astrologer to him and asked him if the danger had passed. The Grand Astrologer gave a shocking and dangerous response, announcing that, even at that very moment, the woman who would become the War King dwelt in the Emperor's palace. The Grand Astrologer might have been a master of the heavens, but not of diplomatic timing, since his comment caused the Emperor, perhaps in the middle of a drink, to collapse into a coughing fit.

Taizong seriously considered killing all the women in the palace. The Grand Astrologer told him there would be little point, since fighting against fate itself would never work. If he took such drastic measures, he would only kill many innocents, while the War King would somehow elude the executioners. Instead, he cautioned the Emperor to leave things be. He pointed out that, if the dangerous woman were already alive on that day, then she would be relatively elderly by the time the three-generation deadline approached. Like a good Daoist, the Grand Astrologer advised that doing absolutely nothing was the best course of action, since, even if the prophecies were true, the War King would have only a few years in the sun before she, too, was taken by old age. Kill off all the prime candidates now, and a new incarnation would rise to take her place, attaining a sprightly middle age at the aforesaid time, and likely to destroy the Tang dynasty completely.

Already feeling the weight of his years, despite being only in his forties, the Taizong Emperor dismissed the Grand Astrologer. If the War King did arise, it would certainly not be a problem for him, although it might be an issue for his loyal son, who even now attended him at his bedside. Resigning himself to fate, the Taizong Emperor returned to his new hobby, which, if the stories are to be believed, involved a beautiful teenage girl he called the Fair Flatterer. In failing health, and with his principal wife already in the grave, the ageing emperor relied on the Fair Flatterer to feel young again. It is perhaps another sign of his approaching decrepitude that he did not stop to consider her real name: *Wu*.[5]

The story of the Emperor and his Grand Astrologer was written down almost a century later, by relatives and former associates of Wu herself, keen to record her memory, to list her mystical qualities and, perhaps, even to admit that some of her later actions threatened the security of China itself. It is thus not impossible that such anecdotes as that of being Taizong and his Grand Astrologer are the medieval Chinese equivalent of 'even-handed' in their treatment of events – both Taizong and Wu were rulers of China, and hence needed to be accorded some sort of magical respect and honour, even if it involved demonstrating their position in the world of fates as being less than perfect. It is worth noting that the prophecies concerning Wu's birth were all promoted by the Empress herself in her later years, as she aspired to and gained a singular distinction, becoming the only woman to rule China as sole sovereign in both name and reality.

Portents of Wu's future supposedly visited her even as a baby. An old well near her ancestral home had begun to put forth water again in her father's youth. In the years before Wu's birth, the well filled once more, and, in the decades that followed, its output increased so much that it became the source of a new tributary to a nearby river. This phenomenon led to a popular song in the period, part of which went: 'the well of Wu fills | from it a sage must emerge.'[6]

Her parents were Wu Shihou, a middle-aged former lumber merchant, and his second wife, Lady Yang. If ages truly match the real dates, then their marriage was strange by the conventions of the time. Shihou had at least two sons by his first wife, and so had already fulfilled the necessities of Confucian doctrine, with heirs who could carry on the ancestral sacrifices after his death, and ensure the continuance of the family line. One might expect, given the conventions of the age and that duty could now be replaced by pleasure, that Shihou might have sought a far younger woman for his number-two wife, but at 42 the Lady Yang was only two years younger than her husband, and bore him three daughters in her forties, of which Wu was the middle one, born in AD 625.[7]

Around 627, when Shihou was appointed as a governor in the Sichuan border town of Lizhou, the family was visited by a fortune-teller. This was no itinerant trickster, but instead a respected face-reader, Yuan Tian-gang, en route to the capital at the behest of the Taizong Emperor himself. As seems traditional, either in China itself, or in imperial biographies in search of legitimation after the fact, the fortune-teller stopped at the Wu residence – possibly even lodging with the local ruler in a manner befitting a fellow imperial servant. Shihou gathered his family for the entertainment of a reading, and Yuan immediately took an interest in Lady Yang.

'This lady', he said, 'has a face that shows she will bear a noble child.'

Sensing the chance to put the fortune-teller's abilities to the test, Wu ushered him over to his sons by his earlier wife. However, instead of making further prophecies of great deeds, the fortune-teller only offered humdrum predictions – that the boys would go on to become provincial governors, but otherwise no great fate awaited them.

The fortune-teller was next brought to Wu's elder sister, Helan, who at the time would have been a child of between 3 and 5 years of age.

'This girl', he said, with either surprising insight or the benefit of the author's serendipity, 'will be honourably married, but will not bring honour to her husband.'

At that time, Wu was still under 3 years old, dressed in boy's clothes and in the care of a nanny. The fortune-teller went over to the baby, but commented that it was difficult for a face-reader to ply his trade when a child's face was scrunched up in sleep. As he looked closer, the child opened its eyes, leading Yuan to comment in surprise:

'The aspect of a man. The countenance of a dragon and the neck of a phoenix, resembling that of [the legendary ruler] Fuxi – indicators of a most celebrated individual.'

Not realising that the baby was actually female, he added: 'If this were only a girl, she could be the ruler of the Empire.'[8]

A decade later, the Taizong Emperor was surrounded by portents of death and decay. Old war wounds were catching up with him, and he felt his age more keenly than most. Wars on the borders continued to bother him. Although he had brought peace and prosperity to China itself, he was troubled by his own immediate family. His eldest son, the putative heir, was rumoured to be a homosexual, and provocatively attracted to the manners and customs of China's central Asian enemies, the Turks.

After a youth spent in wars and great battles, Taizong received an embassy from distant Japan in 630, recognising China as the centre of the world. Thereafter, he began to act less like a frugal, wise administrator and more like an extravagant despot, commissioning fine palaces (one of which he then had pulled down on a whim) and diverting himself with long hunting trips. On several occasions, he left the palace behind for a winter visit to the spas at Blackhorse Mountain, where he would bathe his aching bones in hot springs, attended by his young handmaidens.[9]

For a man of action, used to the chaos of battle and vendettas, peace was proving to be a slow and inevitable decline. Taizong's father, the founder of the Tang dynasty, whom he had forced to abdicate in 627, finally passed away in monastic seclusion in 635. Meanwhile, in what could well have been a cause of even greater grief, Taizong was forced to say a final farewell to the surviving warhorses that had been the companions of his youth. Purple Storm, Red Stripe, Valiant, Black Piebald and Whitefoot Raven, brave steeds that had carried him into and out of danger and bore their own scars to prove it, finally succumbed to old age, leading the bereaved emperor to commission several wall carvings of his beloved mounts. Along with one of the late Tan Fist, which had collapsed under him, shot with nine arrows at a battle a generation earlier, the images of the horses were set in pride of place at the Gate of the Dark Warrior.[10]

All of the above, it seems, was an unsuccessful attempt to distract the Emperor from his true grief. His chief wife, the Empress Wende, a strong, capable woman of the Zhangsun family, also passed away in 636. Mourning her loss, and less scornful of superstition than in his earlier years, Taizong increasingly sought solace among the younger handmaidens and concubines of the palace. Many of the ladies-in-waiting were the daughters of officers or ministers in Taizong's government, who had been only too happy to pack off their daughters for a life of palace servitude, in the vain hope that one of them might become the mother of his heir – though none spoke of it, the future of the Turcophile crown prince was most definitely in doubt.

When Wu herself was summoned to the palace, her own mother recognised how unlikely she was to enjoy much success. Taizong already had many other wives and concubines, and, while the loss of his empress might have hurt him greatly, there were plenty of others to keep his mind off his bereavement. Moreover, he already had fourteen sons, so there was hardly a need for a male heir, and hence little chance that a concubine bearing one now would rise fast through the ranks.

In later years, many authorities, including Wu herself, would make much of her arrival at the court, and the instant attraction that Taizong felt for her. It is implied that the pre-pubescent Wu was a woman of such striking beauty that she was immediately whisked off to become a personal attendant of Taizong. In fact, her arrival at the palace was considerably more mundane. Her own father had died the previous year, and Wu's appointment to the palace may have been a concerted effort by her mother to ensure that her daughters were cared for, possibly to save them from ill-treatment at the hands of their half-brothers. Around the same time, Wu's elder sister Helan was married off to a court official, ensuring that both the elder Wu girls were taken care of, leaving only their youngest sibling, still a child, to occupy their newly widowed mother.

This may have played to Wu's advantage. A pretty young virgin, also mourning the lost of a recently deceased parent, may have held Taizong's attention for a crucial moment longer than the other girls. The Emperor undoubtedly noticed Wu on at least one occasion, for enough time to give her the Fair Flatterer nickname, itself a reference to a popular song of the day and not indicative of anything more than a few minutes in his presence. In fact, the teenage Wu found herself considerably low down in a hierarchy of palace ladies, more a scullery maid than a princess.

The top rank among the palace women was that of empress, now left vacant in honour of Taizong's late wife. As was traditional, she was his one 'true' wife, the mother of his legitimate heirs. Four auxiliary wives occupied the first grade of the other women, known as the Noble Lady, the Pure Lady, the Virtuous Lady and the Good Lady. On occasions when Taizong felt like a change, he might choose to spend his time with the six ladies of the second grade, the wives of Bright Virtue, Luminous Demeanour, Cultivated Beauty and similar honorifics. Below these were the nine Elegants of the third grade and the nine Beauties of the fourth grade. Were the Emperor to sleep with one of his women each day, it would take him a full lunar month just to get through all the top four grades. Even allowing time off for pregnancies, illness, menstruation and sheer exhaustion on the part of the imperial husband, it is unlikely indeed that he would have all that much time for the fifth grade, the nine Talents, of which the teenage Wu was but one member. In theory, he also had access to three still lower grades of women, the twenty-seven girls of the sixth (Treasures), seventh (Ladies) and eighth (Obedients).[11]

However, the palace women were not expected to while away their days in idle pursuits, waiting like oriental odalisques for Taizong to bestow his favours upon them. Although that was undoubtedly part of their function, they were also put to work in the inner palace, the walled enclosure where the emperor was the sole male resident, attended by a staff of eunuchs and the 122 women.

We may assume that the first two grades of wife were those whose role most fitted those of many western fantasies of Chinese courtly life, preoccupied with their own beauty, and perhaps other abilities –

skills of song, dance and the bedchamber, along with politicking and squabbles with their rivals of the same rank.

The lower grades had more routine duties. Day-to-day running of the palace was in the hands of the eunuchs, who were also responsible for the kitchens, budgets and maintenance of the palace gardens. Women of Wu's rank, the Talents, ostensibly answered directly to the empress herself, although, since she was dead, they may have had more time to make mischief of their own. More precisely, the Talents were responsible for bedding and the provision of linen – they were chambermaids, a role that could often put them within easier reach of the Emperor.

Nevertheless, the teenage Wu was one of many girls in attendance on the middle-aged Taizong, and it is notable that we have only one anecdote of her time as a Talent. It is, however, a telling one, since it places Wu not merely working in the palace, but at the Emperor's side in a paddock, engaging him in conversation on his favourite subject, horses. Wu herself recounted a moment of teenage bravado:

When I was serving Taizong, he had a grey horse called Shizicong [Dappled Lion]. It was such an unruly horse that nobody could tame him. I said: 'I can tame him, but I will require three things: a metal whip, an iron rod, and a dagger. I will whip him, then if it does not work, I will strike his neck with the stick and if that does not work, I will cut his throat with the dagger.' Taizong admired my spirit.[12]

At least, Taizong may have chuckled at his handmaid's openly wilful, malicious attitude, something that was unbecoming in a lady of the palace, although it might have struck the middle-aged Emperor as quaintly belligerent. It is an intriguing example, since it suggests not only how Wu may have acted in the Emperor's presence, but also that her charisma, even as a girl, allowed her to get away with outrageous behaviour. It would seem, on the basis of Wu's career over the next few years, that, even if her character only occasionally led her to the Emperor's bed, she still rose through the ranks at the palace through the favour of the other women.

Wu might have remained as a relatively lowly and unimportant serving maid but for a series of scandals that broke out among the Taizong Emperor's children. Prince Cheng-qian, the eldest son of the Emperor and late Empress, had raised eyebrows at court by openly adopting some of the fashions and mannerisms of the barbaric Turks beyond China's western borders. Although the imperial family had a lot of Turkish blood in it – with Taizong himself having a Tartar grandmother and Empress Wende having connections to Central Asia – it was regarded as most unseemly, particularly considering the continuing state of war between the two races.

Prince Cheng-qian had been only 8 years old when his father had become emperor. Although lessons were scheduled for him in the subjects deemed proper for an imperial heir, he lashed out at his tutors and cultivated an air of indifference towards Chinese matters. Lame in one leg because of an unspecified injury or birth defect, the prince was excused at an early age from court ceremonies. As he got older, the limping prince rejected noble pursuits in favour of equestrian activities – presumably because his disability became less obvious on horseback. Teenage rebellion manifested itself in the form of a pronounced interest in matters Turkish. Finding palace ritual and court assemblies to be insufferably boring, Prince Cheng-qian boasted often of his interest in the simple life of the steppes. Surrounding himself with retainers of Turkish descent, he would camp out in the palace grounds in makeshift tents, barbecuing sheep and eating the flesh at knifepoint. The rebellious prince insisted on listening only to Turkish music, danced Turkish dances and imitated nomad thievery by sending his cronies into town to steal livestock from the townsfolk of Chang'an. He even boasted that, upon ascending the throne, he would immediately take off for central Asia, there to hunt, ride and live a carefree life like that of his ancestors.[13]

His tutor eventually lost his patience, and subjected the surly prince to a long tirade about his responsibilities. Forbidden from punishing him directly, the tutor was forced to limit himself to a verbal tongue-lashing. Regardless of protocol or propriety, the tutor may have had other issues at the forefront of his mind. The Prince enjoyed his status only because he was the eldest son of the late Empress Wende. He had an elder brother, the son of a mere concubine, who was fast looking like a more attractive proposition as an heir – not only because he did as he was told, but because Cheng-qian often gave the impression that he would personally welcome exile to a distant frontier post. The last thing the Tang dynasty needed from its imperial family was any reminder of their non-Chinese relatives, and Cheng-qian's little barbarian camp-out was a public-relations disaster. Factions were already moving to recommend that Cheng-qian be replaced. None of this would have reflected well on his tutor, who had dedicated a decade to the dutiful education of a future emperor, at least partly in the hope that a high ministerial post awaited him from a grateful pupil once enthroned. If Cheng-qian were demoted, then his tutor would have literally wasted his time.

The correct way for a noble pupil to react would have been with apologies and promises of reform. Instead, the Prince stormed off in a sulk and later instructed two of his 'Turkish' retainers to break into the tutor's quarters and kill him. However, this news came out only in retrospect, as not even the Prince's henchmen were able to bring themselves to carry out their mission and the plot went undiscovered.

Out of desperation, Taizong appointed a new tutor for the youth, choosing a minister whose reputation at court was founded on his fearless willingness to remonstrate with the Emperor himself when he thought he was acting in error. Although the old man soon died of natural causes, something led to a change in the Prince's outward appearance. At least part of the message had got through, and the Prince began to behave in court in a manner more befitting the heir apparent. However, back in his quarters, he continued to play at a steppe lifestyle, speaking Turkish with his henchmen and continuing to live in as close to a nomadic fashion as the palace grounds would allow. When a palace officer commented on his strange behaviour, the prince punched him.

Strangest of all his activities was the game he called 'Funeral of the Khan', at which the prince would stretch out on the ground pretending to be dead, while his henchmen rode in circles around him uttering cries of mourning. With his younger brother, Prince Han, he would stage mock battles between groups of henchmen, and the pair would speculate loudly about the fun they would have when Cheng-qian was emperor and they could enlist entire armies for gladiatorial events.

Prince Cheng-qian's downfall began in 643, when it came to Taizong's attention that his heir was also a pederast. Cheng-qian had fallen for a 13-year-old dancing boy and begun a homosexual affair with him. Taizong gave orders for the boy to be executed, hoping to shock Cheng-qian into toeing the line. Instead, the Prince swore revenge on his father. He refused to come to court, and spent his days worshipping a statue of his executed boyfriend. He also began to seek co-conspirators in a plot to kill his father.

The Prince's younger brother, his occasional co-sponsor in the gladiatorial skirmishes, agreed to take part so long as he was permitted sexual access to every musician and dancer in the palace, be they male or female. Other conspirators demanded less bizarre fees and promises, but before long Prince Cheng-qian had assembled a disgraced general, some disaffected nobles, and retainers ready to risk their lives in an act of regicide.

On military advice from the general, they agreed that a straightforward palace brawl, like that which had left their father victorious at the Gate of the Dark Warrior, would never succeed in the face of opposition from the guards. Instead, they agreed that Prince Cheng-qian would fake an illness, thereby hoping to bring Taizong to visit him on his sickbed and affording the conspirators the chance to stab the old emperor.

However, Prince Cheng-qian's plot never went into action, as its thunder was stolen by a *second* princely conspiracy. Even as Cheng-qian and his cronies made their plans to murder Taizong, another of Taizong's children was planning a coup of his own.

Prince Zhi was officially serving as an administrator on the eastern seaboard's Shandong peninsula, although he was still relatively young in years and his posting was more of a practical education – his tutors running things in his name and consulting him on administrative matters. This arrangement left Prince Zhi with plenty of time for making new friends, and he fell in with a bad crowd – most notably a maternal uncle who reminded him that, just as Taizong had emerged triumphant from a bitter and deadly sibling rivalry, the time was fast approaching when the sons of Taizong might similarly find themselves at each other's throats.

It came to the attention of Prince Zhi's tutor that he was actively recruiting men for a personal militia. He may have been doing so simply for self-defence, but it certainly did not look good for an emperor's son to be building up a private army. The tutor not only reported Prince Zhi's behaviour to Taizong, but travelled back to the capital personally, ostensibly to plead Prince Zhi's case, but actually to urge the Emperor to write a stronger letter of chastisement to his wayward son. Prince Zhi was deeply offended by the tutor's behaviour and soon had him killed, but not before the tutor had written a letter to the Emperor confessing that he was in fear for his life. A second official in Prince Zhi's retinue turned up dead, apparently murdered for refusing to take part in the execution of his colleague.

Prince Zhi, however, had pushed too far, and realised that it was now only a matter of time before news of his transgressions reached the capital and led to his dismissal. Faced with the option of fleeing or fighting, Prince Zhi chose the latter option, pre-empting his father's anger by declaring a full-scale revolt against the throne. Although Prince Zhi's command centre was briefly besieged, his revolt was swiftly over, thanks to the speedy arrival of loyal government troops and the refusal of many of his own guards to support his actions. The sorry affair ended with a stand-off at Prince Zhi's burning residence, in which the prince was forced to surrender. He was sent back to the capital to explain himself, and most of his supporters were killed.

Crucially, however, once interrogations began in Chang'an, one of Prince Zhi's supporters offered to confess to all his crimes and contacts in exchange for clemency. This remarkable individual turned out to have been a member of both conspiracies and, in revealing his associates in Prince Zhi's, inadvertently tipped off investigators concerning Prince Cheng-qian's.[14]

Taizong was devastated, although, considering his behaviour in his own youth, he should not have been too surprised. The result was a series of purges and banishments that decimated the imperial family. Some, like Prince Han, were invited to commit suicide in private. Others, like Prince Cheng-qian, were dispatched to the far-flung corners of the empire, stripped of their titles and rank, and left to rot out on the frontier. Stuck in remote outposts far from civilisation, few of the cosseted, spoilt princes survived more than a couple of years.

In all, the crisis ended the careers of four princes and many dozens of their retainers. It cost Taizong one of his oldest friends, who was dragged from his presence weeping after the Emperor had offered him a mournful farewell on the day of his execution. More importantly for the career of the Fair Flatterer Wu, it wiped out entire sectors of the concubines and handmaidens of the inner palace. In a moment of rare mercy, Taizong could not bring himself to execute the womenfolk as others might have done, but they still found themselves banished.

We will never know of the rivalries unseen, the vendettas never begun, the competitions for affection that might have resulted if those women had not been removed. The aftermath of the princely conspiracies saw unexpected figures catapulted into the spotlight by rapid promotions. It also saw a conservative backlash among the old guard, as Taizong and his ministers fretted that the Tang dynasty would be seen as a joke. It was time, they decided, for the Tang dynasty to present an image to the world of military triumph and domestic security, sufficient to invite the continued respect of tributaries, and the continued fear of potential foes. It was time to go to war.

TWO

The Favour of Rain and Mist

At the time of the princes' conspiracy, the Fair Flatterer Wu was still only 17 years old, and serving somewhere in the imperial palace. Her official biographies are reticent on her teens and early twenties, but it is reasonable to believe that she was a witness to the uncovering of the conspiracies and the shocking aftermath. She had no role in the Turkish antics of the Prince, and was nowhere near the abortive revolt in Shandong – for possibly the last time in her life, she was in the midst of conspiracy and intrigue without actually playing any active part in it herself.

In later life, Wu herself would deliberately understate her role at the court during her teens and early twenties, in order to disassociate herself from Taizong – a suspected sexual relationship with the father would have made married life very awkward with the son. It is thus difficult to ascertain her status during the late 640s. At one end of the scale of possibilities, she may have still been little more than a chambermaid, one of several dozen servants attending to Taizong. However, considering that this legendary

○

XING – STAR
The simplest of Wu's writing reforms was the word 'Star', which
she replaced by a simple circle.

beauty would have also been reaching the peak of her youthful attractiveness, it is likely that she enjoyed a more intimate relationship with Taizong, at least on a couple of occasions. More importantly for Wu's future career, the beautiful teenager was resident in Taizong's palace at the same time as Gaozong, the boy who would shortly be selected as the new heir apparent.

There were several older male children of Taizong, but Gaozong was the only one who was a son of the late Empress Wende – this made him a much better prospect in the eyes of certain ministers, particularly his own maternal uncle Zhangsun Wuji, who saw in the boy his last available means of exerting control at court in the next generation. Accordingly, even though several other candidates seemed better choices on paper, Gaozong enjoyed strong support from Taizong's closest advisers.

Prince Gaozong was literally born into a different age, after his father ascended to the throne, and hence was raised as a princeling in great luxury, but initially without much hope of ascending the throne. More critically, he was only a teenager himself, no older than 15. Traumatised by the death of his mother when he was only a child, he appears to have believed, or been led to believe, that he was somehow responsible for it. He had been raised in the palace in great luxury and, contrary to custom, perhaps through concern over his bereavement, perhaps because he genuinely was Taizong's new favourite, had never been spirited away from the 'inner palace' that was occupied solely by women and eunuchs. His father doted on him, and seems to have kept him close. Although Chinese histories do not state it outright, it is likely that the young Gaozong had the run of the palace, and would not have been able to avoid noticing Fair Flatterer Wu, by now a beautiful girl a couple of years older than him, on whom he may have had something of a crush.

Gaozong was a shy prince; the only recorded incident in which he stood up to his father is the occasion he tried to resist the concubines chosen for him when he reached his mid-teens. He does not seem to have got on well with his principal wife (the later Empress Wang), a selection approved by ministers, although he hit it off to a far greater degree with Xiao Liangdi, a pretty southern girl, pale, thin and far more genteel and refined than her nouveaux northern associates, and able to turn the Prince's head. When she gave birth to their first child, Taizong himself came over to the eastern palace for the ensuing party, in which even the Emperor himself got up to dance.[1]

But such carefree moments of celebration were becoming rare for Taizong. He remained deeply sickened by the petty backstabbing of court life and, as he settled into middle age, began to yearn for the simple soldier's life of his youth, when enemies had been clearly marked and physically accessible.

Even as Gaozong was confirmed as heir in 643, Taizong and his closest advisers were already plotting a new military campaign to recapture their glory days. News had drifted in of a bloody coup in the neighbouring kingdom of Koguryo, where a minister had murdered his sovereign and placed a puppet ruler on the throne. Koguryo was now threatening to invade its own neighbours, the south Korean kingdoms of Silla and Paekche, giving Taizong the excuse he needed to arrange an invasion.

Taizong's reasons for invading Korea had little to do with his alliance with Paekche. His real motivation lay a generation earlier, in the collapse of the dynasty that had preceded the Tang. Taizong's cousin, one of the last rulers of the Sui dynasty, had exhausted his empire in an unsuccessful attack on Koguryo. If Taizong were to succeed where his relatives had failed, it might help negate some of the setbacks he had recently encountered. It would be regarded, by friend and foe alike, as further proof that the young Tang dynasty still had some fight in it.

Taizong planned a two-pronged assault. The bulk of his force would take the long route into Korea, marching north along the coast, crossing the Liao River into the disputed Liaodong peninsula, and then crossing the Yalu River, ready to face the line of Koguryo forts that guarded the frontier. A second force, comprising a navy of 500 troop transports, would cross the Yellow Sea and arrive ahead of the army, making landfall behind the forts, perilously close to the Koguryo capital at Pyongyang. This, Taizong hoped, would cause the defenders to panic, and at the very least pull troops out of their

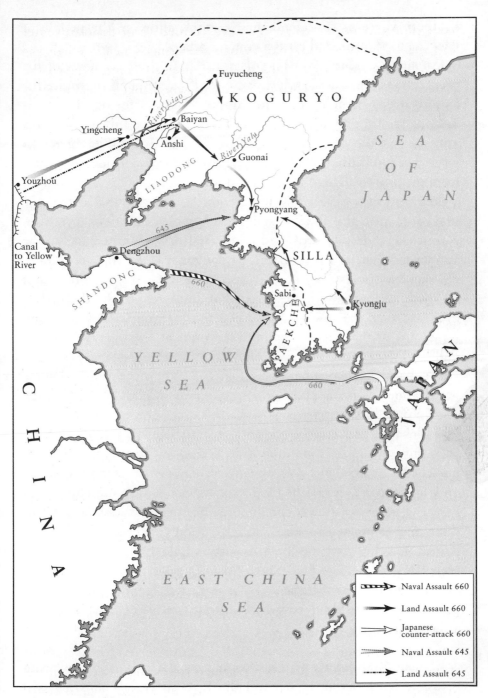

The invasion of Korea.

southern ventures to defend their capital, allowing the people of Paekche to regroup and press a counter-attack.[2]

In many ways, the first line of attack comprised the news of the preparations themselves, which were terrifying enough to inspire the Koguryo government to send ambassadors offering tribute if Taizong would only call off the assault. However, Taizong was less interested in the usurper's bribe than he was in conquering Korea when his forerunners had failed. He refused to consider the offer from the usurper. There was no need for Taizong to go along himself – the front lines were 1,000 miles from his capital, and neither the sea route nor the land-based march would be easy for him. Nevertheless, despite profound ministerial protests in Chang'an, he announced that he would be accompanying the army. Late in 644, Taizong left some trusty officials in charge at Chang'an and set out on the long journey for the coast. For some reason, he decided to take Gaozong, the newly selected heir to the throne, along with him – perhaps in the hope of giving the youth at least a taste for the military lifestyle, or of keeping him out of trouble.

It remains unclear where Fair Flatterer Wu was during all these preparations. Taizong and Gaozong certainly did not head off to the front alone, but journeyed as part of a great entourage of guards, retainers and, presumably, servants. A battlefield was no place for a lady, but nor did Taizong immediately dash off to the front line on horseback. At first, and possibly in the company of selected retainers and serving maids, he headed east to the major metropolis of Luoyang, a seat of power for the previous dynasty. Tellingly, it was there that he chose to make a proclamation concerning his aims in Korea, boasting that the Tang dynasty would bring victory, where their Sui predecessors had failed. Taizong framed his war as a just one, designed to punish the regicide in Korea. Standing in a former power base of the Sui dynasty, he was also unable to resist a potshot at his predecessors:

I am now about to proceed to the northern borders to bring justice to the country beyond the Liao [River]. The army will suffer neither loss nor toil. Those who tell how formerly [the Sui

32

Emperor] Yangdi cruelly sacrificed his soldiers without success, should know that the king of Korea was a righteous ruler, who loved his people. Their nation being united and peaceful, a ruthless invading army could not prevail against them.[3]

Now, argued Taizong, things were different. After spending the winter in Luoyang, he left some of his courtiers behind and proceeded at a swifter pace north-east. At Dingzhou, close to modern Beijing, Taizong ditched the rest of his entourage, including the crown prince Gaozong and any remaining courtiers. If Fair Flatterer Wu still formed part of the group, she would have been left here, as Taizong galloped towards the east with a squadron of cavalry. Nor was Taizong the only old soldier reliving his glory days – his brother-in-law and friend Zhangsun Wuji also accompanied him.

By the time Taizong reached the Liao River, his advanced forces had already taken the major risks on his behalf. His general Li Shiji crossed the Liao further north than the Koreans had expected, breaking through the 100-mile border fortifications at Kaemosong and taking the border town after an eleven-day siege. This effectively cut off much of the Liaodong peninsula from any reinforcements that might come up from the south-east, reducing the risk for a Chinese army in the region. By accident or design, Taizong only caught up with his troops after they had headed south-west towards East Liao Fort, the place where his predecessors had met with defeat. Li Shiji conquered a 40,000-strong army and laid siege to East Liao, dutifully waiting for Taizong to arrive in the second week of June.

Now ready to witness the triumph of the Tang in person, Taizong gave the order to pelt East Liao's south-west tower with incendiary arrows, which, coupled with a strong gale, caused sufficient fiery distractions to allow Tang troops to take the walls. Safely established as the man who had accomplished what the Sui dynasty could not, Taizong advanced east to Baiyan, which immediately surrendered. Several other towns and forts capitulated at Taizong's approach, offering him the hope that Korean subjects irritated by their usurper were prepared to welcome the Chinese as liberators. His troops, who had been hoping to loot the towns for themselves, were less impressed and were mollified only when Taizong offered to reimburse them with suitable riches from his own pocket.

Heading further south, Taizong lured a second Korean army into an ambush and laid siege to Anshi, the last major town in the region. In a boastful letter back to Gaozong, he noted: 'When I am at the head of the army, what else should we expect?'[4]

However, Taizong's advisers were expecting more. As the siege of Anshi dragged on, they urged him to bypass the town and forge on ahead, while news of his earlier swift victories was causing panic in the countryside, and while the Koreans in the south were still disorganised and afraid. But Taizong remained cautious about over-extension; it was, after all, inattention to the rear that had ruined his predecessor's chances, when a Sui army had failed to take Pyongyang and run into difficulties as it retreated. Weather and supplies were also becoming an increasing worry. Taizong's invasion force was relatively lean, but still required massive supplies for its men and horses. The siege of Anshi dragged on for two months, leaving Taizong perilously little time to get home again before winter set in.

Given the chance to put all his old military knowledge to use once more, Taizong was in his element. He spent days surveying the town from every angle, watching for signs of suspicious activity and predicting his opponents' next move. On one occasion, he heard a commotion of screaming birds inside the town and guessed, rightly, that the besieged troops were slaughtering some of their last chickens in order to prepare a celebratory banquet for a special mission. Sure enough, that night saw a counter-attack from within the town, for which the Chinese, thanks to Taizong's wisdom, were already laying in wait.[5]

But, beyond such petty victories, the siege of Anshi was not going well. Taizong may have seized a strip of territory in north Korea, but he was nowhere near his stated aim of unseating the usurper in Pyongyang. Meanwhile, the separate naval force had caused a degree of damage further down the coast but had failed to do anything more than nip at the Koreans' heels. With autumn already turning cold, Taizong set out for home, greatly disappointed, trying to ignore the victorious commander of Anshi, who made a sarcastic appearance on the battlements to wave goodbye.

On paper, Taizong's foreign wars continued regardless. The following year saw a series of small skirmishes in Korea, as detachments of Chinese troops used their new holdings in the Liaodong region to launch attacks on nearby towns. But neither Taizong nor their former leaders were with them. The two generals who had performed so well before Taizong's arrival were reassigned to the west, where, despite Chinese spin-doctoring to the contrary, several Turkish tribes saw the Korean campaign as a failure and took the opportunity to rise up in revolt.

There would be no more campaigning for Taizong. He was now nearly 50, and his Korean adventure had taken a severe toll. A decade of disappointments, from the death of his wife to the conspiracy of his sons, and to his failure to achieve one last astounding military triumph, was only part of it. There is some evidence that he never quite recovered from the attempted poisoning of his youth, and that he was troubled by periodic relapses, gaining in frequency as he aged. It would also appear that he had, despite attempts to insulate himself from true hardships, still suffered during the retreat from Korea. Although he remained protected from attack, little could keep him truly safe from cold weather, draughty tents and days of exposure on the march south through worsening autumn. Although Taizong seems to have regarded his expedition as a bracing diversion, he was never fully well again.

Taizong took two years to die. His interest in court matters remained strong, but he was increasingly absent from imperial audiences. He became unable to hunt on horseback, and made several unsuccessful trips to restore his health in remote villas. He remained mentally fit, able to consult with his ministers, but physically feeble. By late 648, he was bedridden and unable to care for himself – the conqueror of the world, himself conquered by old age.

Perhaps in the hope that news would not get out of Taizong's decline, access to him was limited. Ministers were excluded, along with most servants. Gaozong dared not leave his father's side for a moment, dutifully sitting by his bed and nursing him through his illness. On these long vigils, his only companion was Fair Flatterer Wu, the Talent who had been drafted in to serve as the Emperor's unofficial nurse and sheet-changer.

Much has been written about what may have happened during the Taizong Emperor's illness. The annals of the dynasty itself simply report that Gaozong 'saw and admired' nurse Wu as she attended to his father. The nature of Wu's work left her looking markedly different from the usual ladies of the court. Her make-up was greatly reduced from the ornate applications of the other palace ladies and her clothes were far simpler and utilitarian. She also wore a sorrowful expression, which the prince may have assumed was out of dutiful concern for her imperial master. In fact, Wu was far more likely to have been worrying about her own position. She was still a mere Talent and, as Taizong's health continued to fade, she would have known what would happen next. The days were long past when an emperor's wives were expected to accompany him into the afterlife, but, equally, it was deemed disgraceful for anyone but an emperor to touch a woman who had known the arms of the ruler of the world. Consequently, on an emperor's death, those women who had borne him children would be sequestered in a palace and live a luxurious retirement, whereas the rest of the court ladies were expected to shave their heads and enter a Buddhist nunnery for the rest of their lives – for the 22-year-old Wu, this could have seemed like a fate worse than death.

We will never know exactly how it played out. Laws and customs of the time dictated that a son having sex with one of his father's wives, even one who may never have consummated her 'marriage', was an act of incest. In fact, such a situation was expressly mentioned in one of the ancient Confucian books of protocol, which stated: 'Brute beasts are without propriety; therefore father and son share the same hind.' The proscription is from the *Book of Rites*, another compendium of laws and admonitions that is usually attributed to Confucius himself, as editor if not as author. Such Freudian tensions would have been all the more disruptive at the time, as they would have brought back memories of a similar scandal in 604, when Taizong's cousin, the Sui Emperor Yangdi, infamously celebrated his accession by having sex with two of his late father's concubines. Since the Tang dynasty was at least partly founded on the idea of not making the same mistakes as its predecessor, Gaozong's behaviour was dangerously provocative.[6]

For Wu, the young prince may have been the only adult male she had encountered since she entered the palace, a welcome change to the sickly, ailing man whose bedpan she was obliged to empty. Despite rulings against adult men in the inner palace, Gaozong had trampled on tradition in order to make a public display of his affection for his father. Most importantly of all, Wu was a wilful, ambitious girl, not afraid to boast of extreme measures, prepared to suggest that it was better to kill a rebellious horse than let it fight on. She was the epitome of all-or nothing, one of the most beautiful women in the world, and soon to be facing decade after decade of monastic seclusion, unless she took drastic steps.

Folklore recounts that Gaozong got up at one point to relieve himself, coming back out of the water closet to find that Wu had followed him in to the antechamber. She knelt on the floor before him and offered a water bowl for him to wash his hands. As he did so, he inadvertently splashed her face with water and commented that the 'clear waters have marred your powder'.

Wu flirtily replied: 'I accept Heaven's favour of rain and mist,' making a poetic allusion to sexual intercourse. A later, and considerably less reliable, source has Gaozong initiating the wordplay, flicking water at her from the bowl and musing aloud that he has been thinking of an old story in which a prince has sex with a goddess. Wu then replies with a couplet of her own, in which she suggests the pair of them sneak behind the curtains to make love.[7]

Whatever the exact circumstances, it is widely accepted that Wu and Gaozong were intimate before her 'husband' Taizong was dead. No mention is made of it in the Tang annals of the time, although it was certainly a matter of scurrilous gossip during Wu's own time and would later be levelled against her as an accusation by one of her rivals.[8] At the time, however, it seems that only Wu and her lover were aware of the incident.

Fictional accounts of Wu's life have her cuddling up to Gaozong in the afterglow, sobbing that she was torn between her loyalty to the dying Emperor and to the passions of his son, and that in having sex with Gaozong she has become a sinner and a criminal. Gaozong supposedly unhooked his belt and gave it to her as a keepsake, promising that, when he became emperor, Wu would become empress. This part of the story rather ignores the fact that Gaozong already had a wife of his own.[9]

THREE

The Family Matter

Taizong finally passed away in the sixth lunar month (early July) 649, and Gaozong was duly crowned as his successor within a couple of weeks.

Those women who had borne children to the late emperor went into honourable retirement in a secluded part of the imperial residence. Those other wives and concubines who had not given him a child presented more of a problem, since they could not be permitted to return to public life, to know the touch of another man. Instead, the women of the late emperor were bundled off to a nunnery, there to shave their heads and live out their days in prayer. Like presidential victors taking over the former residence of their opponent, the wives of the new emperor moved into the inner chambers, but Wu was not among them. Instead, as one of the outgoing former incumbents, she was sent off to the nearby Ganye

SHENG – BIRTH
Until the times of Wu's reforms to the writing system, the word for
'birth' had resembled a thrusting shoot, pushing up through the
ground. Wu altered it so that the original character was partly walled
in by a vaginal enclosure. During her reign, the definition of 'birth'
favoured that which did the pushing, not that which was pushed out.

convent, and not expected to be seen at court again. A poem she is supposed to have written around this time suggests that she spent the rest of the year dutifully waiting for Gaozong to make good on his promise, and had heard nothing from him by the following spring:

Watching red turn to green, my thoughts entangled and scattered,
I am dishevelled and torn from my longing for you, my lord.
If you fail to believe that of late I have constantly shed tears,
Open the chest and look for the skirt of pomegranate-red.[1]

Wu had started to believe that she had been forgotten, cast aside by her former lover as he threw himself into the affairs of state, and busied himself with his many concubines. However, back in the capital, the inner palace life of Gaozong was far from harmonious or happy. Gaozong had several concubines of his own, as well as his chief wife Empress Wang, a woman of a good family with strong ministerial backing. Unfortunately for her, she lacked one essential quality for imperial well-being – she had failed to provide the throne with a male heir. Since it was the duty of the top-ranking wife to provide an heir, she was forced to assume the shaky expedient of adopting one of the new emperor's four sons by other women.

Such situations are often the cause of great political drama. The new crown prince was one Li Zhong, a reasonable enough choice, and one that enjoyed the support of all the Emperor's chief ministers – a statement loaded with implications of its own, since many of them were relatives of the concubines. While the men of the Tang dynasty may have been nominally in charge, many of their aristocrats and ministers were drawn from noble families of the former Wei dynasty, a ruling class distantly descended from central Asian conquerors who had ruled China a century earlier. The Taizong Emperor's favourite aunt, his chief wife, and his most powerful daughters-in-law were all daughters of the old Wei aristocracy, nominated and manipulated by their male relatives.

However, an heir so easily made could also be unmade, and this possibility was not lost on Xiao Liangdi, the 'Pure Concubine', who rated herself as the Emperor's favourite, and hoped to persuade him in time to revoke the Crown Prince's status and make her own son Gaozong's heir.

Like Empress Wang, she was a rich and privileged girl of middling looks – had she been a true beauty, we might expect that she would have been snapped up by the former emperor, or by his elder sons when they were in the frame to succeed him. Instead, she ended up as a bedmate to the Emperor's fourth son by Empress Wende, a relatively lowly position, suddenly thrust into the limelight after his elevation to the status of heir. Empress Wang, however, was not one to take her promotion with grace. Her role as the new emperor's chief wife seems to have been defined more by relatives and power-brokers than by any elements of her own personality, which by all accounts was haughty and brusque. We might also infer much from the fact that her husband had taken it upon himself to desert her in order to care for his ailing father, eventually to have an affair with the dying man's nurse, with Empress Wang nowhere in sight.

If only Empress Wang had had a son of her own, her position would have been safe; she could have behaved any way she liked, and the rules of Confucian propriety would have ensured that her boy would have been the first choice as the new heir. Instead, she had let her family and ministerial sponsors down, and with heartless diplomacy, they had settled on Gaozong's eldest son, a child born of a relatively lowly concubine. This initially pleased the Empress, as it temporarily removed Xiao Liangdi's own son from the frame, although Xiao Liangdi had ample opportunity to work on the Emperor whenever she attended him in his chambers – the fact that her own son was something of a child prodigy only made him appear more appealing as a potential heir, and irritated the Empress Wang even more.

Xiao Liangdi also had a better relationship with Gaozong. Xiao Liangdi now had the support of the ministers. Xiao Liangdi would only need to wait around, and stay pretty and beguiling, until Empress Wang made a mistake, and then Empress Wang might find herself suddenly downgraded. Considering that Empress Wang had insulted a lot of her fellow concubines on the way up, it was unlikely that she would find much support on the way down.

This strange but rather common set-up in the world of the Chinese imperial court was to lead Empress Wang to go in search of new allies and new weapons in the undeclared war against her rival Xiao Liangdi.

A year after the death of the Taizong emperor, his famously filial son travelled to the Ganye temple. There, while supposedly praying to the spirit of his father, he encountered a shaven-headed, weeping woman who revealed herself to be the Fair Flatterer Wu, that same beautiful girl who had offered him such comfort during his father's final days.[2]

That, at least, is the official story, although it seems confused. First, it is not at all clear that all Taizong's women *would* be exiled into obscurity – on the death of his own father, Taizong had released many of the lesser palace women from their obligations and allowed them to return home. If Gaozong had sent all his father's women into seclusion, then we would surely be discussing a convent of some size and repute, large enough to take 122 new arrivals, and prestigious enough to be worthy of imperial ladies. And yet it is difficult to pinpoint exactly where this Ganye convent would have been – sources have offered several candidates, including one in urban Chang'an, but its location remains undetermined. Even more strangely, why are sources so keen to stress that it was a Buddhist temple? The religion of choice in Taizong's period, if it was anything at all, was *Daoism*, while Buddhism, an occupation of the departed Wei dynasty, did not gain true prominence again until later in the rule of Empress Wu herself. It could be that Wu's place of temporary exile was not that of the other concubines at all, but a special dispensation, perhaps to keep her close to her lover, the new emperor, like a modern mistress sequestered in a nearby apartment. Certainly, if there was ever a cessation in her affair with the new emperor, they were back together within a couple of years, since she had given birth to his son by 652/3. Her hair, supposedly, magically grew back.

Extravagantly long hair was *de rigueur* for ladies of the Tang court, necessary in order to allow the ornate knots, braids and pinnings of a Tang hairstyle. The closest modern analogy is the hair of a modern Japanese geisha, which is invariably now a wig in order to save time in the applications of oils and engineering. We can thus expect Wu to have had fantastically long and well-kept hair reaching down to the ground. If it were shaved off, as would normally be the case for entrants to a nunnery, it would take several years even to approach its former length. But by 652 or 653, sources have Wu back in the court of the new emperor, giving birth to his child and with her hair at a remarkable, documented 7 feet in length.[3] Did she ever cut it all? Was she wearing it, geisha-style, as a wig in order to get back in, and if so, was this part of an elaborate deception in order to set her up as a 'new' arrival. It seems unlikely – we know that there were enough members of the Taizong court remaining to remember her when she arrived at the Gaozong court, and neither Wu nor the Gaozong Emperor made any attempt to conceal her identity.[4] The simplest explanation would seem to be that Wu never shaved her head. Instead, she was sent away to the convent as propriety demanded, there to wait until her lover Gaozong found the opportunity to come to the temple on ostensibly 'spiritual' visits.

Most surprising of all is the insinuation in Chinese histories that Wu's return was not solely the decision of an infatuated young man, determined to have the one woman in the empire that was supposedly denied to him. If all Gaozong wanted was occasional sex in a private love-nest, then he already had it. But his troubled wife, the Empress Wang, reacted with considerable pragmatism to the news that her husband was having an affair. She realised that, if Wu was enough of an obsession for Gaozong to defy convention and propriety, then she was wasted shut away in the Ganye convent. For the Empress Wang, friendless and under threat, the Fair Flatterer Wu would be far more useful in the palace itself. Empress Wang had already resigned herself to not being her husband's favourite – Gaozong spent increasingly longer periods at the palace of Xiao Liangdi, where the woman continued to beat down his defences with tales of her son's great intelligence, his superb academic record and how ideal he would be as a better crown prince than the current incumbent. Every night that she kept Gaozong occupied would be another night he was kept away from Pure Concubine Xiao Liangdi, and, should Wu prove so alluring as to completely replace the Pure

Concubine in the Emperor's affections, then Empress Wang had the ultimate trump card – she was still the Emperor's chief wife, whereas Wu could always be outed as a fallen woman, undeserving of her place at the palace.

Empress Wang believed that she had found the weapon she needed, and it was she who suggested that Gaozong bring his lover back out of exile.[5] Wu's return to the palace was quiet and stealthy, her true identity revealed to only a few handmaidens. Her official position was that as the lady-in-waiting to Empress Wang herself, who looked forward to seeing the Emperor making many more visits to her own chambers, if only to sneak time with his illicit lover. The Empress used this gesture of magnanimity as a means to show Gaozong that she could be more accommodating than he realised – telling him that there was no need for him to sneak away to his lover, and that she would understand perfectly if he wanted to see her at the palace.

It is a sign of the depths of the hatred that the Empress felt for Xiao Liangdi that she was prepared to fight with such a dangerous weapon – one does not need to be a genius to see that the Empress risked making her own situation even worse, introducing a second favourite to the palace, and one who was already pregnant with Gaozong's child.[6] With the birth of Wu's son Li Hong, the secret of her identity was out, leading to extensive gossip behind the scenes, although nobody seems to have dared to challenge the Emperor's decision outright.

Nor did the Empress Wang keep Wu as her handmaiden, instead having her promoted from her original fifth-grade Talent status to the lofty second grade of Concubine of the Luminous Demeanour.[7]

Wu, however, was a far better player of intrigues than her sponsor. Knowing her arrival at the palace to be fraught with scandal, she took every opportunity to endear herself to the other girls at the palace, and made a point, when the Emperor sent her a gift of food or some other trinket, of sharing it with the other palace ladies.[8]

Chinese tradition paints Wu at this time as a form of Cinderella figure, charming her courtly associates with her generosity, while the Empress Wang and her mother parade like ugly stepsisters around the palace, revelling in their official powers and acting with boorish insensitivity towards their inferiors and servants. Empress Wang's plan had worked – Gaozong's interest in the Pure Concubine Xiao Liangdi seems to have tailed off, with circumstantial evidence for this in the absence of any new royal offspring born to her. Instead, Gaozong was spending more of his time with the Fair Flatterer Wu.

Able to see his mistress with his chief wife's full approval, Gaozong indulged himself to the best of his abilities – to such an extent that Wu spent most of the ensuing three years pregnant, giving birth to three (or possibly four) children before the end of 656.

The Pure Concubine Xiao Liangdi was set aside, and so marginalised that she was even driven to seek help from Empress Wang herself, approaching her old enemy to ask if she was aware just how much sway this new arrival had over the man they were all forced to share. The record of her complaint manages to contain slurs on Wu's character, family and morals, which many historians might regard as fair comment. However, its closing words also come perilously close to questioning the reason of Gaozong himself, a sure sign of how angry Xiao Liangdi had become: 'I have heard she was one of the staff of the Taizong Emperor, and not of a particularly good family, either. What has become of His Highness, that he is infatuated by such a woman?'[9] In an unlikely alliance, Empress Wang lent support to Xiao Liangdi's claims, the two women uniting in their wish to remove Wu from the palace. But Gaozong would have none of it, particularly since many of their accusations were made to seem ludicrous by Wu herself. She was able to pre-empt many of their comments and had ready answers for their tests, thanks to the network of palace women, all of whom liked the friendly Wu far more than her rivals.

But Wu was not the sole object of Gaozong's affections. In fact, the previously shy youth had grown into a man of strange appetites – it was not enough for him to be committing technical incest with the former concubine of his father. He also appears to have seduced her sister. Wu's elder sibling Helan, now a widow with two small children, made regular visits to see Wu at the palace, in the course of one of which she also caught Gaozong's eye.

As if Wu's position at the palace was not difficult enough, Gaozong risked a second scandal, sleeping with both her and her sister. For some reason buried in his psyche, there was something about 'family matters' that Gaozong found erotically appealing. To make matters even worse, Helan appears to have become pregnant.

According to the official dynastic histories, the impressively hypnotic Wu managed the remarkable but not impossible feat of giving birth to two children in the same year – a son and a daughter. Records concerning the son, Prince Xian, seem deliberately vague, and the annals neglect to assign him a birth date. It would seem that the boy was actually Helan's son, the exact details of his birth kept unclear either to preserve Gaozong from further scandal, or perhaps as part of an abortive scheme to claim that the boy truly was Wu's, and therefore to provide her with another heir-apparent of her own to bargain her way into the Empress's place.[10]

If, however, that had been Wu's intention, the plan was shelved in favour of something far more drastic and shocking, the details of which have made it one of the most scurrilous incidents in Chinese history.

In late 654, Wu gave birth to a baby girl – recorded in some chronicles as her third child, although more likely to have been her second. Protocol required that her former ally the Empress Wang, as the overseer of the inner palace and lead wife of the Emperor, should pay her a visit and check on the child. This the Empress did, although, when she arrived, Wu was not in the chamber. The Empress picked up the child, played with it for a while, and pressed her cheek against the baby's. She then left the room.

Shortly afterwards, Gaozong himself came to visit Wu. She took him over to the baby's cradle, only to find that the child was cold and dead. Shrieking in anguish, Wu demanded to know who had been the last to touch the baby. With understandable timidity the handmaids revealed that the last person in the room had been the Empress Wang.

Of course, we only have the story as told long after the event, by parties with a vested interest in the way the participants are portrayed. Popular myth in China holds that the murderer was Wu herself, who waited until the Empress had left before heartlessly strangling her own newborn daughter, purely to bring down her main rival. However, not even Wu seems to have been capable of such a terrible deed – in later life, despite all her faults, she avoided causing direct harm to her own children. It seems far more likely that the girl's death was a much more mundane tragedy, but one that Wu was prepared to use to her own advantage. Her official story, intimated when Gaozong was present to see the evidence, and then reiterated once the maids had confirmed who had visited, was that the Empress herself had killed the child – posthumously named the Princess Anding.

Whether the girl's death had been calculated or not, it hit Gaozong hard. He had arrived at Wu's chambers expecting to see his new daughter, only to walk into the middle of a crime scene, with his chief wife as the prime suspect. Although Empress Wang was never tried or convicted of murder, the incident caused her to lose immense standing in the eyes of her husband, particularly since she had only recently been accusing her former handmaid of any number of supposed crimes.

It was the final straw, and Gaozong resolved to have the Empress Wang demoted, with the intention of raising his beloved Wu up in her place. The decision, supposedly, had nothing to do with the recent scandal over the dead baby, and was instead based on a much more prosaic concern, that the Empress Wang had yet to provide the Emperor with a male heir. Clearly, the current adopted Crown Prince was no longer suitable, and Wu had somehow managed to even sour the chances of the Pure Concubine Xiao Liangdi's child prodigy. However, the demotion of an empress, and the subsequent selection of her replacement, were both major undertakings, which the Emperor would be unable to attempt without the backing of his ministers.

The chief minister was the Emperor's own uncle Zhangsun Wuji, brother of the late Empress Wende, and a descendant of the aristocracy of the departed Wei dynasty. It was Zhangsun who had the final say in such important matters of state, and Gaozong hoped to bring him around. His first attempt to ingratiate himself with

Zhangsun was a disaster, recorded in the Tang annals as a dinner party with a hidden agenda, in which the Gaozong Emperor arrived at Zhangsun's residence with Wu at his side. Although they had met before, Wu was reintroduced to Zhangsun and remained on her best behaviour all evening, playing the part of the cultured and genteel lady of the court. The couple had brought more than a bottle, a veritable brewery of wine designed to get the guests merrily drunk, along with ten cartloads of gifts. Gaozong had also arranged for his court artist to paint Zhangsun's portrait and presented him with the picture, to which the Emperor had personally added a poem, in his own calligraphy. The gift was priceless, a supreme honour, and rather obviously intended to curry Zhangsun's favour. While he was at it, the Emperor took the opportunity to tell Zhangsun that his sons were about to be conferred with new honours, and that even Zhangsun's favourite concubine was going to be receiving some good news about her rank in the near future.

Believing that the wheels of diplomacy had been suitably oiled, the Emperor then mentioned that it was a shame that the Empress Wang had been unable to conceive a child and that, perhaps, the time had come to deal with this deficiency in his primary wife.[11]

Zhangsun pointedly changed the subject, causing Wu and the Emperor to flounce away from the party early, leaving the other guests to enjoy all the riches they had provided. Nor were other attempts to jolt the minister into compliance any more successful. By the strict rules of protocol, Wu's cause was gaining ground – Zhangsun may have refused to discuss the topic at the banquet, but that could easily be explained away as straightforward good manners, avoiding discussion of sensitive issues at a time of celebration. By not refusing the gifts outright, Zhangsun had obligated himself to return certain favours in kind, and without rich gifts of his own, he would be obliged to offer time and assistance. Wu's own mother used this temporary obligation to impose upon Zhangsun in several visits in which she hoped to discuss her daughter's status, but while Zhangsun received her, he did not agree to her insinuations. Eventually, Wu leaned on Zhangsun's assistant, and got him to raise the matter when she was not present. It would seem that the assistant brought it up once too often, leading Zhangsun to lose his temper, shouting that he had no ear for the subject.[12]

Zhangsun had occupied a central position for thirty years, and it was proving difficult to dislodge him and his fellow associates of the late Taizong. Instead, Wu began working on the disaffected and discredited members of court such as Fang Yi'ai, an official who had once been highly favoured by Taizong, but whose star had fallen. His wife, Taizong's spoilt daughter Princess Gaoyang, had been a little too aggressive for her own good, agitating at court for her husband to receive what she regarded as his fair dues. As he was a son-in-law of Taizong, she had regarded him as worthy of numerous posts that had already been granted to others, and had complained about it at such great length that even the late emperor had lost his patience.

Gaoyang, the daddy's girl, was pushed aside, her reputation at court now largely founded on her whining. Like Wu herself, she became the subject of a whispering campaign, with scandalous stories circulating that she had enjoyed a torrid sexual affair with a monk called Bianji, whose hermitage was to be found on her hunting grounds. Meanwhile, her husband Yi'ai had himself taken two young lovers, not concubines but sexual partners unapproved by his family, which led only to further censure. Such problems, of course, only made them more likely to feel some sympathy for the charming Wu.

Wu targeted similarly peripheral supporters, paying special attention to those men whose connections to the imperial family were through women. Another of Taizong's daughters was married to a general who had been a major figure in the foundation of the dynasty, but who had been ignominiously called back from the front line after a military mistake. Still another was married to the son of a general who had not achieved anything like the successes of his famous father. Wu made sure the couple became friends, and commiserated with her over the unfairness of the old guard and the lack of opportunities for modern people. One of Wu's greatest catches was a stepbrother of Taizong himself, whose daughter was married to Wu's brother-in-law.

In all these relationships, Wu found allies who were irritated with the current government. Their fathers and grandfathers had been rebels and leaders, who had brought down the Sui dynasty and founded the glorious Tang. Now, a generation after, the rebels had turned into old men like Zhangsun. Such men greatly reduced the chances of power and fame for Wu's new circle – they naturally favoured their own families, and many had daughters who had married into the imperial family. Promotion and career paths in a state of war or rebellion are dangerous but can be swift. Now that China was nominally at peace, it was far harder to make it, particularly when one's family connections were less powerful than the old guard's.

Zhangsun Wuji was certainly aware of such agitations and factions in the court. In fact, he was so afraid of them that he began to believe that Yi'ai was plotting with one of Gaozong's brothers. The luckless prince was said by many to be the spitting image of his father, and had strong ties to the past through his mother, a princess of the departed Wei dynasty. But that was not enough to save him, and Yi'ai was duly accused of conspiracy and sentenced to death, although he managed to pronounce a curse on his accuser at his execution: 'Zhangsun Wuji, you monopolise power and now you murder the innocent. May my vengeful spirit kill every member of your family.'[13]

Gaoyang was permitted to commit suicide. Wu's campaign to replace the Empress seemed to have stalled, but the damage was already done. Still believing her position to be in danger, Empress Wang made the fatal error in summer 655 of listening to her mother, who suggested that desperate times called for desperate measures. The two women turned to sorcery, and were found to be casting spells against Wu herself – the precise nature of the act is not recorded, although it appears to have been some form of sympathetic magic not unlike the sticking of pins in a voodoo doll. A society that placed great value on religion and the spiritual world, whose very basis rested on the Emperor's divine power, also had space for witchcraft and witch-hunts – the casting of spells against the inhabitants of the inner palace was regarded as a form of high treason.

It should be noted that even here the Empress was found to be relatively blameless. Of the two dynastic annals, the *Old Book of Tang* reports the incident as above, while the *New Book of Tang* is more critical, suggesting instead that the Empress remained innocent, and was falsely accused by Wu. Whatever the reality, it was the Empress's family who bore the brunt of the damage – her mother was forbidden from entering the palace again (a social disaster), her unpopular grandfather relinquished his government post before anyone could attack him directly, and, before long, her mother's brother was packed off to a distant post in the provinces.[14]

A cryptic later statement alludes to the exiled minister being sent even further afield after it was discovered that he had given away 'palace secrets'. Although the Tang dynasty is presented as one of the greatest flowerings of Chinese culture, behind the scenes we can see elements of the bitter infighting between rival factions. The ruling house of the Tang dynasty still needed to contend with rivals, both among the Emperor's own family – his uncles, who had once opposed his father, as well as the mysterious conspiracy of his half-sister – and the powerful clans of both the brief Sui dynasty and the contending Wei that came before it. Nor should we forget that Gaozong had been chosen by the ministers because they believed him to be easy to control. Most of the surviving ministers in the Tang government had been associates of the late Taizong during the revolution that established him. Although he had died relatively young, they were still at the height of their powers, forming an elite club of power-brokers who were the true centre of power for the Tang empire. It is a symptom of Gaozong's true powerlessness that he was able to devote so much of his time to such apparently petty matters as who was his favourite sleeping partner.

With officialdom still refusing to consider demoting his empress for what may have been a series of falsified charges, Gaozong instead decided to show the depth of his feeling by raising Wu up to be an auxiliary wife of the first grade. However, only four such posts were available, and all were currently filled – the Emperor would have to find yet another series of accusations against the current incumbents if he were to get rid of any, and that would require the same amount of red tape and unpleasant diplomacy among the officials. Nor was any ready excuse available to eject any of the current auxiliaries – even the Pure Concubine Xiao Liangdi was keeping her head down, although not necessarily out of any choice; both she and the Empress had been confined to their quarters since the sorcery incident.

Believing he had found a way around all the stifling protocol, Gaozong instead announced that he would create an all-new title, above the auxiliary wives, but beneath the Empress. This new, special grade was to be the Imperial Concubine, and its first and only recipient was to be his beloved Wu. This, too, met with the sternest possible rebuke from several ministers, who were intensely reluctant to introduce a new title at all. That, at least, was the official excuse; the real reason was that they were allies of the Empress's relatives, and that they realised that the creation of any new post so close to her own would, by its very nature, reduce the value of the Empress's own position. The fact such a new title was even being discussed at all is indication enough of the Empress Wang's waning authority at court.

A new plan of attack presented itself, this time born of a power struggle among the ministers. Zhangsun Wuji had enemies of his own, including Li Yifu, a minister whom he planned to have sent away to a new posting, sufficiently far enough from the capital to cut him off from courtly life and any further chances of promotion. Li Yifu, however, worked in the secretariat, and hence was able to see Zhangsun's application to have him transferred before it reached the Emperor. Li Yifu was said to be something of a sneak, gaining the nicknames Li Cat or Sword-in-a-Smile – with such a reputation, it is unsurprising that he found a way of ingratiating himself to the Emperor before Zhangsun's message arrived.

Li Yifu wasted no time. He arranged with a colleague to switch shifts, so that he would be able to attend on the Emperor personally. Once in the throne room, he immediately presented the Emperor with his petition – the demotion of the Empress Wang and her replacement with Wu. It is unlikely that any minister would have dared to mount such an open attack on the Empress, but Li Yifu had literally nothing to lose. A few more hours of inaction, and he would have found himself posted to some forgotten border town anyway.

Gaozong leapt at the chance, and offered to hear Li Yifu's suit, conveniently confirming him in his current job, albeit only for a matter of days, until such time as he could promote Li Yifu for his loyal service. The plan to have Li Yifu exiled into obscurity had failed, and the Tang court was slowly coming round to the idea that Wu would not be leaving soon either.

At the end of the summer, Gaozong called a special meeting for all four chief ministers – an assembly of many of his father's old associates. With a fair idea of what was going to happen at the meeting, one of Gaozong's uncles simply did not bother to come, sending word instead that he was ill. Of the three remaining ministers, two others dared not say a word, and simply sat in silence, leaving the talking to one Chu Suiliang.

Chu Suiliang was not a man of noble birth like the others, nor was he a veteran of the revolution. Instead, he was a simple, humble individual, who had devoted his life to serving Taizong, and regarded his current posting simply as a continuation of the former. Chu Suiliang did not see himself as a loyal servant of Gaozong; instead, he thought of himself as a loyal servant of the Gaozong's *father*, and hoped to use that argument with his ruler.

Hoping to appeal to the Emperor's sense of filial piety, Chu Suiliang reminded him that his dying father had literally taken his son by the hand, turned on his deathbed to Chu Suiliang, and said: 'We have a good son and a good daughter-in-law. We entrust them to you.'[15]

Chu Suiliang did not dare refuse a command of his ruler, but he could imply as strongly as he could that a decision had already been made by the late emperor, and that Gaozong was obliged to do as he was told. Having already passed the point of no return, Chu Suiliang added that Empress Wang had not actually been found to have committed any crime.

It was a foolhardy act, but it worked. Gaozong was caught off-guard, unable to mount any arguments on the spot that would not be seen as contradicting his father's will. He dismissed the ministers angrily, but called them back the following day for another try.

This time, the Emperor made it clear that Empress Wang had to go, stating bluntly: 'The Empress Wang has no male heir. Wu does.' After all the insinuations over sorcery and child murder, it came down to childbirth again, at least officially. However, by making his chief wife's failure to produce an heir the new excuse, Gaozong had inadvertently presented his ministers with a loophole.

Reluctantly agreeing to discuss the matter of Empress Wang's son-less state, Chu Suiliang noted that it was still no reason to favour Wu.

If Your Highness must insist, please choose a new bride from elite families. But surely you should not choose Miss Wu. As You know, she once served in the inner palace of Your late lamented father, and we cannot suppress such public knowledge. His Highness should consider with great care how later generations will remember His decision.[16]

Entrusted or not with his duties by the former emperor, Chu Suiliang had overstepped the mark, and he knew it. The other ministers remained tensely silent as he placed his wooden wand of office at the base of the throne before sinking to his knees and pressing his forehead against the ground in supplication.

'I return my wand of office, and I entreat you to return me to my hometown,' he said, using the official protocol for offering his resignation. He banged his forehead against the floor several times to show the sincerity of his feeling.

Gaozong was deeply angered, reprimanding the minister for his insolence and ordering the guards to drag him from the throne room. But then the ministers were surprised to hear another voice joining his in anger – Wu herself had been listening in secret from behind a screen and momentarily forgot that she was supposed to be quiet, shrieking to her imperial husband that Chu Suiliang should be 'beaten to death'.

With Chu Suiliang removed, an uneasy silence settled on the courtroom, until Zhangsun Wuji could bear it no longer.

'Chu Suiliang', he ventured, 'was merely carrying out his duty as requested directly by Your Highness's illustrious father, the Taizong Emperor. Even if he is guilty [of insolence], he cannot be punished.'

The meeting ended badly, and over the days to come several ministers felt sufficiently emboldened by Chu Suiliang's stand to send their own notes of agreement. Han Yuan, the president of the chancellery, was particularly vehement, pleading that the Emperor should reconsider. He added, in a written memorial, that the Empress Wang was the symbolic mother of the nation. She could not be simply cast aside on a whim. If the state was to be run along Confucian lines, everyone had to respect their own place in the natural order of things, and that included the Emperor himself. He could no more throw away his chief wife than any other family head.

From the thrust of some of the arguments employed, it would appear that the debate grew personal and direct. Han Yuan alluded to the beauty of the Fair Flatterer Wu, but pointed out that beauty alone was no qualification for imperial promotion. In fact, there were several incidents recorded in the annals of beautiful women driving their emperors to distraction and causing the downfall of an entire dynasty. Such disasters, argued Han Yuan, should be compared to ancient times, when a legendary emperor's wife was a great ally and administrative companion to her husband, bringing great benefits to the kingdom, regardless of her dowdy and plain appearance.

Things were getting desperate, and the arguments were managing to annoy everyone; Gaozong was irritated at the insinuation that Wu might cause the collapse of his empire, and Empress Wang cannot have been too happy with the implication that she was not all that attractive.

Matters reached a conclusion of sorts when the long-standing abstainer, one Li Zhi, finally shook off his supposed illness and made it into court. All the other ministers had made their position bluntly clear, both in person and in written memorials. Only Li Zhi had remained quiet on the matter, and it was to him that Gaozong turned for a comment.

Like Zhangsun Wuji and the other ministers, Li Zhi was a remnant of the old order, one of the warriors who had carved out the Tang dynasty in its earliest days, a faithful servant of the founder, and of his son Taizong. Taizong had placed such faith in him that a popular Chinese story recounted an incident in which the late emperor had once donated clippings of his own beard in order make a potion to clear Li Zhi of an illness.[17] Li Zhi was one of the cornerstones of Taizong's inheritance – the late emperor had ordered him sent away to the provinces on his death, a test designed to see if he would faithfully follow his lord in the afterlife, or seize the opportunity to fight back. On receiving the order, Li Zhi had dutifully left the capital, prompting Gaozong to regard him as trustworthy enough to recall and reinstate. His very presence at court was as a symbol of continuity and protocol, an adviser chosen to function in many ways as the voice both of antiquity and of Gaozong's own father. It was thus a matter of great surprise to all concerned, and of supreme triumph for Wu, when Li Zhi was finally called upon to answer, and left with no choice but to say something. Instead of supporting the wise counsel of his fellow elder statesmen, Li Zhi dismissed Gaozong's impasse with a ministerial shrug.

'This is a family matter,' he said. 'Others should not interfere.'[18]

The phrasing may seem lacklustre and everyday, but its very blandness was a crucial moment in the debate. All previous debate had centred on theory and politics – matters of statehood, of succession and propriety. But Li Zhi's comments deflated much of the earlier big issues, rendering them pointless and overdramatic. The Emperor, he argued, was indeed the head of an important family, but his private affairs were no concern of the public.

It was a disingenuous and misleading argument. Nor was it necessarily a sign of Li Zhi's support for Wu – it is much more likely that he knew Gaozong was capricious, and saw no need to make a stand on such an issue when any concubine was always subject to the threat of replacement by a younger model. Considering the official duties of an empress and the power she and her relatives could wield, it was most certainly not an issue to be taken lightly. There was nothing, in theory, to stop an emperor spending as much time as he wanted with a particular bedmate, but that in itself was no need to promote her to an official position. But Li Zhi was a powerful-enough figure in the government for his words to form a reasonable alternative to the other elder statesmen's protestations. Before long, some of the younger advisers were jumping on the bandwagon.

'Even a farmer fancies a new wife if he harvests ten extra bushels,' commented one Xu Jingcong. 'Let alone an Emperor, who controls the treasures of the four seas. People should not criticise Him for wishing to change one empress.'[19] He did not make this comment to Gaozong, but news of it reached Wu's ears, and she ensured that it reached the Emperor's.

Many ministers saw the new argument for what it was – a potentially dangerous trivialisation of the issue, likening the divine Son of Heaven to a cheating husband or a common farmer with a seven-year-itch. But Li Zhi's comments had dealt sufficient damage to the opposition. By late 655, the loyal minister Chu Suiliang had been sent off to a distant posting in the provinces, and other opponents faded away.

In November, Gaozong issued a decree claiming that, despite their long records of deep enmity, Empress Wang and Xiao Liangdi had been caught plotting against the throne and had planned to poison him. Accordingly, they were stripped of their ranks and former status, and their entire families were to be similarly demoted and punitively shipped to the far south to live out their lives in exile.[20] The two women were kept under house arrest, barricaded inside a single pavilion, with only a small opening in the doorway for their meals to be slipped to them. Cunning, poetic insult was added to injury by forcing the two bitter rivals to be cellmates – they now had nobody's company but each other's.

Six days later, a group of court officials took the obvious hint, and petitioned Gaozong to select a new empress, suggesting that Wu would be an ideal candidate.

Despite the arguments that it was a matter of no concern to anyone outside the Emperor's immediate family, the promotion of Wu to empress was couched in terms designed to play up her ancestry and noble qualifications, many of which were either remarkably bent truths, or complete lies concerning her position with Gaozong's mother and father:

> The Lady Wu comes from an illustrious and honourable family, originating in a land famous for its warriors and scholars. She was chosen to enter the Palace for her talent and virtue. She gained the goodwill and respect of all the ladies of her own rank, and served her superiors with honour and merit. When We were Crown Prince and attended on Our late mother, the Lady Wu was constantly at her side both day and night. She was careful and diligent in her duties, and had no quarrels or disagreements with other ladies. The Late Emperor [Taizong], realising her good qualities, constantly praised her and after conferring honours upon her, bestowed her upon Us. Thus it is fitting that she should be raised to the rank of Empress.[21]

The official record now claimed that Wu had been a trusted servant of Gaozong's mother – a woman who had been dead before she ever entered the palace. It made the outrageous claim that she had no enemies, and even managed to suggest that her marriage to Gaozong, far from being a Confucian scandal, had actually been Taizong's idea.

Wu now enjoyed a set of references bordering on the saintly, with a public image that made her sound like the perfect empress, and even compared her favourably with Gaozong's late lamented mother. Even those who had opposed her were now forced to acknowledge her as the chief wife of their emperor, the first lady of China.

Within a few days, she began her revenge.

FOUR

The Treacherous Fox

Wu was enthroned as empress in winter 655, in a major ceremony that caused much bitterness among her rivals. The higher-ranking and longer-serving officials and palace retainers were perfectly aware of the lies in Gaozong's proclamation, and now they were forced to endure an uncharacteristically sumptuous ritual to announce Wu's promotion.

The decree from Gaozong was brought to her with due solemnity by two of the officials who had been first to break ranks and support her claim. After accepting it with the required grace, Wu then made a procession out of her quarters. All the officers of the court were made to stand in attendance to her in the courtyard before one of the palace gates, as were the other wives and concubines of Gaozong. The mass audience also required the attendance of all the wives of the court officials. This had never been ordered before, but seems in keeping with the victorious Wu's desire to gloat upon anyone who may have doubted her chances.

TIAN – HEAVEN
Until the reign of Wu, the word for 'heaven' had shown a line above a human figure. Wu changed the character so it displayed a line above the character for 'irrelevant'.

Having made her point, Wu was then taken from the courtyard to the Temple of the Imperial Ancestors, where she was officially made a member of Gaozong's family. In a traditional move designed to ensure that ranks were in accordance, it was also announced that Wu's father had been posthumously promoted to a dukedom, while many other members of her family were given 'the revenues of a thousand families' – tantamount to baronial estates.

Wu began her reign with a beautifully subtle attack on her former opponents. In a memorial to her husband that had the outward appearance of good grace and statesmanship, she requested that Han Yuan and Lai Ji, two ministers who had so persistently fought against her promotion, be rewarded for their loyalty. In an argument for remonstrative officials that would have melted the heart of Taizong, Wu wrote that the two men had only been acting with due diligence to their ministerial roles, and that, far from punishing their opposition, the Emperor should elevate them to even higher office.

Gullible as ever, Gaozong regarded this as a sweet and good-natured entreaty from the perfect empress, and even showed it to the ministers in question. Far more skilled than he at politics, they saw it for what it was – a timely reminder from Wu that their opposition had not been forgotten at all. Both begged the Emperor to be allowed to retire, but this in itself was often regarded as ministerial good manners, and Gaozong refused.

No, the ministers pleaded, they really *did* want to retire now, if the Emperor would be so kind as to allow it. But Gaozong would hear none of it, and the two ministers found themselves saddled with even greater responsibility. If they thought that Wu was setting them up for a fall, they were absolutely right.[1]

In early 656, Wu's eldest son Li Hong, conceived out of wedlock when Wu was still supposedly a nun, was officially recognised as heir. In order to pre-empt any criticism that her family would exert undue influence, Wu also ordered her half-brothers to be sent away to a distant posting in the provinces. The official spin praised her for her forethought – in fact, Wu had never much liked her siblings, and welcomed the chance to exile them.[2]

Meanwhile, the fallen empress and Xiao Liangdi remained confined in the palace grounds. Likely to have been an area roughly the size of a small apartment, off a small tiled yard, their place of imprisonment would have seemed relatively well appointed in the early days of their sentence. However, from the moment the gate was firmly bolted, conditions began to slide. No more servants brought baths or removed chamber pots; fresh clothes were a thing of the past. Without a constant coming and going of eunuchs and handmaidens, their courtyard incarceration swiftly became squalid and unpleasant.

Reared for their entire lives to pay attention to their looks, they had been stripped of all the expensive accoutrements of vanity. Suddenly, there were no dressers, make-up girls, coiffure experts or bath attendants. Instead, they were stuck with each other's company, broken only by the deliveries of food through the slot in the door barricade. In the year since the first accusations against them, their conditions had gradually worsened, until early 656, when their appearance was dishevelled and unkempt.

However, for as long as they were still alive, there was still hope. Not long after the enthronement of Wu as his empress, Gaozong accidentally wandered close to the pavilion where the two women were being held prisoner – considering his earlier happy 'accident' of meeting Wu at the Ganye convent, we may speculate that he went over there deliberately.

It is possible that he had been unaware of the conditions in which the two women were being kept. Assured that they had been 'dealt with', he could have assumed that they were simply idling away their days in one of the many hundreds of private palaces, not left to rot in an increasingly dirty compound. He may have even expected that life for them had gone on much as before. Instead, he found himself unable even to enter the place of their seclusion, forced to shout through the tiny food opening. In his haste, he forgot that they had been officially stripped of their titles, and called them Empress and Xiao Liangdi.

The Tang dynasty chronicles are not clear on who replied, but one of the weeping women answered him:

'It's You, Your Majesty! But we have been reduced to the status of slaves for our crimes. Why do You address us by our old titles?'

Gaozong, still in shock at the conditions, merely asked them if they had anything to say. Their reply was that, if he thought there was any chance of them escaping from their fate, he should rename their prison the Court of Reconsideration.

Time passed slowly for the two prisoners, until, a few days later, they heard men at the door of their cell. Someone was pulling away the bricks that barricaded them inside. For a moment, the ladies assumed that Gaozong had had a change of heart, and that, at the very least, their conditions would be improved. However, this turned out to be the cruellest trick of all, as the men at the door were revealed to be servants not of Gaozong, but of Wu. They revealed that they had been ordered to subject both to a hundred lashes – a punishment that could easily kill them.

The former empress refused to let her feelings show. Instead, she bowed three times, and said:

'I wish my former husband every happiness in the future. Bright Virtuous Wu has ensnared the love of His Majesty, nothing remains for me but death. Do as you will.'[3]

Xiao Liangdi, the Pure Concubine, did not accept her fate with such a serene air. She yelled at her captors:

'Wu is a treacherous fox, who has bewitched the Emperor and now sits on the throne. I hope I shall be reborn as a cat, and the bitch Wu as a rat, that I may bite out her throat.'

It is unclear whether Wu was around to hear any of this. Chronicles of the Tang dynasty merely record the meting-out of the women's punishment, after which their hands and feet were hacked off, their maimed extremities repeatedly smashed and broken, and their bleeding bodies dumped in vats of wine, where they took several days to die.

'Now those witches can get drunk to their bones,' Wu is supposed to have said, a strange comment with a meaning seeped in ironic retribution. 'Intoxicated unto the melting of the marrow' appears to have been a contemporary poetic term for an orgasm – Wu's chosen means of execution for her two bedchamber rivals was a brutally literal enactment of sexual ecstasy. The closest possible analogy in a modern English vernacular, deprived of such classical niceties, would be: 'Fuck them both to death.'[4]

Her final words to the two would-be sorceresses, spoken to them as their lives finally ebbed away, comprised the news of her decision regarding their posthumous names. Traditionally, people received 'temple names' designed to encapsulate their fortunes in their previous life, and to offer a direction for their next. Careful consultation was required in order to ensure the right level of good fortune and guidance. In the case of the former empress and the Pure Concubine, however, Wu was prepared to make a radical exception. She had decided that the former empress would be known in the afterlife simply as Python, while the Pure Concubine would henceforth be referred to as Owl. Such names, it was believed, would guarantee their reincarnation as the named animals, in what may have been a deliberate attempt by Wu to thwart the cat-curse uttered by Xiao Liangdi.[5]

Wu's position was now considerably stronger. Her eldest son, Li Hong, was now the heir to the throne, and she was pregnant with her third (or fourth) child, another boy. The former crown prince had been a son of another concubine, who had been adopted by the sonless Empress Wang in order to hang onto her position as chief wife. With the Empress Wang dead and dishonoured, the boy stood no chance, and he was stripped of his inheritance, given a made-up noble title and sent away to a provincial posting.[6] However, Wu remained haunted by the deaths of her rivals, and reported many nightmares and hauntings, in which she was convinced she was beset by bleeding apparitions in tattered, stained court gowns, their ankle-length hair matted and filthy through neglect. Wu was troubled enough by her guilt to order the banishment of all cats from the palace. Within a few months, she had decided that Chang'an itself was a bad location and persuaded her imperial husband to relocate the entire court 200 miles west.

Wu's superstitions may have been the most minor of considerations. There were plenty of other reasons to move the court to Luoyang, not the least its fame as a capital city for several earlier dynasties, its prominence in the Buddhist world and its more central location, affording better access to eastern China. There may even have been concerns that Chang'an was too exposed to attack – foreign traders were not the only people who might use the Silk Road as a means of transportation, and Gaozong may have wanted to put a little more distance between himself and the front line of his ongoing wars in central Asia. However, the reason traditionally cited is Wu's fear of vengeful apparitions, particularly the two women whose agonising deaths she had ordered.

While Chang'an remained an important city on the Silk Road, it was abandoned by the court of the Tang dynasty for much of the next four decades. Gaozong and Wu had other business further east, and it seems that neither wanted to linger in a city that had seen bloodshed in the palace for three generations.

Wu's years of continual pregnancy finally came to an end, making it possible for her both to join the exodus to Luoyang and to deal with the rest of her enemies in the court. Anyone whose rise to power had been achieved through the sponsorship of the former empress was in a precarious position, but some of the old guard hoped that Wu's cronies would be the first to put a foot wrong.

They almost got the scandal they wanted, when Li Yifu, the 'sword in a smile' minister who had first suggested the elevation of Wu to empress, was implicated in a scandal of his own. Developing a perverse obsession with a beautiful female prisoner in the local jail, he had leaned on the governor to secure her release and then set her up as his mistress. When Li Yifu was subsequently investigated for corruption, it became apparent that the entire case would rest on the prison governor's testimony, although such a realisation proved to be of little use to the courts when the governor was found dead in his office.

Although the governor appeared to have hanged himself, investigators were convinced that the 'suicide' was far too convenient for Li Yifu not to be involved in some way. Li Yifu was accused in the presence of Gaozong, but simply remained silent and did not answer any accusations. When Gaozong did not speak either, and with the sole witness for the prosecution already dead, the case collapsed, and with it the reputation of one of the Tang dynasty's greatest investigators, who was demoted and banished.

Li Yifu, it was widely believed, had literally got away with murder – Wu's supporters were untouchable, whereas those who had opposed her now risked betrayal at every turn. In a ludicrous series of events, the upstanding minister Han Yuan petitioned for the return of the banished Chu Suiliang, who had been sent away to run a military outpost far to the south. Instead of receiving a favourable reply, Han Yuan and his associate Lai Ji were accused of conspiring with the distant governor to stage a revolt, and of forging documents to get Chu Suiliang moved to a military town with better prospects for revolt and revolution. In fact, Chu was probably quite blameless, as were his supposed co-conspirators, since the 'forged' order was most likely to have come from Wu herself, who conveniently forgot to mention her involvement when the matter came to trial. No explanation was offered as to how Chu Suiliang's troops would have organised a rebellion, or indeed how such an uprising would have presented any threat to a capital 1,000 miles away.

Chu Suiliang's punishment was yet another posting, so far to the south that it was outside China proper in Thanh Hoa, in what is now Vietnam. On a frontier notorious for deprivation and disease, Chu Suiliang sent one last begging letter to the court, hoping to remind Gaozong that he had been one of the crucial supporters of Gaozong during the selection process to make him crown prince, but such ancient history was of little concern now. Gaozong ignored Chu Suiliang's pleas, and by 658 the ageing minister had died.[7] Lai Ji and Han Yuan, who had once begged the emperor to be allowed to retire, were also banished to the provinces, the former to a town south of the Yangtze, the latter to the far south-eastern island of Hainan, with sentences that specified they should never be allowed to set foot in the capital again.

The move to Luoyang presented Wu with further opportunities to purge her staff. Her supporters also searched for every available opportunity to strike back at those who had opposed them before the elevation of their patroness. One, Xu Jingcong, heard rumours of a secret society formed by the palace librarian, Wei Jifeng, and a few other employees. The exact nature of the society is unclear – it may have been nothing so dangerous as a few friends meeting for drinks and chess. But, considering the past behaviour of Tang dynasty princes, the news that associates of minor officials and princelings were meeting in secret sounded to some suspiciously like the formation of a faction, ready to agitate for some unwelcome change – the recall of an exiled minister, perhaps, or the return of one of the banished princes. Whatever the group's motives, a victorious Wu supporter would immediately suspect the worst – that their plot would be aimed at somehow undermining Wu's authority.

Xu Jingcong was tasked with investigating, and subjected the librarian to a series of interrogations and torments so threatening that the poor man was driven to suicide. He was foiled in his first attempt, but successful in his second, saving him from further investigation by Xu Jingcong, but also providing his tormentor with the opportunity to make new accusations.

It was, Xu Jingcong reported to Emperor Gaozong and Empress Wu, something of a surprise that such a low and relatively unimportant official should have so much to hide. There was only one possible explanation, that Wei Jifeng had taken his own life in an effort to protect the real mastermind, a conspirator far higher up the chain of command. Knowing that only he and the dead Wei Jifeng knew the contents of their last conversation before the librarian's death, Xu Jingcong even claimed that his victim had confessed who was really behind the secret society – the first minister, Zhangsun Wuji.

If ever a sign was needed that the old order was gone for ever, it was this accusation. Zhangsun Wuji was one of the last of the old warriors who had fought for the foundation of the Tang dynasty, a lifelong companion of the late Taizong Emperor, and Gaozong's maternal uncle. A veteran of numerous battles, from the Gate of the Dark Warrior to the recent invasion of Korea, he was a true statesman, and his suspicions about Empress Wu were well known. It was Zhangsun who had presented such opposition to her elevation, and Zhangsun who continued to haunt court occasions like Banquo's ghost, making it abundantly clear that he regarded new ministers like

Xu Jingcong as little more than uppity fops. None would have dared challenge Zhangsun while Taizong was alive; now he was accused of conspiring against Gaozong himself, on the flimsiest of evidence.

As a newly promoted minister and one of the prime architects of the 'family-matter' solution, Xu Jingcong had endured particular scorn from the elder statesman, and now took his revenge. Reporting the findings of his interrogation, he frightened Gaozong with tales of ancient precedents. There was simply no time, he lied, to present Gaozong with all the evidence, of which there was plenty. Instead, it was his sad duty to reveal that the librarian's society had only been a front for a much greater conspiracy. Xu Jingcong had uncovered a dagger aimed at the heart of Gaozong's empire, a cancer that had already spread further than anyone expected, and time was of the essence. Xu Jingcong claimed that there could be literally mere minutes to spare before Zhangsun realised that his plans had been discovered and leapt into action.

'Zhangsun Wuji', he warned, 'was instrumental in the incident at the Gate of the Dark Warrior, and has exerted the authority of a prime minister for thirty years. Once he learns that his plot has been discovered, his reaction could be dangerous. Your Majesty must capture and execute him at once.'[8]

Gaozong protested that it was hard to believe, but Xu Jingcong pressed on, with the assistance of Empress Wu. There were plenty of precedents in history, of long-serving uncles usurping the throne of their nephews. Why, within living memory there was the sad tale of the last days of the Sui dynasty, when many of the imperial family had been massacred by a turncoat. If it could happen to Gaozong's second cousins, it could happen to Gaozong, unless he acted quickly.

With great reluctance, the weeping Gaozong was persuaded. He did not even call Zhangsun Wuji in to answer for himself. Instead, he took the advice of Xu Jingcong and sent officers to arrest Zhangsun Wuji, strip him of his rank and titles, and transport him to the distant southern frontier. The fact that he had not ordered his immediate execution suggests that he still wanted to see the evidence. This, however, only allowed Empress Wu's supporters to gain even greater ground. Xu Jingcong produced a long list of co-conspirators, some of whom were already dead, and many others already in exile. By all means, said Xu Jingcong, the government should recall these suspects to explain themselves, although he secretly made sure that the trip home, arduous enough at the best of times, was made unbearably difficult for them. Han Yuan, who had only just reached the place of his distant exile after several months' travel, received a message soon after his arrival, ordering him to come back; the effort involved would kill him long before he reached Chang'an.[9]

Xu Jingcong ensured that, in the absence of any actual evidence, there would be plenty more guilt by association. Zhangsun Wuji reached the place of his exile, only to be hounded into suicide by interrogators who followed him in order to obtain further details of his alleged plot. As soon as Zhangsun hanged himself, Xu Jingcong took the news as further proof of his guilt, and dispatched executioners to meet other suspects on the road. They were stopped in their tracks, informed that their guilt was no longer a matter of debate and beheaded. Considering the distances involved and the speed of communications, it seems remarkably suspicious that news of the suicide of a man in the far south of China could somehow reach Chang'an, and then head south again in time to intercept Xu Jingcong's other victims. It would seem, instead, that Xu Jingcong was ready to act on Zhangsun's 'suicide' before news of it could ever reach him. If there were any questions asked about his supreme efficiency, Empress Wu was there to smooth things over with the distraught Gaozong. Meanwhile, her cronies hunted down all the alleged 'conspirators'. While the evidence may have been cobbled together in an extremely doubtful manner, the executions were carried out with great thoroughness. In the case of Han Yuan, Wu's men even dug up his grave, to verify that he had died before they could kill him themselves.[10] By the end of the purges, potential victims were doing their tormentors' work for them. Lai Ji, once a court minister, then forced into southern exile, then transferred to the far west, then accused of fomenting revolt in his new posting, finally gave up. The old soldier left his armour behind, drew his sword and led a suicide attack on a Turkish camp, plainly wishing to die. His last words were: 'With this, I repay the blessings of the state.'[11]

Empress Wu's supporters had now successfully removed all the elder statesmen who stood in their way, destroying the network set up by the dying Taizong to ensure his son an untroubled reign. Gaozong now ruled without any 'institutional memory', with few of the old guard surviving to advise him with the benefit of hindsight. Instead, he was surrounded by new appointees, many of whose claim on promotion had been founded on their support for the elevation of Wu to empress.[12]

None of this, however, immediately affected the standing of the Tang dynasty abroad. The campaigns against the Turks in the west had extended the borders of China far into central Asia, dominating more of the Silk Road than ever before. States as far afield as Kashmir and Nepal recognised the supremacy of the Tang dynasty. In the provinces, where the system and appointees of the previous emperor were still largely in place, things were running smoothly. It was only at the centre of power, at its very head, that the danger lay.

Gaozong and Empress Wu kept their court on the move in the late 650s, in a processional through the neighbouring provinces that presumably ensured that the majesty of the Tang dynasty was still being noticed closer to home. The movement, looping out from Luoyang into other major metropolises, including a stay back amid the ghosts of Chang'an, also served to keep foreign ambassadors on their toes. When Japanese diplomats arrived with gifts and greetings from the land of the rising sun, they were kept on the move with the court, thereby ensuring that they did not immediately head back to Japan. Although this may have seemed like an extravagant and welcoming court protocol, it was also designed to keep them from getting home in time to report Gaozong's latest project, a major new assault on Korea.

Empress Wu made the most of the moving court, scoring impressive points in her hometown by actually bringing the entire court there, and lording it over her former neighbours and friends in a banquet at her old home, with her imperial husband in attendance.

All, however, was not well. Although he had not endured his father's harsh, tough youth on the front line, Gaozong was still a weak and sickly man. He had been troubled all his life by recurring spells of dizziness, described in contemporary accounts as *feng-xuan*, or 'gusts of confusion'. Although it is impossible to say for sure, modern authors usually translate the term as 'epilepsy', although Gaozong's own medics identified more unusual symptoms, including temporary blindness. Since Gaozong remained cogent in the early stages, but was unable to read and unsteady on his feet, one might also diagnose relapsing – remitting multiple sclerosis.

Whatever these spells may have been, late in 660 they took a turn for the worst. Shortly after returning to Luoyang from his visit to Wu's hometown, Gaozong suffered a debilitating attack, with effects more similar to a stroke than an epileptic fit.

Wu refused to leave Gaozong's side when doctors were summoned to examine him, and fumed silently behind her modesty screen while three surgeons examined him. One timidly suggested that Gaozong was suffering from a build-up of blood and, offering a typically medieval remedy, suggested bleeding the Emperor to relieve the pressure. The distraught Wu flew into a rage, yelling that any talk of cutting the imperial flesh was punishable by death. It was Gaozong himself who stood up for the physicians, reminding his wife that they were only doing their job.

In a strangely human moment in the saga of Empress Wu, she is recorded collapsing in tears when Gaozong announced that the bloodletting had indeed cleared his vision a little. Breaking the protocol of remaining behind the screen, she personally approached the doctors to thank them with jewels she had brought in her own hands. It is palpably not the act of a cruel and heartless despot – considering Wu's previous behaviour, one might almost expect her to have been personally responsible for the Emperor's illness in the first place, but it would appear that she was genuinely concerned for his well-being. But, as the Emperor began his slow recovery, he continued to suffer from losses of balance and an inability to focus his eyes. Before long, he asked his beloved Wu to help him read over his court circulars and proclamations and help him with imperial business. Graciously, she accepted.

FIVE

The Supreme Sacrifice

Seventy miles to the west of Chang'an (modern Xi'an), is the Famen temple, an ancient repository of Buddhist lore and treasures, sitting on the famous Silk Road to India and the west. Established long before the Tang dynasty, it was dominated in later centuries by a towering Ming dynasty pagoda, which finally collapsed in 1981 after heavy rains and ground tremors. As restoration work began, workers discovered its last secret in 1987, a richly decorated underground vault containing the most sacred of Buddhist relics.

The Famen temple had always been said to be the repository of some of Buddha's finger bones, four of which turned out to be safely intact among the many other treasures from the secret vault. Locals, it seems, had known of it, but conspired to keep it secret during the upheavals of the twentieth century. It was sealed up before the Japanese invasion in 1939, and left mercifully unopened during Mao's Cultural Revolution, in which Red Guards were

YUE – MOON
During Wu's reign, the word for 'moon' was changed to a partial enclosure around the character for 'putting forth' – possibly 'that which rules birthing'?

warded off by the sight of a Buddhist monk, who burned himself to death before them.

The Ming pagoda is now restored, while the temple precincts have been remodelled to look the way they would have done in the Tang dynasty, when the temple enjoyed imperial patronage.

Gaozong's grandfather, on his hasty retirement from office, had arrived in the last days of his reign to greet the monks as a fellow Buddhist. He worshipped at the temple, made donations of funds and treasure, and thereby established a new tradition – that, once each generation, the ruler of China would come to pay homage to the relics of Buddha.

Famen's richly appointed modern museum has large-scale paintings depicting the visits of early Tang monarchs.[1] The first shows Gaozong's grandfather, the Gaozu Emperor, wearing a monk's robes but carried in imperial pomp towards the temple. The second, set sometime in the 660s, features the arrival of Gaozong himself. He is depicted as a frail, bearded man, supported by fretting attendants, barely able to walk, struggling along the last few metres of his pilgrimage, needing help even to climb the steps. Rank after rank of courtiers and officials are arrayed behind him, waiting expectantly. Standing off to one side, in ostentatious finery, seemingly with her own entourage, is Empress Wu. She stares haughtily at her husband as he makes the agonising journey towards the temple. A careless viewer might even assume that Wu, standing tall with a commanding presence, was the subject of the image, and not the hunched, robed figure edging across the foreground.

The nature of Gaozong's disability in the 660s is unclear. He does not appear to have lost the power of speech, nor his sexual potency, since Wu would bear him two more children, a boy in 662 and a girl around 664.[2] However, Gaozong came to rely heavily on Wu in the early 660s, as she became the conduit through which all court documents passed. No proposal or memorial would be 'read' by Gaozong unless Wu had read it to him, giving her supreme control over the information he had when he made his decisions. Gaozong still had the last word, but Wu controlled every syllable of his vocabulary.

The chief concern of the Tang court in the early 660s was the new invasion of Korea, undertaken in part to build on the 645 campaign that had cost the late emperor Taizong so dearly. Preparations had been under way for over a year, but Gaozong's illness struck just as the campaign entered the active phase. The excuse this time was a request for help from the south-eastern Korean state of Silla, which was facing attacks from its neighbours Koguryo and Paekche. Paekche, once an ally and supposed tributary of Tang China, was now flouting its disobedience.

The invasion plan was only a slight modification of that used fifteen years earlier by Taizong. Su Dingfang, a veteran of many battles in central Asia, was put in charge of a fleet of troop transports, which crossed the Yellow Sea in mid-660, smashed through defences at the mouth of the Kum River on the Paekche coast, and then sailed upriver to Sabi. Joined by allied troops who had marched overland from Silla in the east, Su Dingfang's troops captured both the Paekche capital and its royal family, whose capitulation brought the entire Paekche region under Tang control.

With the approximate area of modern South Korea now under Tang control, the Chinese army was able to attack the northern kingdom of Koguryo on two fronts. Su Dingfang returned to China to raise a new army, purportedly of Chinese conscripts, although he appears to have recruited many of his troops from the families of Korean expatriates, who had gratefully fled their own kingdom as 'prisoners' of Taizong's army a generation earlier. Su then took his second force back to the Korean peninsula, sailing up the Taedong River and laying siege to Pyongyang itself in late summer 661.

The Tang troops became increasingly bogged down in Korea. Gains made the previous year in Paekche were far from sturdy, and occupation troops were forced to deal with a series of uprisings. Su's well-used fleet of transport ships was soon back again with 7,000 reinforcements from Shandong, while Liu Rengui, a resourceful commander in allied Silla, was obliged to mount several expeditions in 662 with both local and Chinese troops to come to the aid of beleaguered occupying forces in Paekche and Koguryo.

By 662 Su Dingfang had been forced to quit the region around Pyongyang to fight insurgency elsewhere in Korea. Meanwhile, the Paekche rebels had successfully sought aid from Japan, leading to a major naval battle at the mouth of the Kum River between Chinese and Japanese ships. With the Japanese defeated, the Chinese finally felt able to proclaim themselves the masters of both Silla and Paekche, and ready to deal with Koguryo to the north.[3]

Back at the Chinese court, Gaozong was still recovering – he appears to have regained most of his faculties by the time of the defeat of the Japanese fleet, but, for much of the Korean conflict, it was Wu who was running the Chinese government. The annals of the Tang dynasty report that Gaozong found his empress to be an able administrator, more than capable of running things without any input from Gaozong at all, and that, even as the Emperor regained his strength, Wu was left to make more decisions. Circumstantial evidence, particularly the birth of Wu's younger children, suggests that Wu and Gaozong enjoyed much time together, and that the Empress kept herself by his side, even when Gaozong's illness had faded.

As Wu might have argued, sex with her was an important part of Gaozong's continued recovery. We can see elements of her character in the allegorical Tang dynasty tale found in Sun Wei's *Biographies of the Goddesses*. Claiming to refer to an ancient story, it features a warrior struck low by a debilitating illness, who prays for recovery to the image of a female deity. The goddess herself appears and attempts to seduce him, only to have the warrior resist her advances. It is only after his death that the disappointed nymph reports to the Emperor that her *yin* essence could have saved the man, whose faltering *yang* would have been bolstered and improved by sex with her.[4]

A cryptic comment in the Tang histories refers to Wu's willingness to 'abase her body and endure shame in order to conform to the Emperor's will'. Whatever she let the Emperor do to her in the bedroom, it gave her power over him in the throne room, although it is difficult to work out what it was she would do that the Emperor could not get from any of his other concubines.[5] Considering the detailed sexual manuals available to Chinese couples since ancient times, the prim attitude of Wu's critics seems strange. There is a suggestion, at least partly supported by later catalogues of Tang erotica, that Wu may have enjoyed sharing her husband with other women. She is alleged to be the central figure in an erotic illustration, now lost, depicting an emperor having sex with a woman who is supported and assisted by two serving-girls. A note to the picture suggests it is a 'secret dalliance' (*bixi*), known only to the inhabitants of the Emperor's harem, but it does seem remarkably tame to induce such scandal. Emperors had, after all, been enjoying sex with multiple partners for centuries, and bisexuality was no surprise among the lonely women of the harems of many dynasties.[6]

Another possibility may lie in a more technical issue – the traditional Chinese medical belief that sex was beneficial to emperors only if certain rules were followed. Multiple sexual partners were required, both to ensure propagation of the dynasty and to prevent one concubine achieving any hold over him. The pseudoscientific explanation for this involved the female essence, or *yin*, and the male essence, or *yang*. *Yin* essence was of great value in maintaining an emperor's health and vitality, but, in order for the sex magic to work, he would need to bring his female partner to orgasm without having one himself. Female ecstasy would impart *yin* essence to her sexual partner, while abstention from ejaculating would allow the emperor to maintain his own *yang*. This, claimed the sexual manuals, was the real reason for an emperor having multiple sexual partners. However, as one manual put it: 'If a man continually has intercourse with one and the same woman, her Yin essence will become weak, and she will be of little advantage to the man.'[7]

Could this be the terrible activity that has led to centuries of erotic supposition about Empress Wu? Prurient public interest might have made Wu a legendary figure of erotic excesses, but much of the scandal about her may have been based on a misunderstanding. Those who criticised her during her lifetime may have been leaning, like Liu Rengui, on traditional protocols. If this were the case, then her true offence, such as it was, was her continuous presence by Gaozong's side, to the presumed exclusion of many other sexual partners. To a Chinese physician of the period, Wu's prolonged dalliance with Gaozong was not merely unseemly, it was also dangerous. Gaozong was a sick man, still recovering from his 'gusts of confusion', while she was taking far more of his semen than was her right, turning her from a source of *yin* essence into a veritable succubus, draining the precious life force from his body, even as her own *yin* essence continued to fall. Wu's terrible, unnameable perversion, the source of centuries of speculation and reams of pornography, may have been the one concept that would have truly shocked and scandalised Tang dynasty courtiers: *monogamy*.

As Wu's personal grasp on power tightened, she was able to sacrifice a few of her earlier pawns. One such victim was Li Yifu, the corrupt 'sword-in-a-smile' minister, whose floundering attempts to keep his job had initiated the downfall of Gaozong's former wife, and who had proved to be untouchable in the scandal over the pretty prisoner. Believing himself still to enjoy protection from Empress Wu, Li Yifu had continued his old ways, as had his sons, whose behaviour came to the attention of Gaozong.

In what began as a quiet word, presumably with Wu in silent attendance behind her screen, Gaozong suggested that Li Yifu should rein in his sons' excesses before they led to trouble. Li Yifu, however, made no attempt to answer the accusations, instead demanding to know who had dared to slander him to the throne. He then left the throne room without apology, plainly expecting Wu to smooth things over with her husband. Instead, Wu did nothing, and before long Li Yifu was convicted of gross misconduct and banished to live out his few remaining years far to the south.

While Wu remained confident in her hold over Gaozong, there are signs that the disapproval of others was not unknown to him. Liu Rengui, the same general who fought so valiantly in the Korean campaign, proved that his bravery did not merely extend to the battlefield.

Wu and Gaozong had taken to spending their days canoodling on a large couch, surrounded by large mirrors in order to allow them to view their lovemaking from multiple angles. General Liu arrived for an audience with Gaozong and found the Emperor sitting alone on the couch. It was a rare moment when Wu was nowhere to be seen, and General Liu took his chance. Noting the multiple images of Gaozong, doubled and redoubled in the mirrors, General Liu said: 'There are no two suns in the sky, nor two rulers on the earth. Now your servant sees all around numerous Sons of Heaven. Is this not a sinister omen?'[8] Liu did not mention Wu by name, nor did he criticise Gaozong. He carefully hid behind a question about a matter of protocol, not suggesting anything directly, but planting the thought in Gaozong's mind that images of multiple emperors might be tempting fate with allusions to pretenders and revolt.

It seems that Wu's hold over Gaozong lessened when she was pregnant, since it would have inevitably led to his occasional seeking of alternative sexual partners from among his many, and presumably now rather idle, concubines. In particular, Wu seems to have had a very personal, physical charisma about her – Gaozong might have been able to think for himself when Wu was absent, but was powerless to resist her when she was in the same room.

This peculiar relationship left Wu vulnerable to attack, and Gaozong to suggestion, whenever Wu was indisposed. Around the time of the birth of Wu's youngest child, her daughter Princess Taiping, a minister attempted to lodge an official protest about Empress Wu and almost succeeded.

A palace eunuch presented evidence to Gaozong that Empress Wu had been secretly seeing a Daoist priest, admitting him into her chambers and offering him courtesies unavailable to the highest minister. The priest was permitted the run of the palace, and no guard was able to stop him. Although the eunuch could not be sure, he believed that the Daoist was performing ritual sorcery. Considering that Wu either had just given birth or was about to, it is entirely possible that these 'sorceries' were aimed at securing the health of the mother and baby, but Gaozong and many of his courtiers still recalled the embarrassment of the fall of his former wife. On the assumption that the spells being cast by the Daoist were malicious in nature, it was only a small jump of pseudo-logic to suggest that, since they were being cast within the chambers of the Emperor's own palace, Gaozong was their target.

Gaozong called upon one Shangguan Yi for consultation. Tellingly, the minister was a former adviser to Gaozong's discredited and exiled son, the former crown prince who was eking out a miserable existence far to the south. This should have been a warning sign for Gaozong, who may not have realised that the eunuch who presented the original evidence was also a former servant of the exiled prince. Had Wu been anywhere nearby, she would have sniffed out the implied conspiracy immediately, but she still remained elsewhere.

Shangguan Yi confirmed Gaozong's worse fears, claiming that Empress Wu did appear to be sponsoring a series of sorcerous curses upon the throne – considering Gaozong's ill health of recent years, such an accusation would immediately have been seen as further evidence that Gaozong's 'gusts of confusion' had been magically induced. Still troubled by the affair of the late Empress Wang, whom he still believed to have similarly conspired against him, Gaozong lost his temper. In this case, Wu's own achievements worked against her, since her elevation had set a precedent for removal of an empress. No longer would Gaozong have to sit through endless meetings and discussions on whether an empress could or should be unseated. Instead, he ordered Shangguan Yi immediately to draft a document dismissing Empress Wu from her lofty position.

However, while Wu was not present at the meeting between Gaozong and Shangguan Yi, their conversation was sure to reach her. She found Gaozong with the decree laid out in front of him at his table of documents, requiring only an imperial seal for it to become a public proclamation. But any bravery or independence Gaozong may have exhibited in her absence immediately collapsed. While Wu protested her innocence and, once that was established, berated him for his lack of trust, he pleaded with his irate wife to forgive him. Eventually, he blamed the entire affair on Shangguan Yi's advice.

It was time for Wu to set her minions on her enemies. Xu Jingcong, the faithful tool of Wu's ambition, had successfully brought down ministers in the past with no evidence at all. The previous associations of Shangguan Yi, the eunuch and the exiled prince presented him with an embarrassment of accusatory riches, which he exploited to the full. The palace conspirators were flung in prison, where they eventually died. Shangguan's family were enslaved and their property confiscated, and, far to the south, the exiled prince was ordered to commit suicide. Wu had successfully headed off another plot against her and ensured that her own son, Li Hong, was still the heir to the throne.[9]

Wu had not merely eliminated another set of enemies at the palace. The Tang dynasty annals also identified the fall of Shangguan as the final defeat of Gaozong. Never again would Gaozong be able to mount any successful opposition to his wife's will – although they would continue to argue on occasion, future attempts by Gaozong to rein in Wu's excesses would meet with ministerial obfuscation from courtiers who were largely loyal to Wu. Wu now controlled new appointments to the court and ensured that, as the old guard died off, they were replaced with officials loyal to her:

> From this moment forward, whenever the Emperor held court, the Empress attended behind a curtain. There was no matter of state, great or small, which did not reach her ears. All true power under Heaven resided in her: demotion or promotion, life or death, reward or punishment. The Son of Heaven sat with folded hands. In court and country, they were called the Two Sages.[10]

After the dangers presented by Shangguan, Wu would not make the mistake of becoming pregnant again, and she ensured that she could remain by Gaozong's side constantly. She even became quietly complicit in Gaozong's latest sexual conquest. Wu, it seems, was no longer enough for the Emperor, and he had recently begun a clandestine affair with a palace lady by the name of Guochu. The affair was hushed up because it would have created yet another public scandal – Guochu was Wu's niece, daughter of Helan. Not content with flouting Confucian etiquette by taking his late father's concubine, Gaozong could also now boast of having had sex with a mother and daughter – although, since Helan had passed away by this point, not at the same time. To add insult to injury, Guochu was using Wu as a means of access to the palace, arriving ostensibly to pay her respects to the Empress, only to sneak off for sex with Gaozong. Although Wu was unhappy with Gaozong's new attachment, initially she made no move to stop it – it could have been more convenient to her as a lever to use against him in future. For now, Guochu was a useful distraction for Gaozong, although Wu plainly did not intend to allow her to stay around forever. It would not have been lost on her, for example, that she herself had once seemed to be a harmless sexual diversion for Gaozong, only to turn on her sponsor Empress Wang. Wu would certainly not allow Guochu similarly to turn the tables on her.

Wu was still not completely safe from attack. She might have defeated several enemies who attempted to use hearsay against her, but protocol could still be an effective weapon. One possible charge, often levelled against imperial wives, was that their influence over their husbands could often lead to the creation of a new faction – relatives of the Empress, riding her coat-tails to government office. In order to demonstrate her wish to keep the Tang dynasty free from unwelcome influences, Wu gave orders for members of her own family to receive postings far from the capital.

There was, of course, more to the story than that. On paper, the removal of Wu's cousins and nephews to far provinces seemed like the act of a true stateswoman. In fact, Wu was settling a personal score, and doing so in a manner that made her appear to have the country's best interests at heart.

Wu and her sisters had never got along with their half-brothers. The boys had been the children of their father's first wife, and resentment seemed to be mutual between the two halves of the family. The sons never liked their stepmother, or the unwelcome female relatives she had brought into the world, and the irritation must have grown particularly great after the hated middle sister had somehow become empress. Such a fact adds extra spice to the story of Wu bringing the travelling imperial court to her ancestral home – it must have made her half-brothers furious. In the aftermath, Wu's mother had taken the opportunity to goad one of her stepson's children about it, and the boy had replied with an insult aimed at both her and Wu. By sending the men of the Wu family away to the provinces, or, in one case, keeping him there, Wu was enacting revenge for many childhood torments.

However, showing off to her family was not enough for Wu. With the Emperor obeying her every word, her family chastised and her son as heir apparent, she wanted to show off to the whole world. This continued desire for approval, it is believed, was to lead to her participation in the most powerful religious ceremony in Chinese history.

The 'Feng-Shan', as it was known, was an intensely complex, powerful and, above all, expensive religious ceremony, conducted by emperors at the foot and summit of the sacred Mount Tai in eastern China. The Feng and the Shan comprised dual reports direct to Heaven and Earth, in which the Emperor, instead of simply offering seasonal sacrifices and bowing to his deities and ancestors, would actually lodge formal announcements of his successes. The Feng-Shan represented the pinnacle of imperial achievement, and as such could not even be attempted until an emperor was sure that his domain was safe, secure, happy and prosperous. Ancient folktales, set during China's legendary Golden Age, make several dozen mentions of the Feng-Shan, making it seem relatively commonplace. However, incidences in recorded history were considerably more unusual – by the Tang dynasty, there had been only three verifiable Feng-Shan sacrifices, and the last of those had been six hundred years previously.[11]

In the centuries since the collapse of the Han dynasty, China had been too fragmented for any single ruler to lay claim to true success. Emperors might have seized control on earth, but none dared to put a Feng-Shan ceremony into motion. Doing so without being absolutely sure of having the Mandate of Heaven was hubris in the extreme and liable to lead to misfortune and calamity. During the short-lived Sui dynasty that had preceded the Han, two emperors had discussed the possibility of holding the Feng-Shan sacrifice. They had even attempted dry runs at it, going through the motions of several aspects of the ceremony, without committing themselves to the full set of required rituals.

Both Gaozong's father and grandfather had toyed with the idea of arranging a Feng-Shan sacrifice, but neither had taken matters all the way. The Emperor Gaozu, unassuming at the best of times, had deemed himself to be unworthy. So, too, had Taizong during his youth, although as he aged he appeared to be seduced by the idea. He was, however, talked out of it twice by his trusted minister Wei Zheng, and once by the appearance of an ominous comet.[12] When the subject next came up, it enjoyed the support of most of Taizong's ministers, but the Emperor's sense of worth had been so greatly deflated by the failure of the Korean campaign of 645 that he had lost interest. When he could not even chastise a usurper in a neighbouring vassal state, it was clearly not his time to proclaim to heaven that he was the uncontested lord of the world.

The Empress Wu had no such scruples. She was proud enough of her husband's achievement to think a Feng-Shan sacrifice was a worthy crown to his career and seems to have been agitating for it since her promotion to empress in 655. The first sign of preparations came in 659 when Gaozong appointed Xu Jingcong to look into the possibility of holding the Feng-Shan. Since Xu Jingcong was Empress Wu's staunchest ally in court, it seems obvious where the real impetus may have originated.

Xu worked periodically on the project throughout the early 660s, during which period Gaozong was in no fit state to leave his bedroom, let alone walk up a mountain to report to the gods. When China enjoyed five bountiful harvests in a row, it was taken as another sign that the time was right, although exactly how the dynasty should act was still unclear.[13] The Feng-Shan sacrifices occurred so rarely that there were few records of what they comprised. Since Taizong's ministers had already conducted extensive research and consultation during the 630s, their reports were dusted off for examination. Curiously, the Feng-Shan ceremonies were not mentioned at all in the classic court manual of protocol, the famous *Book of Rites* said to have been compiled by Confucius himself. This left many ministers doubtful that the Feng-Shan rites were an ancient custom at all, and led many to suspect that they were some sort of vulgar super-ritual, cobbled together from half-remembered folktales and bloated extrapolations of pre-existing ceremonies.

However, Wu pressed her case, expecting that, with his health still in doubt, Gaozong would ask her to assist him in the supreme sacrifice just as she assisted him in the courtroom. Eventually, late in 662, ministers set a tentative date of 664 for the Feng-Shan, only to cancel it within weeks, citing the ongoing Korean campaign as one of several factors affecting current worthiness. By 664, however, the plan was set in motion, and the court diary included a new addition. In 665 the court would set out from Luoyang to the east, beginning a long journey across newly built roads and renovated bridges, with its ultimate destination the sacred Mount Tai. In early 666 Gaozong was scheduled to carry out the Feng-Shan ceremony.

It was a colossal undertaking. Not only did the route need to be planned in advance for maximum ease and comfort, but witnesses needed to be summoned from all over the known world. Nor could any of the attendees burden the local population – on this occasion, the entire court procession would have to be self-sustaining, as, if its passing caused stress or discomfort to inhabitants of the surrounding region, their ill-will might ruin the ceremony.

Gaozong and Empress Wu spent several days preparing for the ceremony in a retreat at the base of Mount Tai, beginning with 'rest and relaxation' followed by 'intense seclusion' – likely to have meant three days of sexual abstinence, which, for that couple, would have been tough.

The ceremony itself, based upon the researches conducted by ministers for Gaozong's father, took several days. A preliminary sacrifice at the base of Mount Tai would alert the spirits to the coming big event – that is, assuming that any local deities had not noticed that their sacred mountain had transformed into a religious building site for weeks before the occasion. The Emperor was then obliged to ascend the mountain on foot – a crucial part of the ceremony, and one that earlier celebrants had flouted to their cost. Considering his stroke and recovery, it was also a peculiarly cruel thing to force upon him, but he agreed to do it.

Once at the summit, he would make further sacrifices at a giant altar, before ceremonially burying his report – several massive jade slabs, inscribed with the achievements of his dynasty and the state of the empire. The slabs were to be slotted into a specially designed stone coffin and then entombed in sacred earth, symbolically making Mount Tai just that little bit higher than it had been before the Emperor's arrival.

At the beginning of 666, the players in the ritual had all assembled, undergoing varying degrees of purification and rehearsing their roles in the great religious drama about to unfold. Ambassadors from every vassal state of Tang China had gathered at Mount Tai to act as witnesses of their ruler's greatness, along with prisoners from Gaozong's recent territorial conquests, whose spirits would be offered as symbolic sacrifices to the gods. It was only once everything was ready to go, with no hope of turning back without massive loss of imperial face, that Empress Wu raised a point of order.

They were, she observed, just about to get everything wrong and call disaster down upon her dynasty. Wu argued, first to Gaozong, and, once he acquiesced, to Gaozong's ministers, that the Feng-Shan ceremony had never been correctly held before. Court protocol had missed one vital aspect, which was that the Emperor and his officials were physically qualified to perform only half of it – the sacrifice to Heaven from the mountaintop. This, Wu argued, was fine, because Heaven was masculine: a *yang* element attended by male spirits. Earth, however, was unquestionably *yin*, a female element attended by female spirits, and, for the Feng-Shan sacrifice truly to work, the Earth sacrifice at the bottom of the mountain would have to be carried out by women.[14]

Said Wu:

For I notice that at the worship of the Earth[,] the spirits to share the offerings are the [ghosts of the] previous empresses, while the service is rendered by the men ministers; this in the opinion of your humble wife may be due to a lack of forethought . . . Moreover, one does not suppose that the spirits of the empresses

84

will condescend to show themselves in men's presence; it is as against common sense as it is inconsistent with the august conception of the sacred functions.[15]

We may only speculate why Wu had neglected to bring this up beforehand. But she had cast-iron arguments in her favour, not the least in the facetious suggestion that previous Feng-Shan sacrifices had all been incorrect. If they had been performed correctly, she argued, then the dynasties that performed them would surely have been truly perfect. If they had been truly perfect, they would never have lost the Mandate of Heaven, and the Tang dynasty would never have come into being. When this was put to Gaozong's ministers of protocol, some reluctantly conceded that Empress Wu had a point – ancient rituals were distinctly divided into male and female ceremonies, and it did seem logical that the supreme sacrificial ritual should require the participation of equal male and female celebrants. It was one of the greatest victories in Wu's career, insinuating her presence into a ritual that had heretofore been the sole territory of great emperors. When Gaozong reported to Heaven, Wu would now be at his side, in ceremony as in the court, as his nominal equal but actual superior.

Wu's stance on the ceremony had other implications. Just as the Emperor had male assistants for his part of the rituals, Wu required women to act as her servants. Celebrants were hastily drafted from the entourages of other attendees, the wives of ambassadors and the Emperor's serving girls. As the Emperor's part of the ceremony finished, the menfolk were obliged to clear the mountain, and forced to watch from a distance. Eunuchs carrying parasols and long silk screens walked on either side of the women – whether for modesty or to protect them from the elements is unclear. The women then commenced the Earth ritual of the Feng-Shan sacrifice, offering food and wine in a ceremonial banquet. As their singing voices carried across the base of Mount Tai, those out of earshot of the Emperor voiced their deep disapproval. This was, by its very nature, one of the most important religious ceremonies in the history of the world, and Wu had hijacked it.[16]

SIX

The Poison Chalice

Following the Feng-Shan, a number of prisoners of war were taken to the tomb of Taizong. In olden times, they might have been sacrificed, but, for the Tang dynasty, it was enough that their spirits alone were bestowed in a symbolic offering on the ghost of Taizong. Their souls now presumably the property of Taizong, the still living bodies were permitted to return home. Honour had been served, and the campaign supposed to have caused Taizong's early death was now coming to an end.[1]

As if Heaven itself was on Wu's side, China's fortunes continued to rise. For a while, the Chinese position in south Korea had looked doubtful, with general Liu Rengui complaining that the allure of a foreign posting was swiftly wearing off. Few of the soldiers in his command had expected to have to remain in Korea for longer than a year, and now, in the second year of their commission, they were still flinging themselves at the Koguryo border with little sign of success. Meanwhile, back in China, new recruits were increasingly hard to find – soldiers signed up for booty and fast promotion, not endless

CHUN – PRINCE
During Wu's reign, the word for 'prince' was altered so that it was composed of the characters for 'one who keeps a peaceful mouth'.

months in a foreign country, particularly when a series of orders prevented them from looting.[2]

In the year 666, a few months after the completion of the Feng-Shan sacrifice, the Korean usurper Yon Kaesomun finally died. With no clear heir among his sons, civil strife broke out in Koguryo, offering China and her south Korean allies a sudden opportunity. Tang troops began skirmishing on the Liao River frontier in 666, but the true assault did not begin until the following year, when the venerable Li Shiji, a veteran of the Taizong administration, was called back into service to lead a new invasion. Although there was no doubting Li's skill as a commander, much of his army's progress seemed charmed. Seventeen Korean border forts swiftly surrendered with barely an arrow let loose, allowing Li a lightning advance into Liaodong. Here, for the first time, the Chinese had secured enough of an area to make it possible to spend the winter. Instead of retreating into China, Li was able to wait right on Koguryo's borders, ready for an early assault. In spring 668, he was back on the offensive, sure in the knowledge that he would not have to waste months in retreat with the onset of winter. This fact allowed him to press his attack for a few crucial extra weeks in early autumn, leading to the surrender of Pyongyang itself in October 668. Korea became, at least officially, a Chinese province, although China's hold on the peninsula was often loose, and by 676 the Chinese headquarters were back in the Liao River valley, suggesting considerable gains by Korean rebels.

Nevertheless, in the early to mid-660s, the news from abroad was generally good, although not for Wu. The imperial entourage had returned from Mount Tai with a number of new members, two of whom were Wu's deeply unwelcome cousins, Weilang and Huaiyun. As per Wu's original plan, their father had died soon after arriving at his place of remote exile, but the brothers had somehow inveigled their way into the imperial party on the way home, and made it back to the city. Wu may even have allowed them back herself, hoping to put them to use in a new project.

In summer 666, Gaozong and Wu came to another banquet at the home of Wu's aged mother, at which her cousins were present, along with Guochu, the niece with whom Gaozong was continuing to have an affair. Partway through dinner, Guochu suddenly began choking. While Gaozong watched in shock, his secret lover collapsed in violent convulsions and died at the table. In the chaos that ensued, Wu pinned the blame on the two cousins, alleging that they had been hoping to poison *her*, and that it was only an accident that the food intended for her had ended up on the dish of the unfortunate Guochu. The brothers were dragged off for a swift execution, and, as was her wont, Wu exacted further revenge on their afterlife by ordering that their surname be changed on their tombstones from Wu to *Fu* – 'Viper'.[3]

After such a terrible offence, it was plain that no male members of the Wu family should be allowed anywhere near the palace. The rest of Wu's male relatives were downgraded to commoner status and sent to the far south – and, Wu undoubtedly hoped, a lingering death from tropical afflictions.

The death of Guochu is a turning point in historical accounts of Wu. Previous treatment of her in the Tang dynasty annals had been unafraid to report the accusations of others concerning her activities and alleged crimes, but had shied from any form of agreement. However, the poisoning of Gaozong's lover marks the first moment when the chroniclers of the Tang dynasty itself are prepared to suggest that Wu herself was behind it. Her cousins may well have been the ones to put the poison in Guochu's food; more fool them, for, if they did so, they would have played right into Wu's trap, perhaps carrying out her dirty work in return for her promises to bring them back to court. Whatever the means that the poison found its way into Guochu's food, the Tang dynasty's own history lays the blame for it at the feet of Wu herself.[4]

At least part of this change of heart may have taken its cue from Gaozong, who plainly suspected Wu, although he was too afraid of her to confront her directly. He was seen commiserating with Guochu's brother Minzhi, comforting the tearful boy, who would shortly be officially adopted into the Wu family to carry on the ancestral sacrifices on behalf of the exiled menfolk – Wu may have hated her male relatives, but she was still obligated to her father's spirit to honour her ancestors. The thought of Wu poisoning Guochu was all the more terrifying to Gaozong for several reasons. He was heard to wonder aloud how Guochu's mother had died – there is no proof of the involvement of Wu in her sister's death, but it had aroused Gaozong's suspicions.[5] Wu's apparent willingness to kill off her own relatives did not bode well for Gaozong, particularly considering the degree of access Wu enjoyed to his private chambers. Most chilling of all for Gaozong would have been the fear that Wu may have been attempting to poison *him*, indirectly, through Guochu. It is alleged that one of Gaozong's favourite activities with Guochu was drinking her breast-milk by suckling on it like a baby. This practice may even have been undertaken at the suggestion of his advisers, who would have known the folktale that a diet of human milk could keep a man alive for a century. If Wu had introduced poison to her sister's body, could she have intended it to reach Gaozong through this unexpectedly intimate route? Moreover, if Guochu had breast-milk to provide, then presumably she was pregnant with Gaozong's child, representing a far more powerful threat to Wu than Guochu alone, and leading to her removal.[6]

Whatever the truth behind the demise of Guochu, Gaozong did not have any more children after that fateful banquet. He may well have had other bedmates during the early 670s, but, if he did, none of their children was carried to term. Wu, meanwhile, was left with the issue of Minzhi, and whether or not the youth might plot revenge. If Wu could use her nephews as pawns, then so might the timid Gaozong.

However, Wu need not have worried, as Minzhi managed to ruin his chances without any outside assistance. A spoilt child, doted on by his aged grandmother Lady Yang, he reacted with complete lack of interest to her death in 670. This was a source of some surprise to Wu, who mourned her devout mother for many months, even composing a poem during a visit to the Shaolin Temple in which allusions to old buildings and precincts hid a deeper sense of loss, and of purpose:

A mountain of flame flew over the serried fields,
Of Flower Terrace no trace is left
But Lotus Tower maintains its glory.
Truly it depended on those with benevolent means
To aid the Almighty One's power of perfecting the world.[7]

Wu was, it seems, genuinely heartbroken at the passing of her mother, proclaiming 'even tears of blood will not bring her back'. Minzhi, however, gave it little thought, instead preferring to hang out with the women who were caring for Wu's 6-year-old daughter, Princess Taiping. These palace ladies, like Wu in her youth, were technically concubines of the Emperor, although the chances of them ever making it to his bed were remote. Minzhi took full advantage of their exclusion and supposedly seduced all of them. His activities went unobserved for a while, with the full scope only becoming apparent after he was accused of raping the fiancée of the Crown Prince. Minzhi's habits had gone unnoticed, or at least unpunished during the lifetime of his grandmother, but, with the old lady now dead, there was nobody to protect him from the wrath of Empress Wu.

Minzhi soon had greater cause to mourn the passing of his grandmother, as, with nobody to stand up for him, he was banished to the far south. No mention was made of his assault on the girl; instead, his failure to observe mourning customs was cited as the reason. He conveniently 'committed suicide' en route to his new home. Some chroniclers suggest that he was entirely blameless, and the tales of his seductions and assaults, coming as they did entirely from Wu's own household, were manufactured at Wu's own request. His crime, suggested the *New Book of Tang*, was no more than to appear suspicious of Wu, thereby encouraging her to launch a pre-emptive strike against him before he amassed any evidence concerning her poisoning of her sister.[8]

Wu might also have had cause to fear her husband Gaozong. But Gaozong was soon neutralised by another powerful attack of his 'gusts of confusion'. This time, the stroke left him virtually paralysed, unable to walk unaided, half-blind and able to speak only with extreme difficulty. There would be no more concubines for

Gaozong, nor would there be any opportunity for him to enlist potential allies against his wife, as Minzhi may have been. Instead, he was held prisoner in a crippled body – though no subject would dare to utter such heresy, it might have been better for him if he had died. It might, too, have been welcomed by his ministers, since, if Gaozong had died, they would have been able to appoint his successor. Instead, with the Emperor still tantalisingly alive but incommunicado, they were obliged to obey the orders of his representative, Empress Wu. Gaozong would live on for another decade, still nominally emperor, but with Wu now openly taking on his duties. It was presumably around this point that she ceased taking audiences behind a screen, and openly sat before the ministers. When the Emperor tried to speak, only the Empress dared to attempt to interpret his indistinct mumbles. As the sole reader of his wishes, she informed the court that he had asked her to take over his affairs of state, and, after refusing several times as protocol required, she had reluctantly agreed.

Wu's next problem was a new omen. After several years of good harvests, the climate took a turn for the worse, and north China was plunged into a terrible drought. The adverse conditions also caused problems outside China, leading to pressures on the border from central Asian tribes and further conflicts. The inhospitable southern colonies suddenly found new importance, as the state re-routed food supplies north to fight off famine. Gaozong's ministers imposed a programme of increased austerity, encouraging the urban population to hold off on wasteful activities, including unnecessary ceremonies. Even the palace was encouraged to tighten its metaphorical belt, with the larger audience halls shut down in order to save on lighting and heat. Neither was in as short a supply as food and water, but, in reducing the amount of fuel required to hold meetings in the large halls, the government was able to reassign fuel transports for food and also to reduce the amount of water kept in outdoor cisterns in case of fire.

Amid such strict prohibitions, Wu unwisely ordered that her mother's funeral should be an expensive occasion. In a city where music and celebration were discouraged, the Lady Yang's funeral cortège turned into a major state event, complete with attendant rituals that would usually be applied only to a member of the imperial family – Lady Yang had been posthumously upgraded to imperial status, as had her late husband, but that was no excuse for such a huge event in a time of shortages. Despite her indulgence of Minzhi, Lady Yang had enjoyed a long and productive old age and had become one of the period's most generous donors to Buddhist temples, presumably leading to a large number of extra voluntary attendees from the many religious institutions that had benefited from her charity. Lady Yang's funeral procession was led by a band of musicians, along with ceremonial officials and a military escort. Ministers, officers of the court and ladies-in-waiting all received an invitation they could hardly refuse, only adding to the size of the event, and to the embittered complaints whispered in its aftermath.

Wu had hoped that the funeral event would serve as reiteration of her power and of the influence she enjoyed over the state itself. She might, simply, have been hoping to give her mother a good send-off. Instead, such an overt extravagance only set the people against her, creating new rumours that her role as Gaozong's regent was responsible for the current bad weather.

Wu made a public display of contrition, even going so far as to offer her resignation to Gaozong. As might be expected from a man whose every word needed to be filtered through Wu as interpreter, Gaozong refused it, and Wu was permitted to stay on in her role as regent.

Not wishing to make the same error again, Wu began to cultivate many sectors of Chinese society. The scholar class, source of many of the ministers and officials of the palace, was a prime target for her, since such men were the interpreters of tradition, and tradition was largely Confucian and chauvinist. Wu took steps to become a patron of learning, sponsoring several literary and educational projects. Although some were neutral in tone, others seemed aimed at encouraging an appreciation for the role of women – Wu's regency saw the writing of several biographies of famous female historical figures, all part of Wu's programme to make female rule seem less of an abomination.

Wu was also behind a series of wide-ranging reforms promulgated in 674.[9] In a capital city whose success was founded upon the silk trade, Wu reduced taxes on silk, and exempted silk workers from compulsory government service. She applied similar reforms to the farming community, in an effort to reduce the risk of future shortages, and to butter up the scholars – a 'scholar', after all, was often a farmer whose holdings were so large that he could afford to hire in help and thereby devote his time to literary researches.

Seemingly still spooked by the shortages of previous years, Wu announced a second decree related to the zone of uncultivated land around the city walls. This green belt had been left untouched in part because a large section of the north city walls adjoined imperial land, either the palace itself or the walled imperial parkland to the north. Wu now turned this land over to farmers, in the hope that more food could be stockpiled in case of future drought.

Wu's third decree capitalised on military successes in Korea, central Asia and elsewhere, demobilising many detachments of the Tang armies. It was attached to a proposal for peaceful resolution of conflicts, echoing Wu's late mother's Buddhist faith and perhaps also a disdain and dismissal of warfare itself. As an addendum, Wu would later abolish the special tax that paid for border troops, generating greater good will from the population, but also forcing the imperial government to pay for military expenses out of general funds.[10]

Wu's fourth and fifth decrees ratified the previous austerity campaign that she had flouted in her late mother's name. Despite her disregard of the order when it was a mere matter of ministerial decree, she now jumped on the bandwagon, announcing that the imperial government would cut back on non-essential public works. She also forbade wasteful investment in temples or monasteries, a strange decision that may have hidden a cunning ruse. On the surface, it would enjoy support from Confucians, who regarded Buddhism as a dangerous foreign influence on Chinese tradition and did not enjoy seeing public riches pouring into the coffers of abbots and monks. In putting a cap on Buddhist donations, Wu would have suggested that she was not a pawn of the monasteries and still recognised the relevance of Confucianism.

Many of the decrees seem to have been inspired, at least indirectly, by Wu's loss of her mother, and a temporary prohibition on new temples would only serve to make the Lady Yang's donations and establishments all the more memorable. It would also, of course, present Wu with a convenient excuse for not donating so much herself, and, if she ever needed to bribe a religious order with a devotional gift, she could always make a new decree announcing that her latest donation did not qualify as 'wasteful'.

Wu's sixth decree would be the cause of much strife in later years, although it was greeted with much excitement by her subjects. It was now legal, in fact encouraged, for subjects to communicate with their ruler. Ostensibly, this allowed any commoner to complain about an unjust law or a corrupt official. In reality, it opened the floodgates for a surge of accusations and counter-accusations. It was now possible for subjects to leave anonymous notes about ministers in a comments box at the palace, affording Wu's agents an increased opportunity to investigate allegations of corruption. The next decree was a half-hearted attempt to discourage false accusations, thereby allowing anyone accused of wrongdoing under the sixth decree to fight back with the seventh. The only winner in such a conflict would be Wu herself, whose agents would have obtained useful information from both parties.

The eighth decree seems to have been a red herring, exhorting the population to pay heed to the works of the great Daoist sage Lao Zi. This does not seem to have served any direct purpose, except perhaps to imply that Gaozong was still in charge, since legend held that Lao Zi was one of his distant ancestors.

It is in the ninth decree that we see the first flowering of what later writers would sometimes term Wu's 'feminism'. The deceptively simple announcement calls for the mourning time for a mother to be the same as that for a father. Confucian tradition held that the death of a father should lead to a three-year period of mourning, the effects of which varied depending on the wealth of the bereaved. Some might take it as an order to wear appropriate mourning clothes for the period, others to abstain from luxuries. In some echelons of the imperial service, a 'mourning period' was more like a career break, taken by middle-aged ministers with some sense of relief and often adjudged to begin in the year of the death and end on New Year's Day on the second year afterwards – effectively making 'three years' last anything from thirteen months to just over twenty-four. Now, 'three years' after the death of her own mother, Wu argued for female parents to receive similar respect from their children. This may have been an attempt retroactively to excuse unrecorded strange behaviour from Wu for the last few seasons, or even to excuse a temporary absence from politics, although the latter seems unlikely – Wu was not the sort of regent to delegate. It may have been a genuine mark of respect to her mother, but, whatever Wu's reason, the decree was a further step towards establishing a concept that would have been alien to the medieval world – equal rights for women.

A further possibility may have stemmed from the idea of mourning as a form of ministerial vacation. By doubling the number of occasions when an ageing minister might need to take leave for personal reasons, Wu also doubled the number of opportunities when she might replace an old and fractious official with a new, more pliable appointee of her choosing. Taizong's old guard were now all dead and buried, but Wu may have still had a few lingering enemies among Goazong's personal staff.

If this was the case, then it adds new meaning to Wu's three remaining decrees, all of which involve ministerial posts. The tenth exempted any retired officials from the need to answer a call to duty and offered legal immunity from prosecution for any past offences. This not only presumably saved the necks of several of Wu's hatchet men as old age approached; it also permitted a number of ageing ministers to retire, secure in the knowledge that they would not be retroactively persecuted for any old crimes. Some would have still remembered the purges overseen by Xu Jingcong, in which Wu's enemies were shipped off to exile on trumped-up charges, only to die en route to hearings supposedly arranged to clear their names.

The eleventh and twelfth decrees made life better for all the ministers who remained – presumably now largely Wu's own hirelings. High-ranking ministers all received a raise in salary, and numerous low-ranking officials were rewarded for their 'long service' by new promotions. Wu's men now dominated the court, leaving Gaozong even more of a figurehead, and greatly reducing the number of ministers who might have hoped to organise a restoration in his name.

There were, however, new problems. In 675, Gaozong suffered a further attack of his illness. Its nature is unclear, since he was too ill to function as ruler, but well enough to be able to communicate, at least to Wu, that he wished her officially to become regent. Throughout the 670s, Wu had been demonstrating an able grasp of government, although many of her decrees and reforms had been in Gaozong's name, and hence not credited directly to her.

However, Wu's request still met with opposition from the ministers, particularly one Hao Chujun. Clinging to Confucian orthodoxy, Hao's argument demonstrated just how tenuous Wu's grasp on power still was. He refused to consider Wu as regent because, despite her achievements, she occupied a commanding position in the palace only because Gaozong was unable to leave it: 'The Son of Heaven rules without, the Empress rules within. This is the way of Heaven.'[11] If, as it now appeared, Gaozong was too ill to continue as emperor, then perhaps it was time for him to abdicate, as his grandfather had done before him. He might then be succeeded by his son Li Hong, now in his twenties and enjoying a reputation as a considerate nobleman.

Li Hong was the son who had been conceived out of wedlock, either during Wu's time as a nun at the Ganye convent, or shortly after her return to the palace. By all accounts, he had grown into a fine young man, brave enough even to stand up to his mother on occasions when he disagreed with her. It was Li Hong, for example, who bravely brought up the subject of Pure Concubine Xiao Liangdi's two daughters. Through no other crime but being the children of the woman Wu had mutilated and drowned in wine, the two girls had been raised in seclusion and were now of marriageable age. It was Li Hong who reminded his mother of this fact and suggested that the girls did not deserve to miss out on married life merely because their late mother had been Wu's rival. With great reluctance, Wu had conceded her son's point, and found the girls low-ranking officials to marry.

A few months later, Li Hong upbraided his mother over her treatment of his brother Zhongzong's first wife. The unnamed woman, a daughter of Gaozong's niece Princess Changlo, had supposedly become a little too intimate with the Emperor for Wu's liking. Nothing improper took place, and, it seems, Wu took drastic steps to ensure that nothing ever did. The girl's parents were exiled to the provinces, and the unlucky girl was confined without food until she had starved to death. Zhongzong did not even dare to visit his wife during her brief sentence, but Li Hong chastised his mother for it, reminding her that it was only recently that she had sponsored the compilation of a series of pro-female biographies: 'I recollect that Your Majesty wrote a book about the lives of virtuous women. It is a poor comment that a virtuous woman should be allowed to starve to death in your own house!'[12]

Eighteen days later, Li Hong was dead. As the official story went, he was staying with his mother and father at their summer retreat, when he suddenly fell ill and died. Naturally, the suspicion of many chroniclers immediately fell on Wu, since it would not be uncharacteristic for her to have arranged a poisoning of a potential enemy. Li Hong's epitaph took great pains to mention that he had never enjoyed good health – this seems like a strange piece of news suddenly to make its way into his biography, when there had been no mention of it before. Was Wu deliberately casting around for a new excuse to justify her son's sudden demise? Or in the days before modern medicine, was it simply that many internal complaints such as appendicitis or diverticulitis might go undiagnosed until it was too late, striking at their victim with sudden agony indistinguishable from poison?[13]

Among the contemporary sources about the Tang dynasty, only the *New Book of Tang* pins the blame for Li Hong's death on his mother. Other sources are prepared, just this once, to agree that Li Hong's death was from natural causes, since, even if one were prepared to believe that Wu could murder her own son, her position after his death could have been more, not less, vulnerable. Gaozong was so weak he might die at any moment, while Wu still had three other sons who stood a better chance of ascending the throne instead of her if Gaozong were to die. They were also demonstrably more malleable – Li Hong had protested on Zhongzong's behalf, but Zhongzong had made no comment about the death of his wife. Two of them were still in their early teens, and might reasonably be expected to require a regent. If Wu really had Li Hong killed in order to make her chances of keeping a regency more likely, then she would also need to kill her second son, Prince Xian.

Cause and effect are difficult things to determine. Hindsight, based on later chronicles, tells us that Prince Xian may not have been Wu's son at all, but a child of her sister's earlier affair with Gaozong, passed off as Wu's baby in the 650s. If that were true, then Prince Xian would have been an unwanted spare for many years, the remnant of a long-forgotten power struggle. Whether he was Wu's son or Helan's, he had been raised as Wu's own, and was made the new crown prince after the death of Li Hong. For some reason, quite possibly self-preservation, Prince Xian spent very little time with his mother, and dwelt most of the time in Chang'an, the city that she continued to avoid – if Wu were going to remove him, she would not be close enough to use poison.[14]

He would not last. There was no way Wu would permit a boy who was not her son to ascend to the throne. It seems likely that she already had Prince Xian earmarked for an early demise. Notably, when the time came to appoint the new crown prince with tutors, Wu happily selected men with whom she was known often to disagree. From a Confucian standpoint, this was an act of supreme statesmanship, in which a truly wise ruler did not shy from men who would argue with him when loyalty demanded it. It followed a famous precedent, since Gaozong's own father had adored his argumentative minister Wei Zheng, and cherished him for his fearless counsel. The Crown Prince's tutors, should he succeed to the throne, would be the prime candidates for his leading ministers, and liable to sideline Wu, making their appointment appear, from the outside, to be an act of political suicide for the Empress. However, such a conclusion would require the Prince actually to outlive his father, and it would seem that there was little chance of that.

In 676, Gaozong (for which read Wu herself) publicly praised Xian for his literary achievements. As an exercise in statesmanship, Xian had penned a commentary on the historical work *The Book of Later Han*, demonstrating a keen grasp of political theory – or, at least, signing his name to a book written by scholars whom he had funded. Such honours, however, hid private intrigues. It came to Xian's attention that Wu had been seeing a fortune-teller, who had informed her that, regardless of his current position, the Crown Prince simply lacked a face suitable for an emperor. New rumours were already circulating that Xian was not Wu's son; none would question the official line until sanctioned to do so, but, if Xian were actually Helan's son, there would be plenty of servants in the palace who already knew it. But, since nobody below Xian's rank could challenge him, the truth of his origins was a weapon that Wu could choose to wield at any moment. If she did not choose to do so immediately, it was probably simply because she would then have to admit to her earlier deception.

Her meeting with the fortune-teller may have been a ruse designed to get an insinuation about Xian's illegitimacy out into the open without declaring it herself. Alternatively, it may have been a private plot that was never intended to reach Xian, since, with or without Wu's knowledge, Xian was enjoying a forbidden affair with one of Wu's own serving girls. The rumour grew with the telling, as palace employees gossiped that Wu had seen a seer, who had informed her that, for some reason none dared speak, Xian was 'less noble' than his brothers. The phrase was beautifully calculated – implying he was still the son of the Emperor, but not of the Empress. If the news ever truly broke, then he would be left with a single chance to save his position; he would have to beg Wu to adopt him, rendering him legitimate after the fact. Far from appointing a potential rival, Wu had backed Xian so far into a corner that he would have little option but to obey her every word.[15]

One day in 679, the fortune-teller met with an unforeseen event. To his great surprise, but not to anyone who knew the intrigues of the imperial family, he was set upon and murdered by 'bandits' outside Luoyang. Suspicion immediately fell on Xian, who denied everything and dared his accusers to provide a single scrap of evidence. It was, however, easier for investigators to lean on the source of Xian's information, the hapless serving girl, who soon confessed, truly or falsely we shall never know, that Xian had personally ordered the thugs to kill his accuser.

Sensing that they were wading far out of their depth, Xian's advisers tried to control his behaviour. But it was too late – now that the truth was out about his liaison with the serving girl, Wu had cause to call for a deeper investigation of the Prince's recent actions. Officials descended on the Prince's quarters in a surprise search, and found several hundred suits of armour hidden in his stables. The discovery was treated as evidence that the Prince had been plotting a coup, and Wu called for his summary dismissal.

Even in his enfeebled state, Gaozong made his displeasure obvious. Perhaps he already knew the truth that, regardless of Xian's guilt or innocence, the boy was his last surviving child not to owe full allegiance to Wu. Nor did Gaozong seem ready fully to believe the new accusations about Xian. Only months before, this had been the golden youth who had so impressed the court with his historical essay. Now, the Empress was calling for his execution for treason.

Gaozong prevaricated for months, and even seemed prepared to forgive Xian – perhaps secretly impressed at his foresight, and even hopeful that the plot had been aimed not at him in particular, but at his wife. Wu fought back by manipulating public opinion. When the suits of armour were ordered to be destroyed, she ensured that they were disposed of in a highly public manner, creating new rumours even as the evidence was officially removed. She then remonstrated with Gaozong with uncompromising force: 'When a son plots revolution, neither Heaven nor Earth can permit it. He conspired to exterminate those who should be dear to him. How can he be forgiven?'[16] Eventually Gaozong relented, downgrading Xian to a commoner, and exiling a dozen of his friends, who made up the much-needed numbers in order to justify talk of such a 'conspiracy', as Xian on his own would not have made much of a revolt. Xian was initially confined under house arrest in Chang'an, but soon quietly moved to a distant province, where, as Wu might reasonably expect, he was sure to have a miserable time.

Luckily, there were still two more imperial princes who might replace the discredited Xian. Wu favoured her youngest son, Ruizong, who was still in his teens, but the obvious candidate was Zhongzong, Ruizong's elder brother. Zhongzong, who had just become a father himself, was duly selected as the new heir, but, in a bizarre move, Gaozong also proclaimed a conspicuous blessing upon Zhongzong's baby son. Zhongzong, said the Emperor, was the new crown prince, but his new baby would enjoy the title of Imperial Heir Grandson.

It seemed that an heir might be required sooner rather than later. The following year was Wu's *annus horribilis*, with torrential rain in Luoyang in the spring, which led to massive flooding, sufficient to drown several sectors of the city and washing away the three bridges in front of the palace. This, in turn, ruined the crops in the surrounding area, which struggled to recover in a summer drought, and then succumbed to a plague of locusts at harvest time. The onset of starvation led to a rapid rise in crime and banditry, and misery was compounded by an earthquake in the autumn. Throughout these signs of divine anger, Wu persisted in the construction of a new altar in imitation of the Feng-Shan location at distant Mount Tai. This version, however, was much closer to Luoyang at Mount Song, where she hoped to initiate a new Feng-Shan. Despite signs of obvious misfortune, Wu pressed for the new pseudo-Feng-Shan to be held in early 683. Her court procession duly wound its way along the mountain passes to the venue, only for Gaozong to suffer a further attack to his health, so severe that he lost his sight completely.[17]

There was something going on behind the scenes. Perhaps Gaozong knew that he was dying and could see that Wu had designs on becoming his true successor. The announcement of an imperial grandson might have been a deliberate attempt to lock in the succession before Wu could raise any arguments. Conversely, the proclamation may have been Wu's all along, representing a secret determination to kill off Zhongzong as soon as possible, and establishing early that his successor would be a babe in arms who would, of course, require an experienced old hand as his regent.

Gaozong stayed on in Luoyang, growing steadily weaker, attended only by Wu and a few select servants. For government officials, now temporarily back in the old capital of Chang'an, the Emperor's silence was deeply suspicious, and many began to suspect that Gaozong was already dead.[18] That, however, was an old trick, and Wu had plenty of her own. Late in 683, Wu's messengers announced that the ailing Gaozong wished to come back to Chang'an. Aged just 55, Gaozong could have passed for a man a generation older. Attempts to put him on a horse for a triumphant arrival were abandoned when he was unable to sit upright. He was all but carried into the palace, where he feebly waved his arm in agreement to a series of proclamations, including a general amnesty that freed many criminals from their sentences. Such deathbed mercies, however, did not extend to his son, the newly exiled Xian, who was pointedly excluded from the list.

Gaozong was now so ill that it was thought unwise to attempt to remove him from his hall of audience. Instead, he was made as comfortable as humanly possible, while his servants kept a bedside vigil. Late that night, he called his chancellor Pei Yan to him and handed him his last will and testament – an act that effectively appointed Pei Yan not only as executor, but also as China's protector in the forthcoming interregnum.

With that, Gaozong breathed his last. His reign was over, and with it, that of his Empress. Wu would now be expected to go into seclusion as the widow of the ruler. Again.

SEVEN

The Hen at Daybreak

The new Emperor Zhongzong had very little time to get used to his role. He had entered his teens as one of the youngest children of a relatively young ruler. His father may have been crippled by his 'gusts of confusion', but, for as long as Wu was at his side, Gaozong's proclamations had continued to issue forth and his rule had seemed consistent. Consequently, nobody in the 670s had any reason to suspect that Zhongzong had the remotest prospect of becoming an emperor himself. The chances were higher that Zhongzong would be forced to live out his life in relative obscurity, an imperial hanger-on, with a modest retinue and a couple of sinecure positions, perhaps in the hope of one day becoming the uncle or great-uncle of the actual successor.

Princelings like Zhongzong might be expected to seek military careers somewhere dangerous, or administrative office somewhere unpleasant and distant. They might also be encouraged to enjoy themselves a little (or a lot), pushed into artistic pursuits that would

CHEN – MINISTER
During Wu's reign, the word for 'minister' was altered so that it was composed of the character for 'loyalty', with its top a little flattened.

offer little threat to the incumbent regime. In other words, Zhongzong spent his entire formative years being studiously taught how *not* to be an emperor.

He was, of course, sternly inculcated with the works of Confucius, particularly the all-important maxims concerning knowing one's place in society. His place, up until his sudden promotion to Heir Apparent, had been that of an unwanted extra, and he had embraced it with gusto.[1]

Zhongzong had not distinguished himself with any imperial office, nor had he written any literary masterpieces like his fallen 'brother' Xian. He had held a single official post, which was little more than a vague badge of office that served little purpose beyond determining where he should be seated during civil banquets. He had demonstrated no aptitude for rule, and instead devoted himself to his hobbies – which, according to the Tang annals, largely featured wine and women.

Zhongzong had already had a taste of his mother's power. His first wife, a princess of some standing, had been thrown into jail by Wu's order in 675, and died there under suspicious circumstances. His second wife, known to posterity as Empress Wei, exercised a hold over him rivalled only by that of Wu over his father. Wei's family were old-time aristocrats, now powerful ministers, and she had, perhaps, even developed something of a grudging admiration for her infamous mother-in-law.

Gaozong's will specified that Zhongzong should take power immediately, but this did not happen. Instead, Wu was able to invoke a clause within it that, in recognition of Zhongzong's lack of experience, left her at least temporarily in charge: 'Should important matters of defence and state be undecided, follow the ruling of the Empress.'[2]

Wu had no just cause to override Gaozong's will. Her decision to postpone Zhongzong's enthronement until after Gaozong's funeral rites seems to have been a calculated act of spite, designed to inform her son who was really in charge. Zhongzong, however, did not take the hint. While his mother remained ominously present during state proceedings, he continued to do as he wished – or rather, as he was told by his wife.

Within a month of his taking power in early 684, Zhongzong and his wife committed a crucial error. Instead of following a careful policy of gradual, albeit sneaky, change like Wu, they jumped straight in with an announcement that created a whole new series of enemies for them. Bending to his wife's will, Zhongzong proposed that his rich and influential father-in-law Wei Xuanjen should be given an important ministerial post.

The suggestion ran contrary to all the policies that Wu had so assiduously pursued during the life of Gaozong. Whereas Wu had dutifully (and in secret, happily) ordered her male relatives away from the capital in order to prevent them from exercising undue influence, her daughter-in-law was now openly calling for a relative to gain powerful political influence.

To Confucian statesmen, it was a very bad sign – as Wu had been told herself on numerous occasions, wives held power only within their palace, not in the government at large. Wu had enjoyed power over Gaozong only in exceptional circumstances, but now her daughter-in-law seemed ready to assert her authority for no good reason. It was certainly not to Wu's liking, nor was it plainly in the interests of the minister Pei Yan, who might lose his new high position.

Zhongzong made repeated requests for the appointment of his father-in-law, until one of his ministers was moved to remind him of the trouble this would cause for protocol, and for his image as emperor. Instead of calmly listening to the advice, Zhongzong snapped.

'We could give Wei Xuanjen the entire Empire, if We wished,' boasted Zhongzong. 'The presidency of the chancellery is a mere trifle.'[3]

Zhongzong's rude comment was entered in the court record, and immediately reported to Wu by Pei Yan. Although it was probably simple hyperbole, taken out of context it could easily be seen as a threat to the entire dynasty. Each for their own reasons, Pei Yan and Empress Wu agreed that Zhongzong's willingness to consider handing over his authority to a relative of his wife, even in jest, could not go unanswered. Wu resolved to act while there was still the opportunity to invoke the clause in Gaozong's will that granted her special powers in a state of emergency. Alone, she could never have made the decision, but Pei Yan felt his own position was under attack, and agreed to support her.

It was, by Chinese standards, a remarkably bloodless coup. Late in February 684, only six weeks into Zhongzong's reign, Wu called for a massed assembly of palace officials, attendants and residents in the largest of the halls of audience. Zhongzong went along with it, perhaps in the assumption that he was being called upon to witness the disbursal of some donations to worthy monks, or the suggestion of some new noble titles. Ironically, he may have even been expecting to hear Empress Wu announce her official retirement and assumption of the lesser role of Empress Dowager.

Instead, the assembly was interrupted by a flurry of red silk, as soldiers of the Yulin Guard marched in. Their chests adorned with symbols of lions, goshawks and falcons, these 100 palace sentinels were the praetorians of the Tang palaces, supposedly loyal only to the Emperor. However, like other imperial soldiers in other places and times, their allegiance often defined the ruler instead of supporting him. It was the Yulin Guard who had backed Taizong in his rebellion against his own father, and now, it seemed, the Yulin Guard had found a new mistress.[4]

Zhongzong did not even register what was happening until it was too late. As Wu proclaimed to a surprised hall that the Emperor was guilty of treason against his own throne, the guards dragged Zhongzong bodily from the dais. Realising at last that he was under attack, the Emperor yelled that he had committed no crime.

'Thou so easily offered up all under heaven to Wei Xuanjen,' replied Empress Wu. 'How is that no crime?'[5]

Zhongzong and his pregnant wife were soon hauled off into exile, where he was informed that he was now a prince again, his six weeks of imperial rule an unfortunate mistake in the history of the Tang dynasty. Meanwhile, Wu wasted no time in placing her last remaining son, Ruizong, on the throne.

As the youngest of her sons, Ruizong was Wu's darling. He and his sister Taiping were her favourites, and Ruizong had remained in Wu's quarters far longer than propriety deemed suitable. Like his father before him, he had been reared in the inner palace by doting nannies and servants and indulged in his every whim. Now, the golden boy was a weak-willed youth of 22, so enthralled by his mother that he did not dare offer a word of resistance. Instead, he remained sequestered in his quarters, while Wu informed a fearful court that the new emperor had a speech impediment and had asked her to speak for him on all matters.

After the scramble for authority of the late 670s, Wu finally had what she needed – a compliant ruler, almost as powerless as the paralysed Gaozong, who would allow her to continue her secret rule without any interference.

However, it was not long before she fell out with her ally Pei Yan. After demonstrating such former interests in Confucian protocol and Daoist religion, Wu began to act favourably towards Buddhists. Like her mother before her, Wu had a great interest in omens and portents, particularly if they were favourable, and word had spread around the country of strange lights in the sky, that had later been found to be resting on a place where Buddhist relics were found. It was not enough, argued Wu, simply to set up a temple on the site, although she did. Omens throughout the land in recent years had all been pointing to a single inevitable truth – that the time was fast approaching when a saviour would come to unite the world.

Some of these omens seem rather frivolous – the sort of Forteana that might find its way into a modern tabloid newspaper, such as the hatching of a three-legged chicken, news of which Wu heard with great relish. Others were more likely to impress the population at large, or at least to frighten them. Weather was bad in 684, with fierce rains and uncharacteristically savage lightning storms. In September and October, the superstitious got an even bigger surprise, when the night sky was lit up by a massive comet, and later by many smaller lights – possibly a coincidentally attendant meteor shower. The 'broom star', as the *New Book of Tang* called it, was seen all over the world, its appearance recorded everywhere from Japan to the *Nuremberg Chronicles*. It was one of the most spectacular historical appearances of Halley's Comet, and Wu took it as a sign that great things were in the offing.[6]

It is not clear when Wu suddenly found religion. Possibly, it was the influence of her mother's death; perhaps it was a cynical ploy designed to capitalise on her many donations to temples and abbeys over the years. But, with her blunt and bold overthrowing of her own son, she began to take a greater interest, particularly in Buddhist prophecies. Prophecy, of course, had played an important role in her young life, when her superstitious mother had obtained a declaration that her daughter would one day rule as an emperor. If there were any truth in the stories about *wu wang* that had been a feature of her youth, then surely such tales could now be seen to be coming to fruition.

From the standpoint of a Confucian minister, Wu's behaviour was anything but innocent. In 684, she established seven ancestral temples in Luoyang, in memory of departed members of the Wu family. Pei Yan and several other ministers raised their voices in complaint, although to the population at large it might have seemed churlish to object to such an apparently pious act. Technically, Wu was not a member of the Wu clan any more – nor had she been since the time of her wedding. If she insisted on building temples and monasteries in the name of a family, then surely she would have been better off dedicating them to the Li family – the family of Gaozong and of the supposedly incumbent Emperor Ruizong? Instead, her decision to venerate her own relatives could have seemed dangerously close to the crisis precipitated by the fallen Empress Wei and the deposed Emperor Zhongzong.

More worrying to Wu's critics was the same year's Act of Grace – which, once again, appeared to be wholly innocent on the surface, and was originally presumed to have been arranged in celebration of the aforementioned charmed discovery of Buddhist artefacts in an unexpected location. Its purpose was supposedly to pardon a number of criminals and to offer rewards and bonuses to hard-working officials who might have been overlooked in previous honours lists. However, its wording and subclauses concealed a series of extensive and far-reaching alterations of names and protocols. In modern terms, it was a massive rebranding of the entire Tang dynasty, which found new names for many ranks and positions, and imposed new designs on the uniforms and insignia of many government postings. Even the flag of the Tang dynasty was altered, ordered to be gold with purple trim.

Name changes and inflation of job descriptions were nothing unusual in Chinese history. In fact, the name of the entire reign period was often altered in order to reflect changing circumstances, offset apparent curses or usher in new projects. Wu was one of the most fickle reign-namers in Chinese history; she had a great love of words and their apparent power and loved to tinker with titles. Back in the days of Gaozong, when a farmer had reported seeing a dragon during a flood, Wu had arranged for the reign's name to be changed to Dragon Inauguration. When someone reported seeing a unicorn (the sign of an earthly saviour), she had swiftly moved to change the reign title to Unicorn Virtue. Whereas other rulers might have the same title for their entire reign, lasting for decades, Wu chopped and changed every couple of years, as if she were fine-tuning fate itself, steering China towards perfection.[7]

But Wu's behaviour (and nobody believed for a moment that it was Ruizong's) seemed alarmingly like the preamble to a change in the dynasty. Wu was notorious for her past attempts to argue for the equality of women and the need for court ceremonial to recognise women as equal partners. Some believed that her new reforms were aimed at wiping out all vestiges of the Tang, ready for her to proclaim herself not merely a regent in the name of a weak emperor, but the ruler in her own right.

It is these cosmetic but influential changes that often occupy historians of Empress Wu, leading into discussions of her crazed desire for power and her determination to become the proverbial hen crowing at daybreak. But it is also possible to see a number of enlightened reforms within Wu's Act of Grace, hotly contested by her bureaucrats, but arguably in China's best interests.

Wu observed that the Chinese population had been expanding at a fast rate, not only through the domestic peace that kept all but the border regions out of danger, but also through the generally bountiful harvests, and a few isolated cases of mass immigration, such as the Koreans who had settled in north-east China as refugees from the Korean wars. Wu argued that much of the new population was invisible to the old census-takers. Accordingly, she appointed a new section of her Censorate, empowered with improving record keeping in the provinces, and weeding out tax evaders. County and prefecture boundaries were redrawn to reflect new populations, unburdening overloaded administrations, much to local officials' gratitude, but also dumping increased workloads on soft postings where influential ministers had previously had it easy.

Those who had been dodging their tax responsibilities might have been irritated by Wu's decision, as might those officials who were now forced to work harder, whereas before they had been less accountable and responsible for smaller areas. Career politicians and civil servants might have welcomed Wu's reforms, with the exception of blowhards of the old Taizong and Gaozong administration, who complained that the redrawing of boundaries seemed aimed at wiping every last vestige of the old regime off the maps and account books, until everything was made anew, in Wu's image.

Similarly mixed reactions greeted Wu's military reforms. Many of her ministers might have regarded her as a fearsome but silly matriarch, ignorant of the ways of war, although if they did they were probably unaware that Wu had been the acting commander-in-chief of the Chinese army during Gaozong's illness. Her observations on military matters were not the idle comments of a palace concubine with ideas above her station – they were based, at least in part, on more than a decade's responsibility for military operations. Wu may never have been to the front line, and she certainly left the day-to-day decision making to her generals in the field, but it may have escaped the notice of some of her critics that she had also been the secret leader of China during many of the supposed victories of earlier administrations.

She was thus more than qualified to make suggestions about the way the Chinese army should be run. Perhaps on her own initiative, perhaps taking a hint from one of the long-serving generals like Liu Rengui, she noted that corruption was rife. Medals and promotions often made their way into the hands, not of the valiant, but of the rich. In several cases, Wu found retired, decorated, high-ranking military officials in the provinces, trading on their alleged heroism and experience, but unable to display any evidence of seeing combat. This, Wu argued, was no way to run an army – it demoralised the soldiers who did the real fighting and, in cases where the holder of a military sinecure was responsible for actual men, could endanger soldiers' lives.[8]

Instead, Wu wanted army officers who knew what they were doing – in fact, she ordered each of her officials to nominate someone based, not on family connections or wealth, but on suitability for the job. In doing so, she caused the appointment of large numbers of new bureaucrats, most of whom would regard her as their benefactor. Her opponents saw this as another cunning move to crowd out her enemies with new cronies; but then again, they would. When examining the sources for Empress Wu, for her alleged atrocities, her strange decisions and her infamous corruptions, we must also consider the reverse – that the state administration of the Tang dynasty had been in a state of constant crisis from the time of its inception, and that Wu was the woman who saved it.

It may have been easy, in 684 almost as much as today, for Wu's critics to forget how precarious the founding of the Tang dynasty had been. The rule of China had been snatched from the previous dynasty by a civil war, the new emperor deposed by his own son, Taizong, who murdered the rightful heir and seized the throne for himself. Wu may have exploited Gaozong's illness, but one might argue that, if she had not done so, someone else could have with far less harmonious results.

Thirteen hundred years after the events, all we have to go on are the insinuations of Wu's successors, and the stories told about her by the children and grandchildren who despised and feared her. The evidence is so thick with lies, some admittedly created by Wu herself, that it is almost impossible to discern which interpretation of these events is the most valid.

Some, however, had already made up their minds. Wu planned on staying in Luoyang for the foreseeable future. In a gesture that scandalised some of her critics even further, she renamed the city Divine Capital (*Shengdu*). What, whispered her enemies, was the Empress now implying? Since she would still require a trusty lieutenant to serve as administrator back in the old capital, she called upon the stoic Liu Rengui, veteran of the Korean campaigns. Liu, that same man who had once complained about the mirrors around Gaozong's couch, was old but clearly still had some fight in him. Wu requested that he go to Chang'an to rule in her name and, knowing that Liu had developed an interest in history in his old age, playfully suggested that things were a bit like the old Han dynasty, when the great founding emperor of that 400-year era had sent his most trusted minister to run the Chang'an region.

However, Liu Rengui was not in the mood for such allusions. In his reply, he graciously declined her offer, and added that, from what he remembered of his readings on the Han dynasty, everything had gone horribly wrong when the Emperor's wife Empress Lü had tried to steal power for herself.[9]

If the stories of Wu's poisonings, stranglings, murders and slanders have an ounce of truth in them, then many had died for uttering less powerful put-downs. However, Wu left Liu Rengui alone. Even more surprisingly, she sent her nephew Chengsi over to Liu with a private note. In it, Wu conceded that posterity had been unkind to the matriarch of the Han dynasty, but that one could not worry about one's legacy when there was urgent business to be done. Instead, Wu wrote, she valued Liu Rengui precisely for the fearless way he clung to what he thought was right, regardless of the consequences. She accepted his arch warning, and promised to bear it in mind. In the meantime, there was the administration of Chang'an, which required someone with the right experience. Surely, Liu was the man for the job?

Despite his previous misgivings, Liu Rengui accepted. We shall never know whether he was swayed by her arguments, or simply wanted an easy life. Some historians have suggested that Liu fully appreciated that Wu intended to seize power for herself, but was persuaded by her letter that, if the Tang dynasty needed to be usurped, it served its own best interests to be usurped by her.[10]

An image of Wu in later life, from the Southern Song dynasty book *Sanlitu* (*Some Ceremonial Pictures*), *c*. 1176.

A detail of an image of Wu from the Qing-era book *Empress Wu of the Zhou* (*Wei Zhou Huangdi Wu Zhao*), published during the reign of Kangxi, the Emperor of Hearty Prosperity (*c.* 1690).

The 'Nipple Hills' that sit either side of the Spirit Road to Wu's tomb.

Wu's tomb, seen from halfway along the Spirit Road.

The ominously blank memorial tablet at Wu's tomb.

The Constellation hot spring bath, built by Taizong in 644, and a favourite recreational spot for his son Gaozong and later Tang dynasty princes.

Taizong's beloved horse Tan Fist, depicted with nine arrows protruding from him on one of the bas reliefs from the Gate of the Dark Warrior, later relocated to Taizong's tomb.

A statue of a minister from the grave site of Taizong.

A building in the Famen temple, restored to Tang dynasty style.

The relatively humble grave mound of Taizong.

Palace ladies in flowing robes with Tang dynasty hairstyles, shown here from a tomb in Shaanxi province.

Detail of a Tang dynasty painting depicting a hunting party. From the tomb of Prince Xian.

One of the giant warriors who stand guard over the Spirit Road to Wu's tomb.

The image of a dragon on a gilded metal dish from Wu's era.

Detail of a dish image of a phoenix, the imperial female animal, from Wu's era.

A balding, hirsute man with an aquiline nose lurks behind three chatting diplomats. He is believed to be an envoy from 'Hrom' at the far western end of the Silk Road – an ambassador from the Byzantine Empire. Image from the tomb of Prince Xian.

The statues of Gaozong's foreign allies, left headless by unknown vandals after the death of Wu.

A statue of the pilgrim monk Tripitaka, outside the Temple of Maternal Grace in Xi'an.

The distinctive squat bulk of the Scripture Pagoda (aka the Great Goose Pagoda) in modern Xi'an.

A carving of the Laughing Buddha, i.e. an earlier incarnation of Maitreya, from the grounds of the Temple of Maternal Grace, in Xi'an.

The high vault and deep corridor leading to the underground tomb of Prince Yide.

One of the first cinematic versions of Wu's story, from 1938, starring Violet Koo.

A movie version of Wu shows an anachronistic amount of leg, in the 1960 Shaw Brothers' version of her life.

Wu's nephew, who had been allowed back to court after the death of Minzhi in order to ensure that there was someone to pay homage to Wu's paternal ancestors, was rewarded for his diplomatic mission with a more permanent government posting. Meanwhile, others were less easily persuaded than Liu Rengui, and plotted revolt against the Empress Wu.

Down in the south-east, where the Yangtze River met the Grand Canal, the most public challenge came from Li Jingye, the grandson of the loyal Tang general Li Zhi. Its rationale was a little confused. Some claimed that Li Jingye was intent on restoring the deposed Zhongzong. However, Li Jingye himself claimed to be acting in support of Prince Xian, the former heir, and insisted on parading his royal ward around before his men. This would have come as something of a surprise to Wu and her courtiers, who knew that Xian had committed suicide in 684 – in fact, Wu may well have made sure of it, in order to prevent just such an uprising as this.

She had sent a captain of the palace guard to Xian's residence, supposedly to check the place over and ensure that Xian came to no harm. Instead, the captain locked Xian in a back room until the Prince hanged himself. Although the captain was exiled for his 'mistake', he was back in his old job in the capital within six months – circumstantial evidence thought, then as now, to implicate the Empress in Xian's death. The Prince did, however, manage one final, minor gesture of revenge. He was credited with an authorship of a poem, the *Song of the Cucumber Plant*, which allegorised the deaths of the imperial heirs, and became something of an underground hit after his death:

> A cucumber plant below the Yellow Terrace
> Its fruit is ripe for plucking
> One plucking will do it no harm;
> Two pluckings make the plant look thin.
> It will survive three pluckings still,
> But with the fourth plucking,
> Carry the bare vine home.[11]

113

Presumably, however, the song had not yet reached the taverns of the south, where Li Jingye proclaimed that he was Xian's protector, and that Xian would be restored. Militarily, Jingye's revolt was swiftly crushed. Although he enjoyed considerable support in the region around the mouth of the Yangtze, a Tang retaliation was able to use the river and canals to its own advantage, arriving before Jingye could move north to seek further support. Jingye was his own worst enemy, since he had previously had ample time to do so, but stayed in the south in a misguided and wasteful attempt to seize the old southern capital of Nanjing. The rebels were boxed in and wiped out by December 684, although their uprising had several repercussions.[12]

The rebellion may even have gained Wu new support at court, as it appeared to confirm her own secret fears. Just as Liu Rengui had been prepared to serve Wu as the better devil he knew, it was obvious to the inner circle that the rebels' rhetoric of restoration was utter nonsense. The 'Prince Xian' they claimed to support was an imposter, calling their motives into question.

To the historian, the story of Li Jingye's uprising offers tantalising further details about public opinion of Wu during her own lifetime. It is largely remembered for one of its proclamations – an impressive blast of invective, listing a whole roster of reasons why Wu had to go:

This woman Wu has seized the empire, ascending through false means, unyielding and cold. Formerly, she was a minor servant of the Taizong Emperor, her tasks including the changing of his clothes. But as she grew, she brought discord to the palace of the crown prince. She concealed her relationship with the former emperor; her shadow fell on the walls of the court. She entered the gate through deception, and all fell before her moth brows. She whispered slander from behind her sleeves, and swayed her master with her vixen flirting. She trampled on the pheasant regalia of the empress, and entrapped her prince in incest. With the heart of a serpent and the nature of a wolf, she gathered sycophants to her cause, and brought destruction to the just. She slew her sister, butchered her brothers, killed her prince and poisoned her mother. She is hated by men and gods alike, unwelcome in heaven and earth. Her evil heart is set upon the state, while our beloved prince is sequestered in a lesser palace. Even now, she conspires to create chaos, and hands authority to her minions. I say: No! . . .

I, Jingye, former minister of the Tang, scion of a noble family, recipient of imperial grace, respectful of the dynasty's burden, am desolate with princely sorrows . . . My spirit rises in anger like the wind and clouds, ready to pacify the altars. All under heaven have lost hope, and the Celestial people give me their hearts, raising the banner of righteous rebellion, that we may cleanse the world of such sorcerous disaster. From the hundred families of the south, the three rivers of the north, the iron knights ride forth; the jade ships gather. Land and sea shall reap the red harvest, until the granaries are full . . .

The voice of the host shall rise like the north wind. We shall pacify the south on the points of our swords. Yes! The roar of soldiers shakes the mountains. Yes! Our battle cries rend the skies. Among our enemies, who cannot be broken? Among our aims, what cannot be accomplished? . . .

And what of you, my lords, entrusted with great duties by the late emperor? You who heard his dying command in the hall of audience? If his words still reach your ears, how can loyalty be forgot in your hearts? The earth is not yet dry upon his tomb, yet where is his full-grown orphan son? We may yet transform bad fortune to good, honouring our departed lord by serving his true and living heir. Rise as one to pledge your allegiance. Let not his decrees fade unheard. Look around you, at the world today. Whose is the house that should rule all under heaven?[13]

Wu initially reacted to the attack with sarcastic delight, commenting that Li's speech-writer, Luo Binwang, had been wasted in the provinces, and would have been far better use to the world if he had been hired at her court.[14]

But, most notably, the attack on Wu, while rich with insinuations and daubed throughout with insults, neglects to mention some of the most terrible allegations made about her by later historians. She is blamed for the deaths of her (half-)brothers, that much is true, but also for those of Helan, Lady Yang and Gaozong. While her involvement in the death of Helan is not impossible, surely it would have been in her best interests to keep Gaozong alive – her troubles began only after his death forced her to rethink her previous hold on power. It seems similarly ludicrous to accuse Wu of causing the death of an old lady on the eve of her 90th birthday, particularly when, in terms of Wu's alleged crimes against the Tang dynasty, these accusations are relatively tame.

Surely, if one were assembling a case against the evil Empress Wu, in order to sway crowds of potential rebels, it would have been more productive to accuse her of the crimes that would really have got an audience's attention? There is, for example, no mention made of the mutilation and slow, agonising deaths of Empress Wang and the Pure Concubine Xiao Liangdi, nor of the banquet poisoning of Guochu. Most noticeable of all, there is no talk of the rapid rise and fall of several crown princes in the 670s. Surely talk of such issues, if they were known, would have been ideal rhetoric to encourage a 'righteous rebellion'? Such atrocities, recounted in detail in later dynastic chronicles, are conspicuous in their absence here, making Li Jingye's manifesto of revolution an extremely valuable document. For those who would believe that she was a dutiful stateswoman, much maligned by chauvinist history, the *omissions* in Jingye's speech are primary evidence that many later stories about Wu were libellous concoctions.

However, despite her bravado in the face of such accusations, Wu was shaken by the implications of the rebellion. It was only a matter of days before she began a purge of her own staff, alleging that several of them had been in on the plot. Supposedly evidence had come to light that the minister Pei Yan was sympathetic to the rebels' plight, and had planned to kidnap Wu and spirit her off to an undefined fate during a visit to the sacred Cave Buddha grottoes of Longmen. If this were true, then Pei Yan's bid for power would have been thwarted by accident, when rainstorms led Wu to call off the visit at the last moment. Although Wu claimed to present proof to her inquisitors, none of it is extant beyond a handful of circumstantial points. Pei Yan had a nephew among the rebels and, as an official of Gaozong, he had quite literally been 'entrusted with great duties by the late emperor' and had indeed 'heard his dying command in the hall of audience'. This was enough to make Wu think that the hateful proclamation had contained a coded message to Pei Yan, and implied that, even if he were not directly involved, he had engaged the rebels in discussion before they began their uprising.

Of more hurtful concern to Wu was Pei Yan's behaviour during the revolt. As news had drifted up from the south of Li Jingye's early gain, he had advised the Empress that she could put a stop to the unrest in a heartbeat, simply by resigning. Other ministers regarded this suggestion with some suspicion, leading a chief censor to point out that Pei Yan could not possibly have expected to enjoy higher rank if Ruizong were restored as emperor. Nor would a restored Zhongzong have looked favourably on the minister who had helped drag him from the throne. All things considered, if Pei Yan were suggesting Wu's resignation, he was either a statesman of phenomenal compassion or a man preparing to seize power for himself. Predictably, the ruling favoured the latter option, and Pei Yan was duly executed, along with two of his alleged accomplices.

A stern Wu called her ministers for a large-scale audience, and dared them to try it on in a similar fashion: 'These were officials accorded high respect. Yet they conspired, and still I destroyed them. If your abilities surpass theirs, then make your play. Otherwise, change your hearts and serve me, to save the Empire from further ridicule.'[15] It was a challenge of such force as to invite a footnote from the chronicler of the Tang dynasty himself, who commented that only a sovereign who had been greatly shaken would have spoken in such a way to her courtiers.[16]

In the wake of Li Jingye's revolt, Wu determined to nip such conspiracies in the bud. Her censors were given increased powers to root out wrongdoers, and the definition of unseemly encompassed increasingly larger areas of dissent. Wu's secret police force, the Office of Prosecution, was feared all over the empire, and officials

117

were soon arresting people simply for expressing dissatisfaction with the current regime.

Wu helped matters along by revising her 'suggestion-box' scheme to devastating effect. For the rest of her reign, a great bronze urn stood in the palace, with four slots for differing purposes. The first allowed visitors to offer recommendations for people (themselves included) suitable for government positions. The second was marked for anonymous criticisms of Wu's government. The third was a place for subjects to complain about any wrong that had been done to them by others, and the fourth supplied a handy drop for any interesting news about omens, portents or conspiracies.

The effects of Wu's reforms have been largely swamped by complaints about the abuses to which they were put by some of her agents. And yet Wu the evil usurper, the architect of a four-year reign of terror, did not appoint agents solely to harass her subjects. Nor, as some accounts imply, was the urn a free-for-all for toadies and cronies – there were, at least officially, penalties for improper use and perjury.[17] Some were put in charge of charities, tasked with providing for the old, the sick and the orphaned.[18] Such men, however, receive barely a footnote in studies of Wu's reign, since she was far more widely known and longer remembered for a different kind of appointee.

Wu's great urn flung open the doors of government – ostensibly making it possible for commoners to advance to great heights, limited only by their own abilities. In practice, it created a climate of fear, in which no official was safe from anonymous sniping. Nor was Wu's policy limited to the environs of the capital city. Concerned about possible rebel action fomenting in the distant south, she soon reformed the rules for informers, obligating provincial officials to transport anyone with interesting information to the capital. In theory, it meant that every subject in the empire had access to the great urn. In effect, local governors, fearful of the implications if they were found to have dismissed information on a conspiracy that was later found to be true, shipped every crackpot, snitch and sneak in China to Luoyang, creating a new subgroup in administration that came to be known as the 'cruel clerks'.[19]

One of Wu's ministers complained in 689: 'All year, I have seen secret denunciations in every corner. We imprison men by the ten thousand, and most are still denounced for their participation in [the rebellion]. But on close analysis, less than one percent of the accusations are true.'[20]

Wu's bronze urn might have encouraged openness, but was no less open to corruption than the old system of nepotism and patronage. Subjects with nothing to offer except slanderous accusations might inveigle their way into the government, and then naturally gravitate towards the job they did best – in fact, the only job for which they were qualified – searching for more corruption. The surviving aristocrats and bureaucrats were crowded out in the late 680s by commoners, many of whom doubtless performed long, anonymous and worthy service to Wu's administration. The celebrities of this era, however, are men like Zhou Xing and Lai Chunchen, embittered investigators for the Office of Prosecution who were determined to root out evil-doers and, where evil was in short supply, to bully innocent victims into confessing. In particular, Lai Chunchen, who would later write the ominously titled investigation manual *The Classic of Entrapment*, bore intense resentment for the gentry of old and took great pleasure in engineering their downfall.[21]

EIGHT

The Hall of Illumination

In the southern quarter of modern Xi'an stands one of the few buildings to have survived from the time of Empress Wu. The 'Great Goose Pagoda', as it is now known, seems strangely alien. It lacks the festive adornments of other Chinese pagodas and has none of their sweeping, uplifted eaves. Instead, despite being the tallest building in what was medieval Chang'an, it still seems curiously squat. It is an impressively solid building, with stone walls several feet thick, its interior seeming in places more like a bank vault than a place of worship.

It stands in the grounds of a more traditional temple – even the locals often seem to forget that the 'Great Goose Pagoda' is merely one building within the precincts of a much larger complex, originally founded as the Temple of Maternal Grace. It is also noticeably rich. Rocket-shaped urns hold the remains of ancient monks, and votive tablets in a side chapel contain the names of devout Buddhists stretching back to the Tang dynasty. Another side chapel is walled entirely in multicoloured jade – a giant wall carving

YING – MUST
During Wu's reign, the word for 'must' was altered to use the
character for a branch of government, wielding an ominous stick.

120

that tells the story of Buddha's life, from his conception to his transcendence, painstakingly realised and pricelessly situated. Just outside the temple gates stands the statue of a lone Buddhist monk, his robes simple and unassuming, a staff in one hand, while his other gives a blessing.

The statue is an image of Xuanzang (*c.* 602–64), sometimes honoured with the holy name Tripitaka, a devout Buddhist who travelled far to the west and returned with holy scrolls from the birthplace of Buddha himself. He is a saint in the Buddhist tradition, a man who defied Emperor Taizong for the sake of his religious beliefs, and returned from more than a decade of travels to be fêted as a religious hero.

As a local celebrity and a Buddhist sage, Tripitaka met the famous leaders of his day. He diplomatically turned down posts in Taizong's government in 645 and 648, and personally gave the Emperor copies of some of his translations, which entertained the dying emperor on his sickbed – when a teenage Wu would have been in attendance.[1]

It is likely that Tripitaka met Wu in the 650s if not before, and may have been an associate of Wu's late mother, who devoted herself to so many good causes. He died long before Wu's grab for imperial power, and could have had no knowledge of the uses to which Empress Wu would put his life's work and teaching. It is highly unlikely that he would have approved. Tripitaka was a man of heartfelt religious conviction, but in the 680s his teachings would be stolen by a former make-up salesman as part of Wu's project for power.

Although Buddhist tradition was not native to China, Buddhist beliefs had gained great influence among the population. Buddhism was another exotic import from along the Silk Road – a religion that offered solace in suffering and the hope of a better life in the next world. Even the imperial court was not immune to it – the emperor was supposedly the high priest of China's native religion, yet there are many references to Buddhist concepts, even at the imperial court. When the Pure Concubine cursed Wu in 656, threatening to come back as a cat, she did so using fashionable foreign terminology – the concept of reincarnation.

But while many, Wu's mother included, might have hedged their bets by giving generously to Buddhist causes, the official religion of the Chinese state remained the intricate ancestor worship of China's distant past. Family ties extended into the afterlife; sacrifices were made in the hope that one's ancestors would intercede on the spiritual plane with spirits of equivalent rank. As China was beset on its borders by Turks, Khitans and Tibetans, so the spiritual realm was dogged by hungry ghosts, and spiritual allies were needed to hold them off. However, such otherworldly concerns were largely discounted and ignored by the scholar class, who preferred to focus on the world around them. Like Confucius himself, the ancient sage whose writings defined Chinese protocol and attitudes, the ministers of the Tang court were less interested in the supernatural than in the natural – they believed that, if everything in the real world knew and embraced its position in the natural order, then the supernatural world would keep similarly in line.

Confucian orthodoxy placed high value on knowing one's rightful place in society. After a brief experimentation with the Machiavellian intrigues of Legalism at the time of the First Emperor, Chinese governments had returned to the sayings of Confucius, making the works accredited to him the bedrock of political philosophy for 800 years.

Confucianism posited a Golden Age in the distant past, a time where gods walked among men, and the world existed in such a state of perfection that everything functioned in perfect harmony. This perfection, it was suggested, had fallen apart because human beings had failed to observe their correct place in nature. Ranks were of crucial importance, as were rituals and behaviour.

In her forties, Wu had exploited this obsession with protocol to her own ends, in her argument that she should be permitted to participate in the Feng-Shan sacrifice. Despite the mutterings and complaints of Confucian officials, she had made a forceful and controversial point. Confucian tradition prided itself on its ongoing effort to replicate the Golden Age of ancient times, but there was far more to Wu's participation than the desire for attention of an imperial wife. Wu's interference had dragged the radical notion of gender into the Confucian tradition.

After several thousand years of experiments, changes in customs and refinement of rituals, Confucian philosophers had still failed to replicate the state of perfection of the legendary kings.[2] Wars were still fought, friends still quarrelled, and Confucians still argued over what they were doing wrong. Rulers and their advisers were educated using Confucian books, rituals were tweaked and moved, and astrologers attempted to gain better insight into the will of Heaven. But Confucianism was not itself a religion – it was a philosophy of statehood that attempted to make sense of the rituals of the ancient Chinese court, and it treated women, as did Confucius, largely as a necessary irritation.

Women had a role in Confucian society, but it was one of subordination to men. Wu's behaviour, particularly at the Feng-Shan sacrifice, suggested that centuries of Confucian scholarship had misread the ancient legends, and that women were, if not actually supreme in times gone past, at least equals of the men. Heaven was only 'above' the Earth, after all, in a physical sense – both required sacrifices and rituals of appeasement, and one could not exist without the other.

Now Wu was moving towards an even more radical suggestion, that her many years as an acting ruler should come to an end, and instead be replaced by her elevation to full sovereign powers, not as a regent or consort, but as the actual monarch of all under Heaven. In this assertion she enlisted additional support from an unexpected source – Buddhism.

Local omens were all well and good – the three-legged chicken had gone down well, and now had a matching portent in a farmer's report that one of his hens had spontaneously changed sex.[3] This would have been particularly galling to those Confucians who had warned of a 'hen at daybreak'. In 687 an earthquake caused a mountain to develop a new peak. Wu treated all these things as good signs, although some of her courtiers regarded them as the exact opposite. In a memorial to Ruizong, one official suggested that the new, 'lucky' mountain was not a good omen at all, but an earthly affliction, as if the unnatural elevation of a woman to a position of power had caused the earth itself to break out in a rash. Ruizong, of course, was not the final recipient of the memorial, and an angry Wu banished the official to the south.[4]

The problem with standard omens was that they were subject to interpretations by Confucians – a self-sustaining state apparatus of stuffy old men, clinging to traditions set down in half-understood ancient books. Wu saw herself as an innovator, cutting through centuries of ossified tradition, whereas the Confucian scholars saw her as a flighty and dangerous female. It is here, perhaps, that we can see a little of Wu's motivation for what later generations of Confucian historians have called her 'reign of terror'. Her infamous urn did not merely serve to introduce gossip and scandal, but it also flooded the court with new appointees who had not, in her eyes, been tainted with the prejudices of a Confucian education.

Beyond the Confucians, there was one group of holy men who might be expected to offer alternate wisdom, and that was the Buddhists. Buddhism had been around in China for several centuries, travelling along the Silk Road from the west in much the same manner as exiled Persian princes and rare perfumes. In the years before the foundation of the Tang dynasty, it had proved particularly popular with the barbarian tribesmen who had ruled parts of China, who saw in the foreign religion a mirror of their own position as rulers in a foreign land.

Buddhism, however, may have lost a little in translation in its initial arrival. Indian monks, unsure of their Chinese, or local aspirants, unsure of their Sanskrit, had garbled and diluted some of the teachings. In places, Buddhism seemed to take on many aspects of China's native religion, but there were those among the truly devout who wanted to seek out the pure truth. Doing so would involve taking a hazardous journey to the west, along the Silk Road, across legendarily impassable deserts and uncrossable mountain ranges, to the distant lands that few had seen and from which fewer had returned. Some, however, were prepared to take the risk.

The most famous of the travellers was the monk Tripitaka, a man from the Luoyang area who had sneaked out of China in 629, after dreaming that he had been ordered to make a pilgrimage to the west. In doing so, he was technically breaking a law of Emperor Taizong, who had forbidden Chinese from travelling outside the empire while wars raged against the Turks. At the border, as in many of his foreign adventures, Tripitaka was able to prevail upon the Buddhist brotherhood of the people he met. Buddhist border guards agreed to look the other way; Buddhist families took him in, and, as he moved ever westward, he enjoyed the support of an invisible network of Buddhist believers. Moving among the peoples of central Asia, Tripitaka wandered as far west as Samarkand before he turned south for India, the homeland of Buddhism, eventually arriving in 630.

His original destination had been Gandhara, an old centre of Buddhist religion, although, when he arrived, its capital Peshawar had fallen into decline. Instead, he pressed on through India, drifting from monastery to monastery, in a leisurely pilgrimage that took in the places of Buddha's birth and death, and eventually led him to the scholar-town of Nalanda, where he spent at least two years. He eventually arrived back in China at some point in the 640s, where he became something of a local celebrity, weighed down with hundreds of priceless Buddhist scriptures.

Tripitaka had enjoyed a degree of patronage from Gaozong, which, considering Gaozong's 'gusts of confusion', probably meant that Wu had sponsored him herself for some years. But Tripitaka had no interest in politics or worldly matters, instead wishing only to find a place where he could live in peace and translate the scriptures he had brought back with him.

In 652, just as the young Wu's convent career had come to a scandalous close with her return to Gaozong's palace, Tripitaka got his wish. The Temple of Maternal Grace, originally built in honour of the late Empress Wende, was now augmented with the Scripture Pagoda, a massive, reassuringly solid building designed to hold the precious scrolls in fireproof safety. It was so secure that, despite centuries of earthquakes, floods, alterations, annexes and at least one fire, it is still standing at the beginning of the twenty-first century. In 656, at the time of the promotion of the ill-fated Li Hong to crown prince, Tripitaka petitioned Gaozong for assistant translators, and also advised a dozen court ladies who had suddenly expressed a desire to become nuns – were they fleeing the early influence of Wu?[5]

The first record of Tripitaka's direct contact with Wu comes from the winter of 656, when the heavily pregnant Empress asked him to pray for the safe delivery of her baby. Tripitaka agreed, but asked his imperial patron if she would agree to let the child become a monk if it were a boy. The child, originally intended to be named Buddha-Light, was the infant Zhongzong. Although his planned monasticism never materialised, his birthday gifts from Tripitaka included a gilded copy of the *Heart Sutra*, as well as ascetic paraphernalia such as a monk's staff and rosary.[6]

Refused permission to retire by a decree written in Gaozong's own shaky hand, Tripitaka continued to preach at the temple, and devoted himself to the translation of the many scrolls. In some cases, the scriptures were 'all-new' sutras to Chinese Buddhists loaded with new revelations. In other cases, they were new translations of documents that had previously been misunderstood. During this time of revision and reinterpretation, some previously unknown elements of Buddhism came to light. One was the revelation that Buddha had advised severing all family ties – a heretical suggestion for the ancestor-obsessed Confucians, but likely to have been a source of great amusement to Wu, who had been busy severing family ties for years.

Perhaps even more excitingly for Wu, followers of Buddhism realised that the original scriptures had been nowhere near as anti-women as the Chinese translators had claimed. For the local, Confucian-influenced audience, translators had finessed the words a little, suggesting that husbands should 'control' wives, and wives should 'revere' husbands. In fact, the original Sanskrit called for husbands to 'support' their wives, and for wives to 'comfort' husbands – a view of a far more egalitarian world, and precisely the sort of thing that would give Wu additional leverage.[7]

In 664, the year before Wu exiled her half-brothers, Tripitaka died peacefully of natural causes. In his final words to his followers in the shadow of his great stone pagoda, he advised them:

Form is unreal. Perception, thought, action and knowledge – all unreal. The eye, the ear, the mind – all are unreal. Consciousness through the Five Senses is unreal. All the Twelve Causes, from ignorance to Old Age and Death, are unreal. Enlightenment is unreal. Unreality itself is unreal . . . Praise to Maitreya . . . who shall achieve Buddhahood. May I and all conscious creatures soon behold him.[8]

He was referring to the next incarnation of Buddha, the saviour who would come to mankind in the latter days of the law, amid drastic omens. In that regard, it was perhaps an innocuous suggestion to look to the future, although some appear to have heard it differently. Some, even in the palace, took Tripitaka's words to mean that the Last Days were already upon the world, and that the saviour of mankind, Maitreya the Peerless, Maitreya of the Golden Wheel, Sage and Holy Emperor, would soon arrive to usher in a new age of divine peace. Turning such a prophecy to Empress Wu's advantage, however, would require a series of events set in motion by a pedlar.

The key figure in this period of Wu's life was the man alleged in some sources to have become her lover. Xue Huaiyi was a seller of cosmetics in Luoyang, a profession that carries little stigma in modern-day English but that bore undertones of sorcery and lasciviousness to the medieval Chinese.

Although some cosmetics sellers were wholly innocent purveyors of rouge and lipstick, others appear to have had an edgy, criminal association. It was, after all, but a short step in the Chinese mind from selling perfumes to selling potions and poisons. A woman's boudoir in Luoyang, regardless of the reputation and deeds of the infamous Empress Wu, was a place of secrets and intrigues. Concubines, subsidiary wives, serving girls and prostitutes all competed for the attention of their menfolk. The most obvious methods were mundane – the sweeping-up of long hair into elaborate styles, or the selection of suitable robes and accessories. Others involved the use of face creams and salves, often utilising mysterious and occult ingredients, such as bird's blood or exotic herbs.

Selling cosmetics turned a man into an amateur alchemist, mixing neutral solutions using harmless ingredients such as rice flour, and then adding cerussite (lead oxide or 'white lead') for face paint, cinnabar (mercuric sulphide) to make rouge, or alum (aluminium sulphate) and garlic to make nail polish. The discerning lady of Wu's era would pluck out her eyebrows entirely, drawing them back as hazy patches of greenish shadow high on her forehead. These 'moth-brows', as they were known, were sometimes ornamented with dots or designs in the centre of the forehead, symmetrical beauty marks. When a face-reader or soothsayer was in town, ladies might add swipes of litharge (another lead oxide), imparting a yellow aura to their faces that might encourage prophecies of good fortune.[9]

Beauty was a drug, and men like Xue Huaiyi were its dealers. Keeping their clients supplied led to associations with all levels of Tang society and many of its more dangerous sectors. They would buy hair for wigs from impoverished peasants, or shave it from the heads of powerless slaves and prisoners of war. Fences, unable to sell off distinctive stolen property, might grind down jade pendants or melt golden trinkets, hoping to sell them off to a pedlar who needed them for his latest concoction. Cosmetics might be used in court to accentuate the looks of women who were already regarded as beauties, but at the sharp end of the sex trade they had other uses. Disfigured whores and mutilated slaves used powders and creams to cover up scars and punitive brandings, or to mask criminal tattoos. All these elements of female society, from its desperate underclass to its genteel aristocracy, were united through their reliance on and trust in the men who sold them the things that kept them beautiful.

Nor did the pedlars of cosmetics stop with mere skin creams. They would also sell potions for internal use – concoctions designed to render one beautiful from the inside out. There were cloves and camphor to stave off bad breath, and tinctures based on melon seeds and tangerine peels, said to impart a fresh glow to the skin of the woman who took a spoonful three times a day.[10]

Pedlars like Xue Huaiyi had an intimate knowledge of their clients. On occasion, they might be invited behind modesty screens to demonstrate methods of application, or consult on rashes. Merely by association and sales, they knew secrets that no lady should allow her enemies to hear – who needed aphrodisiacs, who had haemorrhoids, who was laid low with menstrual cramps or diarrhoea. Through this situation of uneasy trust and delicate secrets, a dealer in cosmetics might also become a dealer in other items – we may, perhaps, speculate as to the exact nature of some of the 'sorcerers' who had supposedly consorted with court ladies in the past, and perhaps even presume to guess where court ladies obtained their drugs and poisons.

Xue Huaiyi came to Wu's attention because of his association with a minor princess, Qianjin, a younger sister of the late Taizong. The woman was in her fifties and dwelt in the same palace as Wu. Considering Wu's earlier habit of forming alliances with marginalised women of the court, it is likely that they were acquaintances and, in a sense, friends. It would, of course, have been unseemly for an imperial princess to associate with undesirables; instead, Qianjin sent her maid to get the necessary potions or creams from her dealer. Over time, Princess Qianjin came to rely on him and, eventually, met him in person.

Once again, for an unmentioned reason, Qianjin had cause to recommend Huaiyi to Wu herself, calling him a man of 'unusual talents'. No detail is given as to what these talents were, but Wu soon came to rely on Huaiyi herself, and eventually had him brought into her palace.[11] Gossip surrounding the nature of their relationship is based largely on Wu's incidental behaviour. Huaiyi had the run of the palace, and was permitted into the inner sanctum of the women – a privilege granted to no man but the emperor (and during this period of Ruizong's seclusion, not even to him), and a few very young princes. For a man to be allowed to attend directly on Empress Wu, protocol demanded that he be castrated, although Wu pointedly refused to allow this.

Instead, she declared that Huaiyi the travelling potion salesman was now Huaiyi the Buddhist monk, installing him as the abbot of the White Horse monastery in the countryside, where she would be able to call upon him during supposedly devotional visits. She also forced her son-in-law, the luckless husband of Princess Taiping, to 'adopt' Huaiyi in a bizarre arrangement whereby Huaiyi became the man's adoptive *father* – taking his surname, demanding his respect and, presumably, now able to deal with Wu on a more equal and proper footing, in everyday matters such as seating arrangements at dinner. As gossips noted at the time, and have continued to do so ever since, if Huaiyi was nothing but a perfume salesman, it seemed like a ludicrously intricate way to ensure he was on call.

Many previous rulers of China, giddy with the notion of their imperium and fearful of encroaching old age, had turned to drugs and alchemy in middle age, in attempts to cling to the notion of potential immortality. But even if such thoughts had occupied Empress Wu, there is no evidence that Huaiyi would have been any help to her. If he were a dealer in drugs as well as cosmetics, he certainly demonstrated no aptitude for actually making them. Instead, Huaiyi was already known in Luoyang town as a carouser and a ruffian, devoid of any obvious intellectual skills or technical knowledge. Thus, while it remains possible that his value to Wu was medical, some have assumed that his use to Wu was far more physical, and that the pair became lovers.

Wearing the surname of Wu's son-in-law, and robes bestowed upon him by the Empress Wu herself, Huaiyi cut a swathe through the Tang court. He had a retinue of self-appointed fellow 'monks' who were little better than shaven-headed thugs, embracing Buddhism in name only, as an excuse to terrorise local peasants with demands for 'alms'. Woe betide the long-haired Daoist priest who ran into Huaiyi and his entourage, who delighted in beating up their spiritual 'rivals' and forcefully shaving their heads. Huaiyi possessed all the bravado and swagger of the criminal in power, shoving ministers aside and setting his followers on anyone who dared to stand up to him.

One official attempted to report Huaiyi's misdeeds to Wu, but was waylaid later on in the streets of Luoyang and beaten to within an inch of his life by unknown assailants. No witnesses came forward to identify his attackers.

In another incident, Huaiyi deliberately barged past a prominent minister, who retaliated by ordering his bodyguards to teach him a lesson. Huaiyi was grabbed and repeatedly punched in the ensuing mêlée, and immediately went to Empress Wu in search of retribution. Instead of punishing either party, she merely advised Huaiyi to stop using the same gate as the offending minister – saving face for the politician, but also permitting Huaiyi still further access to the inner palace through his use of the north entrance.[12]

Beyond suggestions of his sexual prowess, which remain mere hearsay, Huaiyi had one other identifiable skill, or at least he believed so. Amid much irritation among the courtiers, Empress Wu announced that Huaiyi would be the architect of a new imperial project designed to bring eternal glory to the dynasty and the world, the construction of a Hall of Illumination, or *Ming Tang*.

It is unclear what Huaiyi's qualifications were for this task – as a supposedly Buddhist priest, he should not have been holding any truck with Confucian rituals anyway. Nor is it at all clear as to what the task involved. Like the Feng-Shan ritual that Wu had so successfully commandeered during the reign of her late husband, the Hall of Illumination was a legendary symbol of imperial power, the precise design and function of which had been lost over the centuries since the days of China's mythical rulers. Although no one can be sure, it appears to have been a majestic combination of several other buildings. It was a sort of super-temple, a massive palace in which the ruler literally lived out the rituals required of him, or, as Wu would doubtless have pointed out, of *her*.

Emperors were required to perform sacrifices and ceremonies that communicated with and appeased the gods. Many minor rituals were conducted by proxies, although the sovereign himself was expected to turn up for the major events in the calendar of the imperial Chinese year. One might, perhaps, expect the emperor to have to perform a ritual of some state importance once every week or two, throughout the year, with the most critical coming at moments of astronomical significance, such as equinoxes and solstices. However, a Hall of Illumination served to concentrate and magnify the energies of the sovereign who built it, possibly by functioning as a form of ceaseless ceremony. Instead of processing out to a distant, purpose-built altar once a fortnight, the emperor would essentially live *inside* a giant altar in a state of permanent service, adapting his clothes, activities and even diet in order to conform with the prescribed seasonal requirements.[13]

Part of its function may have been as a walk-in calendar in the style of Stonehenge – its windows and spires marking the passing of the year. It was also a fully functional imperial palace, allowing a sovereign to hold audiences and meetings. It may have been none of these things, but that is certainly the impression that Wu seems to have drawn from the scattered references to earlier Halls of Illumination in other sources.

As with the Feng-Shan sacrifice, the Hall of Illumination was not an obsession peculiar to Empress Wu. The late Emperor Taizong had begun discussions about building one when he was still a mere prince. Confucian scholars had periodically bickered and argued over what it entailed for the ensuing sixty years, with widely varying conclusions as to its size, shape and function. The arrival of Huaiyi ensured that, right or not, a final plan was concluded in record time, and construction began.

In far corners of the empire, insulated from the worst of the infighting and scandal of Wu's court, the news of the building of a Hall of Illumination was greeted with great enthusiasm. It was, at least on the surface, the sign of a dynasty so powerful, successful and confident in itself that it was ready to try for state achievements unseen since the days of legend. To those closer to home, although they dared not voice their misgivings to the Empress and her brutish lieutenant, it was a sign of a regime obsessed with its own power, with a pathological desire to outdo everything that had come before it.

The Hall of Illumination, built to Huaiyi's design, was inaugurated at the Chinese New Year (11 February) 689.[14] It was

300 feet square and 294 feet high, comprising two square lower floors and a circular upper storey, itself topped by a 10-foot gilded iron phoenix. Not that anyone dared to speak out about it, but, if a dynasty were promoting the power of its ruler, a dragon would surely have been more appropriate. However, instead of the traditional symbol of an emperor, Huaiyi's design placed a symbol of an empress at the summit of the super-temple. When, shortly afterwards, the phoenix was toppled by a freak windstorm, it was replaced by a glowing 'fire orb' – some form of luminous material, or perhaps more simply an eternal flame, augmented with mirrors and prisms. A later poem about the Hall noted that its beacon was bright enough to be mistaken for a second moon at night, or a supernaturally bright star during the day. If anyone was old enough or well read enough to remember the omens that attended the later days of the reign of Taizong, they might remember the appearance of Venus for strangely long periods in the daytime sky, and the assumption that this meant a female ruler was on the rise.

Within the precincts of the Hall were nine great bronze tripods, each weighing almost 100 tons, in imitation of the Nine Tripods of legend, the owner of which was said to control every sector of the known world.[15] It was a bold and brash statement of mastery, although not all were happy with it. At least one minister risked his life by telling the Empress that she might have missed the point – the Hall of Illumination in ancient times was believed to have been a much more functional and modest affair. Furthermore, once it was built, it was never really used for its religious function. Wu held occasional grand audiences in its main chamber, but never became the live-in high priest that protocol would have required – perhaps she had originally intended that Ruizong, emperor in name only, could be kept suitably busy going through the motions in the Hall's many ritual rooms. Perhaps she simply did not care.

The construction of a Hall of Illumination, like the holding of the Feng-Shan sacrifice, was a sign of supreme dynastic achievement. Posterity, so it was hoped, would record that the ruler of China of Wu's time had surpassed all previous rulers. The ruler, however, was still officially Ruizong, and Wu was acting only as regent. In

686, she had half-heartedly offered to step down, but Ruizong knew his place, and urged his mother to stay on in her role. But from the time of the inauguration of the Hall of Illumination, there were signs that Wu was planning on making her role official, supplanting Ruizong completely and proclaiming herself as the sovereign of China.

The shock such a suggestion engenders in Chinese is largely lost in English, a language that uses the term 'empress' to describe both a sovereign ruler who happens to be a woman (*huangdi*) and a mere imperial wife (*huanghou*). Empress Wu, in fact, was destined to become the only woman in Chinese history to rule in her own name. As with many Chinese nouns, the term *huangdi* is usually assumed to be male, but it is actually neutral. Some English writers on the subject contort the language to make this more apparent, by stating that Wu was the only 'woman emperor', the use of the male title implying just how strange her grab for power would seem to orthodox tradition and protocol.

The Hall of Illumination was only one of the milestones on her way to seizing full power. A highly suspect 'omen' seems to have been created by Wu's nephew Chengsi, who arranged for a stone to be uncovered in the nearby river that bore the telling prophecy: 'The Sage Mother comes among men – an imperium of eternal prosperity.'[16] The discovery of this handy piece of propaganda was to inspire other cronies to go to even more extraordinary lengths.

While the Hall might have secured some spiritual support from native religions, Wu still stood a better chance of appealing to those who had a taste for the new and the exotic – worshippers of Buddha. It had been twenty years since the death of the famous pilgrim Tripitaka, but the words of his final sermon on Maitreya achieved new currency, particularly when Xue Huaiyi seized upon them. Possibly in search of some new way of ingratiating himself with Wu now that the Hall of Illumination was complete, Huaiyi discovered that one of the Buddhist texts he, as a 'priest', should have known about all along suggested that the Buddha's next appearance on Earth would be in the body of a woman. With the aid of seven real monks who genuinely knew their way around the sutras, Huaiyi dug up some supporting clauses in an obscure scripture called the *Great Cloud Sutra*.

In later generations, the *Great Cloud* was often written off as a fake. It is only relatively recently, with the cataloguing and translation of the Buddhist manuscripts found in the caves of Dunhuang, that it has been found to be genuine. There had been five previous attempts to translate it before the time of Empress Wu, and an earlier version had been a favourite read of the late Emperor Taizong. Part of it involved Buddha making a series of prophecies about future incarnations of himself, including, at the very end:

> When seven hundred years have passed after I thoroughly pass away through [my skill in] means, this goddess Vimalaprabha will arise in a lineage of a king of the realm, called Udayana in a city called Definite-As-Endowed-With-Glorious-Qualities on the southern bank of the river Auspicious-Blackness in the district of *Mun can* . . .[17]

Even to the credulous, its relationship to Wu was tenuous at best. Seven hundred years after the death of Buddha would still place the allotted time several hundred years into Wu's own past, but that could be fudged with some creative explication of how long it would take Buddha 'thoroughly' to pass away. More importantly for Huaiyi was the possibility presented by other parts of the text, particularly if their translation from Sanskrit was nudged a little, to make it all the easier to interpret them in the manner he required.

First, it was possible to get agreement from a number of scholars that Buddha planned to come back in his final 'Maitreya' incarnation as a woman. Once that was established, other parts of Huaiyi's deception became easier to arrange. Forgetting for a moment that local superstitions should not mix with Buddhist scripture, a prophecy had foretold that a Sage Mother would rule mankind – was not Empress Wu the ideal candidate?

With the fuzzy logic common to religious cultists, Huaiyi began drawing spurious conclusions from other parts of the sutra.

Maitreya, it was said, would eliminate all evil – was this not what Wu was in the process of doing, through her diligent secret police? Maitreya would dwell 'east of the river' – was not Luoyang east of a river, sort of? Maitreya would build a Citadel of Transformation – of course, that would have to be the Hall of Illumination itself, already up and running!

'Thus,' wrote Huaiyi, 'we say that Maitreya corresponds to the empress. She must be the one, and the meaning agrees.'[18]

Huaiyi's arguments went on like this for several pages, drawing further unlikely parallels, but returning again and again to the subject of the Hall of Illumination. This, he said, was the single, overbearing piece of evidence that Wu was the living god Maitreya, saviour of mankind. The Hall of Illumination was the final proof of her godhood, and Huaiyi the literal architect of her divinity.

As if that were not enough, Huaiyi then began comparing the prophecies of the *Great Cloud* with the inscription that Wu's nephew had 'found' on the stone in the river. No longer, it seems, did the mystical stone simply bear a single line about the coming of a Sage Mother. Instead, Huaiyi detailed a whole screed of bonus inscriptions that previous reports had overlooked: 'Unlike the leopard or wolf, she is called Wu, and is king in Luoyang . . . One with the virtue of Earth will rule with the greatest prosperity . . . none of the common folk will be troubled . . . a bright cat, far away, shall be your guard in the four directions.'[19] 'Virtue of Earth' was a subtle touch – an allusion to Wu's participation in the Feng-Shan sacrifice, when she had argued so convincingly that female (Earth) nature should be on an equal footing with male (Heaven) nature. But Huaiyi showed his anxiety by naming Wu outright, locating her in Luoyang and even refuting the earlier rebel proclamation, by pointing out that she was definitely not like a wild animal, and that the people quite liked her. Clearly on a roll, Huaiyi had even dug up a prophecy from the sixth century: 'A unicorn is born with two horns, and for generations, the people do not know. When it is grown, full in majesty, its sponsors receive offices and posts. Virtuous and loyal ministers are found at court, and the unworthy are banished from the ruler's sight.'[20]

The key word here is 'people' or *shimin*, which happened to be also the given name of the Emperor Taizong, born as Li Shimin. Here, Huaiyi pointed out, was a text written a hundred years ago, that could be read as a predictive biography of Wu. Had she not entered the palace as a girl, and grown to her full powers during the rule of three other emperors? Was her arrival not prophesied to Taizong, and had he not realised its true implications, with Wu herself mere steps away from his throne, even then? The meaning was clear – a goddess walked upon the Earth, and her name was Wu.

NINE

The Brilliant Void

In 688, Wu's nephew Chengsi had ordered the construction of a massive temple in Luoyang, easily the equal of anything built to honour the imperial family. However, it was not dedicated to the Li family, those male-line descendants of the founder of the Tang dynasty; it was dedicated to the Wu family.

Considering the incredible number of prophecies and portents that Wu's supporters were digging up, from dusty old libraries to countryside graffiti, the name Wu was clearly on the ascendant. However, an emperor with many wives will easily find himself with many children. Despite Wu's own remarkable efforts to thin out the imperial family in the 670s, there were still children of the Tang dynasty's founder yet living – sons and nephews of Taizong and cousins of Gaozong. Their claim on power was extremely distant – most were provincial administrators or minor nobility, whose membership of the imperial family was already considerably far down the scale. Given a few generations, they might even expect to

ZHAO – BRIGHT OR SHINING
During Wu's reign, the character for 'bright', which was also her given name, was altered to comprise the emptiness of the void, above which the sun and moon of 'brilliance' shone down.

drop completely off the noble lists, unless they somehow managed to marry a daughter to someone further up the pecking order, or produced a son who achieved promotion through great martial valour. This was simply the way of things in any imperial family that bore a lot of collateral offspring, but Wu's activities had created considerable unease among these minor princes.

The empire was simply not safe in Wu's hands. Even though the official record was one of great prosperity, word still got out that Wu was exceeding her authority. Even those who might have approved of Wu's reforms would endure them for only as long as she was a mere regent. Nobody would complain about a competent administrator, but, with one heir banished and another supposedly unable to speak, questions were asked about what would happen after Wu's death or resignation – she was, after all, now in her early sixties.

If Ruizong genuinely were disabled (although, in fact, he was nothing of the sort), he would still require a regent, but it was no longer possible to presume that the regent would be drawn from his male-line relatives in the Li family. Although Wu had diligently removed her half-brothers from the political scene, her nephews were achieving greater prominence in Luoyang. Two of her great-nephews had married daughters of the deposed Emperor Zhongzong; considering Wu's record, it was hardly a leap of the imagination to suspect that the Wu family was edging ever closer to the throne itself.

Even many of those who had supported Wu in the past disapproved of her latest activities. One vice-minister commented that Wu had successfully removed the incompetent Zhongzong, and that Ruizong seemed perfectly able to govern without his mother's help. He therefore wondered what possible reason there could be to have a regent at all. Although he made these comments in private, news soon got back to Wu, and, before long, the unfortunate minister became the subject of counter-accusations. Overnight, he went from being a trusted servant of the Empress to someone charged with both taking bribes and improper conduct with someone else's concubine. The minister worked in the office that promulgated Wu's decrees, and was thus considerably surprised to find that a proclamation of his guilt had somehow flown over his head and into the public domain. Ruizong himself came out of seclusion to plead for the minister's acquittal – but, for the first time, trumped-up evidence from the regent was found to have greater sway over the law than the word of the Emperor himself.[1]

Ruizong's willingness to poke his head above the parapet shows all the signs of intrigues behind the scenes. He now had three sons (the third, the future Emperor Xuanzong, had been born in 685), and presumably knew of the concerns of his cousins and uncles about Wu's behaviour. However, Ruizong had grown up in Luoyang under his mother's influence and was fully aware of her capabilities. His own personal efforts to wade into the fray petered out, and it was left to others among his family.

Meanwhile, Wu's Office of Prosecution stepped up its activities, perhaps with deliberate designs on eliminating any potential opponents to the ascendance of the Wu family.[2] The secret police operated out of a compound reached through the Gate of Beautiful Scenery, or *Lijing-men*, in west Luoyang.[3] A wag among them renamed the gate by suggesting new characters with the same sound – the Gate of Legal Finality, implying that all hope should be abandoned by any who entered it. The cruel clerks certainly did everything in their power to ensure that a suspect would 'confess' to his crimes, and thereby justify the arrest in the first place. Prisoners were kept underground, in conditions that were not only dark and unsanitary, but at depths designed to ensure they were also unpleasantly cold. When sleep deprivation and repeated interrogations failed to result in a suitable statement of guilt, the clerks would move on to tortures as prescribed in the *Classic of Entrapment* – mud in the ears, hanging by the hair and bamboo slivers under the fingernails. There was also a variant on the process known around the world as 'Chinese water torture', in which a victim was dangled upside down, and vinegar was dribbled into his nostrils. An even more fiendish method involved a metal cage around the victim's head, into which wedges could be introduced that gradually increased pressure on the skull, causing it to fracture.

These investigations were conducted in a chamber containing ten specially designed racks. If a subject still maintained his innocence, he would be taken to one of these machines, the names of which survive as a catalogue of terrors. One device was similar to a European medieval rack, twisting and bending a victim's limbs in progressive degrees. Another used the same process, but without the gradual intensity – instead, heavy counterweights would fall on the ends of ropes, in order to tug savagely at the prisoner's limbs. Another seemed designed to squeeze the breath out of a prisoner by the slow application of weight to his chest. All ten had names that evoke the terrifyingly matter-of-fact nature of the cruel clerk's atrocities: Stop All Pulses, Pant No More, Howling on the Ground, Instant Confession, Horror Supreme, Dying Pig's Rattle and Beg for Instant Death. One, Beg for Family Ruin, demonstrated a confidence that a prisoner would willingly implicate others if he were locked inside it. The last two, It Is True and I Am Rebel, display a cynical attitude towards the nature of these 'confessions', implying that people would agree to literally anything to escape the pain.[4]

The secret police behaved similarly towards members of the nobility and scored some impressive victories. One duke, the former leader of the armies that had put down the rebellion of Li Jingye, was heard to muse that, with things going the way they were, he would be a likely candidate for the next emperor himself. It was, strictly speaking, a statement of fact, since the decimation of Gaozong's children did make it possible that the line of succession would pass to his uncles. However, Wu's nephew Chengsi, who fancied his own chances, turned it into an accusation of sedition, and had the duke banished to the south.

An even more outrageous miscarriage of justice arose in the case of one Marshal Hao, a leading official in Ruizong's household. He was accused of plotting to overthrow Wu – doubly annoying for the Empress, since it demonstrated not only a hatred of Wu, but also a justifiable mistrust that Ruizong and his heirs would naturally inherit the throne after she was gone. Whether Marshal Hao warranted the charge or not, the circumstances of the case sounded fishy. The evidence against him was nothing more than the testimony of a serving girl, who claimed to have overheard his plot. It is also worth noting that he was the grandson of Hao Chujun, one of the ministers who had opposed Wu's regency in the days of Gaozong's incapacitation – someone whom Wu might associate with further barriers to her ascendancy.

Quite probably because of the shaky nature of the case, it was thrown out of court by a panel of judges. This was not part of the plan, and the judges were promptly accused of crimes of their own, found guilty and shipped off to exile in order to allow the defendant to receive a more fitting verdict of guilty. Marshal Hao was dragged off kicking and screaming to his execution, yelling curses at Wu and her family and, in an unexpected development, shouting out 'palace secrets' to the crowd. Although the nature of the secrets was not disclosed, they presumably related to the situation under which Ruizong was kept in seclusion. His guards attempted to keep him quiet, but he was somehow able to seize a branch from a nearby wagon and began attacking them with it. Eventually, his executioners killed him on the spot, without the ceremonial usually associated with such punishments, and thereafter criminals were gagged and bound on their way to executions.[5]

The city of Luoyang was plainly in the hands of Wu and her family. Their enemies were fast diminishing, their justifiable opponents crowded out in court by new appointees loyal to Wu and to the reforms that had allowed their ascendancy in the first place. Nor, clearly, did membership of the imperial family carry any weight with the new regimes – when even the supposed emperor could be overruled, and judges were exiled for obeying the law, the capital was lost.

The last hope lay out in the provinces, where those who regarded Wu as a usurper, and themselves as Tang loyalists, might attempt to organise some form of resistance. Scattered nobles, unable to draw attention to themselves through meeting openly, took the dangerous step of organising a rebellion by post. In the summer of 688, Duke Huang, a cousin of Gaozong, wrote a coded message to other provincial princes: 'I have a worsening internal disease that must be swiftly remedied. If untreated by this coming winter, I fear it shall prove fatal. We must move quickly; respond with all haste.'[6]

Close behind this incitement to rebellion came an invitation from Wu herself, for all members of the imperial family to assemble in Luoyang for the inauguration of the Hall of Illumination. Already doubting Wu's motives, the princes began to suspect that it would be a one-way trip for them to the capital, and that they would find themselves imprisoned, assassinated or otherwise prevented from ever leaving again as the Wu family grabbed hold of the empire.

Duke Huang wasted no time. Believing that the end justified the means, he forged an edict from the nominal emperor, Ruizong, calling upon all loyal members of the imperial family to converge on the capital and rescue him from Wu's clutches. This 'rebellion of the Tang princes', as it came to be known, was thwarted in its early stages by the difficulty of coordinating such a massive exercise without a discernible leader.

Another imperial cousin, the Prince of Langya, briefly seized territory on the Shandong peninsula in the east in the early autumn, with a small force of 5,000 men. However, the forged edict had already fallen into the hands of Wu sympathisers, and imperial troops were en route to other suspected revolutionary hotspots, ready to stifle any sympathetic uprisings. The early successes of the Prince of Langya stumbled when the wind changed during an arson attack on a besieged city, leading many to question whether this was another omen, that the elements favoured Wu more than the imperial family after all. The Prince of Langya was murdered by his own troops as imperial enforcers approached – the men thereby hoping to secure clemency for themselves.[7]

The domino effect took hold. Tang justice was harsh on the families of criminals – although the Prince of Langya was dead, his father realised that he would be implicated in the ensuing investigation, and raised his own rebellion. But his pitifully small force of soldiers stood no chance against the Tang dynasty's armies, and he was left to commit suicide as his men fled the battlefield near Luoyang. His children and their spouses died with him, preferring to take their own lives rather than leave their fates in the hands of Wu's investigators.

They were the lucky ones. The secret police wasted no time in hunting down lines of supply and chains of command. Even as the first rituals were performed in the Hall of Illumination, with Wu conspicuously standing in front of her son Ruizong as he performed his ceremonial duties, the Office of Prosecution was following the paper trails. Evidence was found that two other uncles of Gaozong had planned on backing the rebellion – unlike the Prince of Langya's father, they had hoped that their plans would not be noticed.

In a mystery that finally gave the secret police a real case to chew on, a court official was found murdered. Investigators discovered that he had been responsible for significant amounts of military supplies, which still existed on the imperial inventories, but were nowhere to be found in the storehouse. His killers turned out to be a committee of minor nobles, including Wu's own son-in-law, the husband of Princess Taiping, who had tired of the long-running charade that required him to pretend Xue Huaiyi was his father. He was thrown in prison, and left to starve to death.

Like the revolt of Li Jingye several years earlier, the abortive coup ended in victory for Wu, but this time she was taking no prisoners. She allowed her investigators to pursue every last conceivable lead, in a series of purges that carried on for two years. Even though the unrest had lasted for barely two weeks, the 'cruel clerks' were able to find (or plant) evidence of culpability in the houses of several hundred royal relatives, all but exterminating eleven entire branches of the imperial family. Their suffering was prolonged even into the afterlife, by the removal of their true surname, and its replacement with the word 'Lizard'.[8]

Wu's enemies, many of whom would write the official history of her reign, saw this as one more example of her atrocities. Yet even they were forced to admit some mitigating circumstances, most notable of which was that the plot for rebellion seemed solely centred on those who stood to gain power for themselves. The Tang princes might have enjoyed better success if there had been a popular uprising in their support, but there had been no such thing. In fact, regardless of the instigation of the nobility, and despite the forged edict from Ruizong calling on the faithful to rush to his rescue, the majority of the population reacted with a great degree of apathy. This did not necessarily amount to tacit support of Wu herself, but possibly a lack of confidence in the self-appointed last great hopes of the Li clan.

In fact, it would seem that, even amid the horrors of the investigators' purges of the imperial family, there was tension at court between the vindictive 'cruel clerks' and certain upstanding officials who continued to cling to the letter of the law.

Examination of the actual court records show that justice of a sort continued to function. Where the investigators had secured evidence through torture or plea-bargaining, cases often reached the court with a guilty verdict already established, leaving the judge, or occasionally Wu herself, with little option but to pass sentence. However, in other cases, particularly those where the investigators had bent the rules too far, there were still fearless officials who stood up to them.[9]

One such courageous man was Xu Yugong, a man who had served an entire term as a provincial judge without ever resorting to flogging a suspect to force a confession. Posted to the capital, he personally interceded at court in literally hundreds of cases, pleading directly with the Empress in cases of wrongful accusation. A wry joke of the period observed that, with Xu Yugong on one's case, life was certain, whereas the opposite was true with Lai Chunchen, the notorious leader of the secret police.

These two officials came into direct conflict over the case of a moneylender who had been a creditor of the Prince of Langya. Circumstantial evidence suggested that he had lent the Prince not only cash, but also support in his schemes, even if such support extended only as far as the turning of a blind eye to how the money was being used. The case dragged on, until the moneylender took advantage of one of the periodic amnesties, plea-bargained his way into a sentence of exile and avoided execution. Despite this, investigators attempted to press the case, arguing that the amnesty applied only to lower-ranking rebels, whereas the moneylender was plainly one of the ringleaders.

Xu Yugong refused to allow it and took his case all the way to Wu herself, arguing that an amnesty meant nothing if it could be withdrawn on an impulse. Nor, he pointed out, should the moneylender ever have been in danger in the first place, since he was a mere accessory, and it had already been decided to hunt down only the chief rebels, and the chief of the rebels, the Prince of Langya himself, was already dead.

A confused and somewhat irritable Empress Wu listened to this argument and asked Xu Yugong to clarify certain points of legal definition. When he had done so, she replied: 'Well, you had better reconsider the case' – hardly the decree of an unreasonable despot.[10]

Another loyal official was Judge Dee (Di Renjie), a popular magistrate in his fifties.[11] Posted to the remote western Gansu region, he had enjoyed the support of both Chinese colonists and the local population of non-Chinese. His career suffered a series of setbacks because of the enemies he made at court, and by the late 680s he was serving as a magistrate in a remote southern posting. In the lightning-fast round of promotions that accompanied the purges of the imperial family, he found himself moved into an administrative position that had been occupied by the Prince of Langya's father. Judge Dee arrived to find a prefecture in chaos, with many administrative personnel carted away for show trials, while armies of secret police terrorised the population.

Here we see an interesting snapshot of this period in Wu's reign. Her secret police might have been behaving like storm troopers, but this was not necessarily with her knowledge or approval. In secret, Judge Dee wrote a letter to Wu herself, complaining that he was witness to daily persecutions of innocent citizens, but that, if he protested, the secret police would be sure to frame him for an imagined crime. If, however, he remained quiet, then he would be doing a disservice to Empress Wu, since she would ultimately be held responsible for the crimes that were being committed in her name. Instead of reacting with the umbrage that her enemies would have us suspect, Empress Wu ordered the release of many of the unjustly accused and commuted the sentences of less clear-cut cases from execution to banishment.

Judge Dee would continue to fight for justice against some of the worst of Wu's hatchet men. When a military governor took over the province, Judge Dee stood up to him directly. His case, like that of

Xu Yugong's back in the capital, was that the people were being punished for the actions of a handful of aristocrats. In fact, in the case of his own locality, peasants who had been oppressed and victimised by would-be rebels, forced on pain of death to carry out their bidding, were now being similarly pressured by the investigators. In fact, Judge Dee went so far as to suggest that the secret police were doing more damage in his region than the rebels ever had. With bullish predictability, the governor wrote to Empress Wu, claiming that Judge Dee was guilty of corruption. He was thus rather surprised when the reply came back, ordering him to be sent away to a distant and unpleasant posting, while Judge Dee was promoted with a summons to serve at the court of Luoyang itself.[12]

There is one story of a loyal servant of Empress Wu, a leading officer in the army that had suppressed the southern rebels, who somehow found himself on the wrong side of the censors, and was dragged through the Gate of Beautiful Scenery for 'investigation'. Orders for his execution were duly obtained, and the man was brought out into the courtyard to be beheaded. But Wu had a last-minute change of heart, and sent a messenger to announce that the man's sentence had been commuted to lifelong banishment. The man, however, seemed unmoved by this act of mercy. Kneeling on the ground, awaiting the executioner's sword, he had initially refused to believe that his life had been saved. On another occasion, a doomed Tang prince was led past a funeral cortège and commented that it would have been a wonderful thing to have died of old age or disease.

With the Tang imperial family now considerably weaker, Wu continued on her grand plan to set aside the regency and become a true sovereign in her own right. In early 689, she led a grand sacrifice in the Hall of Illumination, carrying jade sceptres and wearing the robes of an emperor. Her son Ruizong and his own heir merely served as her assistants, as she paid homage to Heaven, the founder of the Tang dynasty and the departed Taizong. In a move that would have confirmed her intentions for any who still doubted them, the ceremony included rituals to honour her own father Wu Shihou. Chinese honorifics extended into the afterlife – it was considered bad form for one's earthly successes not to be passed onto one's ancestors, even if they had died before one's promotion. Consequently, Wu Shihou was already a prince in the afterlife, and now he was rebranded as an emperor, with five generations of his ancestors elevated to princely status. With such promotions in place, it was now possible to argue that Wu was of truly noble blood and deserving of her supreme role. Although few of Wu's close relatives survived, her living nephews and cousins were granted high rank, consolidating the hold of the Wu clan on the throne. Seeing which way the wind was blowing, Ruizong himself asked if his surname might be changed to Wu.

Further portents were announced – there was a sighting of a phoenix, the symbol of an empress, fluttering near the imperial palace, and garbled reports of hundreds of red sparrows, a symbol of great prosperity, on the roof of one of the halls of audience. Wu, however, had taken the omens as far as she might.[13]

Instead, Wu made her own luck. Copies of the *Great Cloud*, laden with apparent prophecies of her advent and dominion, were sent out to all the existing Buddhist monasteries, while many more were set up, with instructions to make the *Great Cloud* the centre of their sermons. For common folk in Wu's China, a religious experience would now revolve around their supreme leader, as did many popular songs and ballads of the day, and local nature rituals.

Wu began to play the part of an aspiring deity, imitating a divine emperor of legend, who had supposedly invented writing itself on the banks of the Luo River. Calligraphy and word-games seem to have been a popular pastime with Wu, and there are reports of her testing scholars' knowledge of obscure characters on idle evenings, drawing seldom-used words to see if her advisers could guess their meaning, and sometimes bluffing by concocting a character that simply did not exist. Now she imposed some of her new creations on the population, creating new ways of writing several commonplace terms, including Moon, Prince and Heaven. Some of her decisions appear rather frivolous, alterations seemingly undertaken merely for the sake of it, to show that, as the supreme ruler of China, she could even control the language itself. Of particular interest is her alteration of the character for 'human being'. Pronounced *ren*, this simple character is composed of a standing figure, and is still, even today, often termed the 'man radical', even though it is gender-neutral. Wu's reforms discarded the old version and replaced it with a new image composed of elements meaning 'one who is born' – perhaps dragging the meaning of life itself back towards a recognition of the feminine principle.

Similarly, Wu changed the character for 'nation', retaining the border that circled around it but filling its middle with her own surname – Wu was now the centre of the nation itself, and its very essence.

Other changes were designed to save the blushes of the population – it was considered rude to use the personal name of a sovereign in everyday correspondence, and Wu's name was, for want of a better word, rather common. Wu found a way around this by simply insisting that her name be written with a different character henceforth – essentially, she created a new and previously unused character, and then banned its use, allowing the old version to continue to be used in daily life. Her given name of Zhao, 'bright', was in everyday use. She came up with a new way of writing it, combining the characters for 'brilliant' and 'void'. This was now her personal name, an image of enlightenment streaming down into emptiness.

Wu clearly had her heart set on being the official ruler, the first female *huangdi*, rather than a *huanghou* acting as a regent. There was simply no point in announcing such changes to the writing system unless she planned on becoming the person whose personal name would need to be avoided in correspondence. In autumn 690, one of her officials took the hint and suggested that, all things considered, it was time for Wu to embrace her destiny and become the ruling sovereign. As protocol demanded, Wu coquettishly refused. Before long, her ministers approached her again, this time with a petition signed by thousands of loyal subjects, including the surviving members of the Tang imperial family, everyone at court who knew what was good for them and representatives of the many temples and monasteries who had spent the previous couple of years poring over the *Great Cloud* and other arguments for Wu's impending divinity.

Wu refused again, since China already had an emperor in the form of Ruizong, and there was no real need to take over. Matters now fell to Ruizong himself, the luckless individual who had supposedly ruled China for the previous six years. Miraculously still alive, despite being the figurehead of several attempts at loyalist restoration, Ruizong knew what he needed to do to keep breathing. He petitioned his mother himself, announcing that, in his imperial wisdom, he had decided that it was time for him to abdicate. There was no fighting fate or preventing prophecy – destiny clearly intended that Wu should be the mistress of the world. Seers had foretold that the advent of a living goddess would usher in an age of divine prosperity, and she was the one.

With carefully orchestrated reluctance and humility, Wu accepted his offer.

TEN

The Sage Mother of Mankind

The Tang dynasty was gone. Wu proclaimed a new dynasty, the Zhou, named for the rulers of China in the distant past – the time of the great sages Lao Zi and Confucius, and the rulers of China in the days when Buddha himself had lived in distant India. The fact was not lost on the classically educated of the court that the first ruler of the ancient Zhou dynasty had been a man called the 'War King' – *wu wang*.[1]

Her motives for doing so have been questioned ever since. She was in her mid-sixties, most of her close male relatives were dead, and, despite his abdication, Ruizong was still her heir – one of a few historical figures fated to be crowned emperor twice. When old age eventually ran its course, she would die, and a son of Gaozong would rule in her place. One might argue that, given a few switches in nomenclature and surnames, Wu's death would find things going on as the Tang ancestors had intended.

Wu seemed happy to accept the portents of the 'fates', assuming her role as Sage Mother of Mankind. Her new dynasty, such as it

生

REN – PERSON
During Wu's reign, the word for 'person' was altered so that it now had components that could be read 'one that is born'.

151

was, seemed designed to preserve the core of the Li imperial family from usurper cousins, not to steal it from its rightful inheritors – although the deposed Zhongzong, still living in exile far to the south, might have disagreed.

Wu did not behave like a conquering emperor – she did not decree a new legal code, as other dynastic founders had done before her, nor were there any lasting reforms beyond those that she had already introduced during her regency. She did not even announce her dynasty's ruling element – tantamount to a general statement of attitude, such as the Qin dynasty's black Water-nature, or the red Fire-nature of the Han.

Compared to her industrious intrigues of the preceding decades, the fifteen years in which Wu ruled China under her own name were relatively uneventful. This, perhaps, is a sign of her realisation that she had pushed as far as it was possible to go. She enjoyed popular support, particularly from Buddhists, but her presence as ruler was still built on fragile foundations. Without the buttress of the *Great Cloud*, she was just a usurper. Without the bold, magical statement of the Hall of Illumination, she was a 'hen crowing at daybreak'. Notably, she issued two proclamations urging the people to set no store by 'superstitions'. The favourable interpretation of omens had got her where she was, but she could not afford to allow any others to twist natural phenomena and rumour to their own ends. After all the 'lights in the sky', new mountains and miraculous inscriptions of previous years, the period of Wu's actual reign remains largely uncoloured by spectacular phenomena. Three comets are known to have appeared in the Chinese sky in the ensuing decade, but, although they were reported in Korea and Japan, Wu's own astronomers were silent on the matter.[2]

Wu's proclamations against superstition, one in 689 and another in 695, seem designed to stem a new series of rumours. She was, however, unable to resist a couple of propaganda coups in the early years of her reign. In January 692, flowers bloomed early in a Luoyang park. Before news got out to the population at large, Wu was able to issue a proclamation:

With urgent haste I inform the spring
Flowers must open their petals tonight
Don't wait for the morning wind to blow![3]

She was thereby able to take credit for the unseasonable flowering, in an incident that has been garbled and reinterpreted by later writers, as a sign of her hubris or of her growing belief in her own divine powers. The same year saw her proclaiming that she had received her first sign of rejuvenation, when a 'new tooth' apparently appeared in her mouth. Her subjects certainly swallowed the auspicious character of her reign and continued to pay her conspicuous homage. Gifts arrived from every corner of the empire, including beautiful curios like a cloak made of kingfisher feathers, sent from the adoring citizens of Canton.[4]

But in general her interest in portents faded fast, particularly after an accident among her pets. Wu claimed to have successfully reared a cat to live in the same cage as several parrots, without harming them. The annals do not record how many parrots or cats Wu got through before she achieved this marvellous equilibrium, but her animal novelty seems to have been based on simple principles. The cat was kept well fed at all times and thereby had no interest in the parrots. Wu brought this 'miracle' in to her court to show off to her cronies, although for some reason, perhaps an over-long absence of fresh food, or the pressure of being admired by so many ministers, the cat suddenly regained its appetite. The entire incident was treated with secret hilarity in the court, but Wu did not see the funny side – it was not merely the sight of pets eating each other, but the possibility for gossips to create new omens out of it. Was the cat Wu, snatching up and devouring the 'birds' of the imperial family? Or was the cat the vengeful spirit of Xiao Liangdi, back to devour these miniature 'phoenixes' before her ghost claimed the supreme phoenix, Wu herself? Meanwhile, snow fell out of season in 693. When allies in Turkestan sent the court a two-headed dog for their amusement and delectation, none dared voice an opinion concerning the poor creature's status as a good or bad omen.[5]

Some of Empress Wu's cronies were wrong-footed by her sudden change in attitude. Paramount among them was Wu Chengsi, her nephew, who still expected the reforms and purges to continue after Wu's accession. He was now married to a noblewoman, the daughter of Wu's confidante Princess Qianjin. Qianjin had herself adopted the Wu surname – a sign of honour, but also one that would have played havoc with the rules of propriety, since, if taken at their strictest, Wu Chengsi was marrying an adoptive relative, and on the verge of incest.

Most affected by the sudden cessation of interest in the supernatural was Xue Huaiyi. Fearing that he would have no more prophecies to interpret or miracles to uncover, Huaiyi sought a new role as a military man. Turkish invaders nibbled at the borders in 694, leading Wu to dispatch an army under Huaiyi's nominal leadership, although its real generals were experienced soldiers. The Turks were duly put down, Huaiyi erected a stone monument to his own genius, and he returned to Luoyang as full of himself as ever.

But even though Wu had forbidden any further interpretation of omens, they were there for the taking, and not always in Huaiyi's favour. Huaiyi built a Buddhist annexe to the Hall of Illumination, a massive 'Hall of Heaven' containing what would have been the world's largest statue of Buddha. Soon after its construction, the hall was wrecked by a freak wind, leading Huaiyi to petition for more funds. Wu granted them, but others surely noted that there appeared to be some element of divine displeasure in the inauspicious events.

Wu did not restrict her charity to the Buddhist faith, although Buddhism was clearly on the rise thanks to her patronage. Giant Buddhist statues, including a colossal one of Maitreya, said to have been modelled on Wu's own features, were commissioned and carved in the grottoes of Longmen. The eating of meat began to fall out of fashion, as a Buddhist disdain for the butchery of animals took hold among the general populace – this is likely to have been more noticeable at court than among the common people, where meat dishes would have been rarer to start with. However, Wu also continued to honour non-Buddhist figures, particularly Confucius, the icon of the misogynist scholar-elite that had spent so long opposing her. Confucius and his most famous disciples were granted new honorific titles during Wu's reign, and, presumably, many of the scholar-elite were brought round to Wu's way of thinking.

She authorised the construction of yet another showy building, the Celestial Pillar, a towering octagonal iron column 12 feet in diameter and 105 feet high, its height as much as doubled by the great metal mound into which it was set. At its top, it flared out into a massive plinth, on which four mighty dragons supported a glowing 'fire-orb' – presumed to have been a globe of highly polished bronze. The edifice, intended as a representation of the axis around which the whole of Wu's world turned, was designed by a foreigner, recorded in the Tang annals as Mao Polo, although his true name and origin are unknown.[6]

Bad omens continued to haunt Luoyang's great religious complex. A special festival in early 695 admitted members of the public to the presence of the Great Buddha statue, where Huaiyi flung handfuls of coins into the crowd. This was supposed to have been a New Year's gesture of public largesse, but several members of the crowd were trampled to death in the ensuing tussle.[7]

Huaiyi's behaviour grew increasingly strange. In what appeared to be a state of religious ecstasy at one ceremony, he slashed his own thigh and daubed his fresh blood on a statue of Buddha.[8] Soon after, he retired to his base at the White Horse Monastery, and entertained himself with the other false monks of his entourage.

Huaiyi seems to have left Luoyang in a sulk because he was no longer the only charlatan who held the Empress Wu's attention. As a result of the truly immense amount of money she had sunk into Buddhist institutions in the past decade, she had attracted all manner of hangers-on and chancers, many of whom had no real religious interest at all. One woman set herself up as an abbess, benefiting immediately from the resultant tax breaks, even though her 'temple' was actually a front for a brothel. Wu appears to have been taken in by the deception, setting great store by the woman's claim to see the future, and to live, like Buddha before her, on a single grain of rice a day. In fact, every evening she was sneaking into the back rooms of her brothel for a banquet with her fellow whores, although none dared breathe a word of this to Wu herself.[9]

With Huaiyi absent, he was also unable to prevent whispers among his enemies. Before long, a magistrate mused that Huaiyi was not merely 'praying' at the White Horse, but plotting the downfall of the dynasty. Despite the earlier favour Huaiyi had enjoyed with Wu, she was in no mood to hear of new revolts in the offing, and approved the magistrate's investigation.

When summoned to court, Huaiyi arrived on horseback, not deigning to get out of the saddle until he had ridden right into the courtroom. He had been expecting a sham trial that would soon acquit him, but, upon the presentation of actual evidence of wrongdoing, he soon climbed onto his horse again and rode back out. When the magistrate complained to Wu, she laughed off Huaiyi's rude behaviour, but noted that, while the monk was harmless, she was not so protective of his followers. Before long, many of Huaiyi's supporters had been exiled, depriving the false monk of many of his favourites.

Seemingly out of spite, he made his feelings known in an arson attack on the Hall of Illumination itself. Perhaps intended to give himself new-found standing as the architect of its replacement, his vandalism was helped by a strong wind that engulfed the hall in flames and also toppled the giant Buddha statue.

The Hall of Illumination was completely destroyed, and with it any faith Wu might have had in her priestly advisers. When the fake abbess arrived to offer her sympathies, Wu turned on her, demanding to know how a supposed prophetess could have failed to foresee the destruction of the most important temple in the world. It was not long before the true nature of the nuns' temple was made public, and an embarrassed Wu ordered the fake abbess and her aspirants enslaved.[10]

Nor did Huaiyi long survive his fall from grace. In an act that has for ever kept the true nature of her relationship with him a secret, Wu determined to deal with him without a trial, or the embarrassment of a public execution. Instead, Huaiyi simply disappeared one day shortly after being summoned to the palace. A few days later his dead body arrived back at the White Horse Monastery, slung unceremoniously on the back of a peasant's cart. The exact nature of his fate was undetermined, although some said that he had been tied to a tree in the palace and beaten to death by one of Wu's remote cousins. A more spectacular rumour claimed that he had been brought into Wu's bedchamber under the pretence of an orgy with Wu's serving girls. There, Wu's daughter Taiping and some of the stronger palace women had tied him down and, as he lay helpless, watched calmly as he was strangled by Taiping's nurse.[11]

Wu had grown impatient with some of the allies who had helped her rise to power – although annals continued to report injustice and corruption in Luoyang, it is notable that, whenever such things reached Wu's personal attention, she proved to be a righteous arbitrator. The magistrates Xu Yugong and Judge Dee, old men who had everything to fear, maintained their heroic stand against the persecutions of the secret police, heedless of the consequences. Both of them were subject to further attacks by the 'cruel clerks', but somehow survived.

In the case of Xu Yugong, he found himself accused of working in league with a governor charged with corruption – in fact, Xu's 'crime' had simply been to suggest that the man was innocent. Whatever evidence Zhou Xing and Lai Chunchen could manufacture, it was enough to discredit Xu. But Wu refused to issue the death penalty, instead sentencing him in the lightest possible terms. She simply fired him from his job, and made her feelings clear by soon summoning him back to court to a new position.

Presumably expecting some thanks from the reinstated magistrate, Wu called him in for an audience, but Xu remained pessimistic. He compared himself to a deer on a hillside, escaping one hunting party only to be a target for the next. Wu insisted that he take up a post as censor, his job a thankless one of pointing out those occasions when court officials (or the Empress herself) were behaving contrary to protocol and tradition.

Clinging to their former power and position, some members of the secret police turned on each other. Lai Chunchen, the cruellest of the cruel clerks and author of the *Classic of Entrapment*, invited his fellow investigator Zhou Xing to a dinner at which conversation inevitably turned to developments in torture. Lai sighed at the difficulties of extracting confessions from victims who were often unwilling to reveal their guilt, and even occasionally unaware that they were guilty at all. Entering into the spirit of things, Zhou suggested conducting interviews before a giant cauldron of boiling water, so that the subject of the investigation was able fully to appreciate just what would happen to him if he failed to offer the investigators all the information they required. Amid the laughter around the table at this cunning ruse, Lai enthusiastically gave orders for a cauldron to be set up in the hall where they were dining. As the waters nearby gradually came to a full boil, the rest of the room took on an icy atmosphere. Lai began to speak of recent prosecutions, and of the case of a general who was thought to have been plotting with officials within the palace. He suspected that some of the general's co-conspirators were still at large, and that some might even be members of the secret police. As the water came to the boil, Lai turned to Zhou and announced that Zhou himself had been named as an accomplice by the general before his own untimely demise. Zhou was under investigation, and he now had one chance to confess everything he knew, before he would be cast into the boiling water.

Zhou immediately agreed that he was guilty of everything he had been accused of. Stripped of his post and exiled to the far south, he was murdered en route by disgruntled relatives of his former victims. The roster of potential suspects was too long to list.

Lai Chunchen might have been an official appointed by Empress Wu, but it is unfair to hold her directly responsible for his many misdeeds. In fact, he was secretly in league with Wu's nephew Chengsi, who continued to believe that the next step in Wu's reforms would be to strip Ruizong of his status as heir, and to promote himself in his place. Thus, in many of the atrocities of the 690s, it could be argued that we are witnessing not the ongoing intrigues of Empress Wu herself, but rather those of her nephew. In one notorious incident in 693, Wu retroactively approved a series of

executions in far Canton, under the responsibility of a member of
the Office of Prosecution. Several years later, she would claim that
she had been misled into believing there had been a conspiracy. In
fact, a minor prosecutor, Wan Guojun, had ordered the wives and
children of suspected criminals to commit suicide. When they had
refused and protested, he ordered them to a nearby riverbank, where
his soldiers killed them. These 300 deaths were matched by several
other provincial incidents in which similar mass murders appeared
as suicides or executions on the files of the Office of Prosecution.
Wu's critics claim she was fully aware of the deception, while her
supporters are prepared to believe that the buck stopped with her
nephew, Chengsi.[12]

Chengsi's desire to follow his aunt onto the throne was highly
unlikely to succeed. But, considering Empress Wu's successful
manipulation of events over the preceding forty years, who can
blame him for thinking he had a chance? His daughter was married
to a son of Wu's confidante Princess Qianjin, perhaps giving him
more of a shot at becoming a regent to an imperial son-in-law, in the
event that another hundred or so members of the Tang dynasty
dropped dead. Instead, however, he took a leaf from his aunt's book
and set his sights lower. Rather than continue attacks directly on the
imperial family, he imitated Wu's assault on Gaozong's ministers
from the days of her youth, targeting any officers who might present
an opposition to him taking a more direct route. Chengsi seems to
have believed that he needed only to remove a few old-fashioned
censors in order to give Wu herself the opportunity to nominate him
as her heir.

One of the prime candidates likely to stand in his way was the
upstanding Judge Dee, who was rounded up with a number of other
officials and escorted to the investigators' head office by the Gate of
the Beautiful Scenery. Lai Chunchen informed his captives that they
had one shot at mercy – under plea-bargaining terms that Wu had
recently approved, anyone who immediately pleaded guilty could
have his sentence commuted from execution to banishment. With
that in mind, Lai Chunchen asked Judge Dee if there was a
conspiracy. Dee's reply was blunt and sarcastic: '[Wu's] Great Zhou

revolution has occurred, and ten thousand things are changing. Old officials of the Tang dynasty like myself are soon to be executed. You bet there's a conspiracy.'[13] Lai Chunchen would have preferred a straight yes or no, but took Judge Dee's response to be in the affirmative. Dee was locked up for processing, although his stance managed to impress some of his captors. One investigator, doubting very much that Dee would be detained long in exile, asked him if the Judge would put a good word in for him on his return, to which the Judge responded by literally banging his head against a wooden pillar while calling the investigator a series of rude names.

The Judge, however, was not going to go without a fight. Waiting for a moment when he was left alone, he wrote a letter to his son on the inner lining of his jacket, and then prevailed upon his captors to take the jacket back to his home, so that his family could take out the winter padding.

On finding the secret message, Dee's son immediately applied for an audience with Wu herself, and showed the Empress the accusing letter. Lai Chunchen was called to explain himself, but argued that the letter was a forgery, since he had no record of the Judge's clothes being sent back to his house. There, Dee's case might have foundered before it could have truly begun, but for a slave who approached Wu himself. The 10-year-old boy was one of many palace servants who owed their position to the alleged misdeeds of their elder family members. Uncaring that his words could lead to his own torture or death, the boy announced that his family was innocent and that he lived his life as a slave solely because of the persecutions and lies of the 'cruel clerks'.

This dramatic turn of events forced Wu to summon Dee to the palace to explain himself. She asked the Judge why he had pleaded guilty in the first place, to which Dee replied that it was the only way he could avoid torture and death. In which case, asked the Empress, why had he then sent a separate petition, demanding that his sentence be upgraded to execution.

Dee, of course, had done no such thing – Lai Chunchen had merely fixed his name to a forgery. With only circumstantial evidence for the defence, and the prosecution's case now found to be resting on doctored documents, Empress Wu permitted the seven accused officials to go free, although most of them were packed off to provincial postings to keep them out of trouble in the near future.[14]

Chengsi's major opponents may not have been killed, but they were at least removed to a significant distance. He tried his luck by sending an associate to petition on his behalf, suggesting to Empress Wu that the time had come to fire Ruizong as heir and replace him with the more deserving Chengsi.

Wu sent Chengsi's spokesman away on several occasions, and records of their audiences show her increasingly irritated with his constant harping on the theme of Chengsi. Eventually, in an unfortunate incident, Wu ordered vice-minister Li Zhaode to have the petitioner flogged. Zhaode was a zealous traditionalist, a stickler for propriety who managed to alienate everyone at court – Wu cannot have much liked him either, since he was an old-fashioned loyalist and a supporter of the Li clan. He despised the upstart nephews and cousins of the Wu clan, and had no time for the 'cruel clerks' either. However, Empress Wu seemed content to sit back while Zhaode and his various opponents tangled with each other in the ensuing months.

Despite his attitude and lack of friends, Zhaode nevertheless offered important advice to the Empress. It was he who suggested to her that Chengsi's father had died in exile at Wu's own order, and that, far from being a loyal relative of the ruler, Chengsi might have been harbouring resentment and vengeful intentions all his life. Although Wu at first refused to believe such insinuations, it was Zhaode who put an end to Chengsi's political career, when Wu permitted him to give a speech outlining the silliness of handing over the throne:

The Imperial Heir [i.e. Ruizong] is Your Majesty's son. From Your Majesty have come forth sons and grandsons who inherit the empire forever. Why would You use a nephew as an heir? From ancient times, I have never heard that a nephew became the Son of Heaven and [then, in return,] set up ancestral temples for his aunt. Your Majesty, moreover, was entrusted with the guardianship of the empire by Gaozong. Should You pass it on to Chengsi, then he will be without ancestral sacrifices.[15]

Zhaode was right. Wu had pushed as far as she could. The next ruler of the empire would have to be a male-line descendant of Gaozong, otherwise she could lose critical remaining support among the scholar-elite. In a repeat of her censorious actions against her half-brothers, she soon announced a series of 'promotions' and provincial postings that neutralised the growing power of her nephews and cousins – those who remained at court were deprived of any real power, and, although they protested vehemently, she refused to entertain their counter-accusations.

With Chengsi's power undermined, the 'cruel clerks' lost their best protector. Before long, a censor's investigation into corruption found that Lai Chunchen had falsified evidence on several hundred occasions, and the surviving leader of the cruel clerks was himself hauled off to execution. His function now well and truly served, Li Zhaode was sentenced to death on the same day.

Two rival court factions had successfully annihilated each other, leaving Wu comfortably in charge. In the months that followed, she kept her courtiers guessing about the matter of succession. In January/February 693, she arranged a ceremony featuring 900 temple dancers, swaying to music that Wu had supposedly written herself. The ritual reaffirmed her status as a living god, but she chose as her assistants two of the discredited nephews who had recently been moved to sinecure positions.

The decision was confusing – now nobody was sure if the nephews' promotions had been punitive or not. The nephews themselves received a mixed message, stripped of any rank with real power but invited to participate in a ceremony in place of the rightful heir, Ruizong. Nor did the exclusion of Ruizong go down particularly well with the imperial heir himself, leading to a series of criminal accusations concerning his own retinue. Soon after Wu's big New Year's ceremony, two of Ruizong's concubines, including the mother of the future Xuanzong Emperor, were executed on suspicion of sorcery.[16] The same year, Wu ordered the public execution of two court officials who had attempted to meet Ruizong in secret. Ruizong himself was put under investigation, although he was saved from answering any direct questions by the actions of one of his servants. During preliminary hearings over Ruizong's alleged involvement in a conspiracy, the servant attempted to cut out his own heart to demonstrate his loyalty to the Prince and, by association, the Prince's loyalty to Empress Wu. It was a messy publicity stunt, but one that Wu found suitably persuasive. Ruizong's position was considered safe, for now.[17]

Wu's behaviour in these years has confused many historians. It is tempting to write it off as the caprices of an ageing oriental despot, although there are still some who are prepared to suggest there was method in her madness. Throughout several preceding centuries, no dynasty had managed to maintain hold on China for more than a couple of generations. The problem, seemingly doomed to eternal repetition, was that rebels would supplant an incompetent dynasty, only to struggle to establish their legitimacy and nobility. In the process of doing so, they would soon be tempted into the usual traps – dynastic alliances with powerful aristocratic families, who would soon begin to exert power from behind the throne. Early meritocracies, valuing loyalty and competence would be crowded out by nepotism and sinecures, until the rot set in. For those who are prepared to accept this view, Wu's behaviour can be read as an attempt to break this cycle.

In founding the Tang dynasty, Taizong and his father had snatched power from their ineffectual cousins. But already by the time of Gaozong, the old aristocracies were exerting their influence. Gaozong, after all, had a mother from the old aristocratic Zhangsun family, and Wu herself had a mother who had prided herself on her family connections to the departed Sui. But, with her seizure of power from her sons, Wu may have seen herself as stopping the corruption in its tracks. Zhongzong, in thrall to his wife and in-laws, had been packed off into exile. Ruizong, unable to stand up for himself, had been gagged, and now was forbidden from holding meetings with any court official. Meanwhile, Wu's reforms, despite the obvious and manifold abuses to which they had been put, also cut out much dead wood from the administration. Official postings were increased in number, but their terms decreased in length, presumably in order to prevent incumbents from growing complacent and forming inappropriate associations. Wu continually exercised her imperial prerogative to hire and fire, promote and demote her ministers – such that 80 per cent of her officials ended their careers in either dismissal or demotion, compared to 33 per cent similarly ousted during the reign of Taizong. But, while antagonistic historians have seen this as a sign of Wu's addled caprices, her defenders have claimed that she introduced a dynamic system of balances on the abuse of power.[18]

Some might argue that dramatisations of Wu's life have missed the point. Later writers have sensationalised Wu's court politics into a stand-off between good and evil, righteous ministers like Judge Dee, fighting fecklessly corrupt officials such as Wu's nephews. But, when we examine the dates of his appointments, we see a strange symmetry that some might prefer to read as a form of oppositional government. When Judge Dee was first appointed as a minister in Wu's court, he was inaugurated on the same day as Yuning, a nephew of the Empress, whose attitude was almost diametrically opposed to his own. In 698, when Judge Dee was promoted to the presidency of the imperial chancellery, Wu's nephew Sansi was appointed to a post of matching rank in the secretariat.

Wu became regent for a dynasty that had broken all the rules it was now trying to enforce. But her actions in government, particularly in the 690s, served to kick away the ladder that had allowed the Tang dynasty to reach imperial heights in the first place. Although revolts and unrest would continue throughout the Tang dynasty, it would nevertheless endure for two centuries after her death, perhaps partly because of the ruthless purges of her reign.

Despite the opprobrium heaped upon her by later generations, Wu was an incredibly popular ruler with the common people. Her detractors, of course, would say that nobody was left alive who opposed her. While she did spend a lot of public money on extravagances like the Hall of Illumination and its replacement, there appears to have been more public money around. China was prospering, the Silk Road was bringing in massive trade opportunities in the west and Wu's tax office was reaping the benefits.[19] Unlike other legendary big spenders, such as the ancient First Emperor, who taxed his subjects into oblivion for the sake of his public works, Wu's big projects seemed easily funded by the increase in revenue. In fact, in 695, Wu even granted the entire empire a completely tax-free year.[20]

That is not to say that Wu's actions made her the darling of her courtiers. She was a formidable figure to her ministers, willing to sack those who displeased her. Although court histories show numerous incidents in which she listened to ministerial advice, such as her famous willingness to take criticism from Judge Dee, she would hear no comment on several matters of crucial importance. The succession was off-limits for discussion, as was any objection to the activities of her personal retinue, which one court wit likened to 'rotten dumplings' – nice looking on the outside but utterly useless for their official purpose. Such issues were discounted by Wu as 'family matters', and as such were out of ministerial purview, despite the unquestionable influence they had on the wider political world – it was Wu herself, it seems, who finally dealt with the matter of Xue Huaiyi, not any of the censors or secret police.[21]

But Wu was not getting any younger – the issue of who would take over after her was becoming a matter of concern, both for her supporters and for her largely silent opponents. Some, however, were prepared to speak out. In Luoyang, Wu had a recurring dream that she was playing a game of Chinese chess, and that she kept losing. Dee was soon on hand to interpret it for her, pointing out that the word for 'chessmen' was the same as that for 'sons'. In Dee's view, Wu would continue to lose in her dreams for as long as she defied Heaven by depriving her sons of their birthright. Instead of having him fired, imprisoned or executed for speaking of such a proscribed 'family matter', Empress Wu merely listened in silence.[22]

ELEVEN

The Office of the Crane

Once each generation, the monarch of the early Tang would come to pay homage to the relics of Buddha at the Famen temple. Wu is the only ruler to appear twice in its paintings – first as the sinister observer of Gaozong's procession (see Chapter Five), then as ruler in her own right. At the turn of the eighth century, the ageing Wu returned to the Famen temple, donating a beautiful silk gown with lavish brocades to its treasure vault, along with more useful items such as gold and silver artefacts. The painting shows her, white-haired and frail, led towards the temple by two beautiful youths, each supporting one of her arms, smiling beatifically, gazing deeply into her eyes and standing just a little too close for comfort.

As far as the Chinese population in general were concerned, the divine Empress Wu was ruling over a period of unprecedented good fortune. Bad ministers, so they heard, were being purged by loyal investigators. Great public works had been sanctioned by the gods themselves, leading to the long-awaited earthly incarnation of a living god. But, just as Wu might attempt to take the credit for

SHENG – HOLY
During Wu's reign, the character for 'holy' was replaced with
components meaning 'long' and 'heavy'.

anything good that happened, a Chinese sovereign was also expected to take responsibility for the bad. Regardless of the ban on discussing superstitions, there were still signs in the 690s that Heaven was not as pleased as Wu's regime liked to imply.

Tax collection was faltering in some of the provinces, where monasteries, vagrants and unregistered citizens all evaded their obligations. Officials had allowed many to slip through the system, and, after the lavish spending of recent years, it seemed that Wu's government was not as rich as it had thought.

Nor was it as invincible. Wu's age of prosperity had relied, at least in part, on the absence of any threat from beyond China's borders. During the early 690s, everything seemed rosy – the Koreans gave the Chinese no trouble, while the riches of the Silk Road spent longer in Chinese territory, courtesy of the long tongue of land, the Gansu corridor, reaching out far to the west into newly conquered provinces. Nor were the Turks any trouble for the moment. A million foreigners entered China during the first half of the 690s, but did so legally and peacefully. Entire tribes of Central Asian nomads were given permission to settle in relatively inhospitable parts of China. One Turkish leader, the khan Qapagan, mounted raids against Chinese borders, but, when repulsed by no less a general than Xue Huaiyi, soon offered his allegiance and was rebranded as a duke on the borders.

Meanwhile, the good weather turned bad again. This sudden strain on the granaries may have been what first alerted Wu's officials to the number of unregistered civilians; unexpected numbers of dole-seekers were arriving in urban offices in search of free food. This became particularly acute in the north, where a Chinese provincial commander had sternly refused to hand out similar provisions to the famine-struck tribes of Khitan, which had been a Chinese vassal state for several decades. The Khitan rose up in revolt, while, in the west, the Chinese faced an invading force from Tibet.

One could argue, of course, that such border problems were a sign of Chinese prosperity, as China's less organised neighbours were forced to resort to violence when faced by a famine. This was of little consolation to China's ambassador to the great khan Qapagan in 696, who had been hoping for an easy and good-natured exchange of gifts and diplomatic pleasantries. Instead, after presenting Qapagan with a few trinkets and sinecures, the ambassador found himself dealing with an emboldened tribal leader, demanding that his area of responsibility be extended over some neighbouring tribes who currently resided within China's north-west borders. Qapagan also wanted a bigger share of the food that he heard was being handed out all over the empire, as well as a massive imperial donation of farm implements, to help his people 'cultivate the land' in which they found themselves. This last request would have been particularly galling to the Chinese, who had secretly been forced to melt down several tons of farm tools in order to complete Empress Wu's great iron pillar in Lüoyang – nor were they that keen on handing such a large quantity of axes, scythes and picks to a ruler who had started throwing his weight around.[1]

Qapagan demonstrated his resolve by attacking a Khitan encampment and carrying off their women. He added insult to injury by demanding the Chinese supply a man of their own; since he was now a duke in the eyes of Wu's court, he had decided that it was time for his daughter to marry a Chinese prince.

Despite her supposed status as a living goddess, Wu was sufficiently rattled by Qapagan's request to grant it. His borders were extended up to the western banks of the Yellow River, and he was supplied with large donations of grain, silk (which served as currency both inside and outside China), ingots of raw iron and 3,000 'farm implements'. Accompanying the bribe was a Chinese prince of sorts, Wu's great-nephew Yanxiu, whom Wu hoped would prove sufficiently royal a bridegroom for Qapagan's daughter.

Judge Dee made his displeasure felt at court, and took the risky step of citing precedents – Wu hated it when her ministers dragged up past rulers as object lessons in behaviour. But Dee had a reasonable point – in the days of Taizong, China's borders had stopped at the edge of the sand. If the Turks wanted to cause trouble, they would first have to cross the forbidding wastes of the Taklamakan or Gobi deserts. Before they even came within sight of the Great Wall, they would face days of thirst and deprivation that functioned as a very effective barrier as they were forced to march through a region where 'not a hair [of grass] would grow'.[2]

Now, through both the expansion of Chinese territory and the granting of lands to these upstarts, the Chinese had effectively met the Turks halfway. They were now obliged to defend worthless provinces, from enemies that now resided on their very doorstep. And, besides, Qapagan would never be satisfied.

Wu ignored Dee's advice, and the minister must have taken little pleasure from the letter that arrived from Qapagan, which showed that he had been more right than he could have guessed. Qapagan wrote:

> The bad grain you sent would not grow. The gold and silver gifts were worthless fakes. The honours you gave my envoys were revoked. The silk was old and frayed. My daughter is a daughter of a Khan, deserving of a husband who is the son of an emperor. The Wu family is not equal to mine, and you attempt to deceive me. Consequently, I have raised an army and shall conquer [north China].[3]

Qapagan had been even clearer with the envoy who had accompanied the unlucky bridegroom. He offered a series of misty-eyed reminiscences about the good old days under the Li family (that is, Taizong and Gaozong), and claimed to be shocked that only two princes (Zhongzong and Ruizong) now survived. Qapagan then claimed that his sense of patriotic duty had obliged him to invade China, in order to restore the Tang dynasty.

The conflict that ensued in the north would prove damaging to Wu's power base. She was obliged to offer concessions to the invading Tibetans in order to free up troops for the defence of the north. She was also forced to make multiple compromises with the inhabitants of the north itself – many of whom had been absconding southwards in order to free themselves from the heavy burden of taxation, compulsory labour on government projects and military service, which was not required of those who did not live in border regions. When even these deals failed to raise an army big enough to deal with the Turks, Wu resorted to conscripting criminals and slaves – a sign of desperation.

Nor did the campaign go well against Qapagan. The army against him had been led by another of Wu's nephews, who badly mismanaged his task and took out his frustrations on the local population afterwards. The arrival of Judge Dee in the province put an end to his persecutions, but only served to remind the court that Wu's relatives were wholly unsuitable for high office.

The greatest change brought about by the Qapagan invasion lay in the identity of the individual who had accompanied Judge Dee to the north. After the failure of her nephew, and after intense consultation with her ministers, Wu had appointed a commander of reinforcements who was guaranteed to enjoy the support of the people, the approval of the court and, it was presumed, the endorsement of the gods – her eldest son, Zhongzong.

Zhongzong had spent an unhappy time in exile in the south, constantly fretting that he would somehow be implicated in the next purge and receive a curt command to kill himself in the next mail parcel from the capital. He had, in fact, toyed with suicide of his own volition, only to be talked out of it by his loyal wife, the former Empress Wei, an ambitious woman who fully intended to be empress again.

Troubled by the invasion on her borders, Empress Wu had supposedly dreamed of a parrot that had bright plumage but two broken wings. Despite her ban on superstition, she had asked Judge Dee what he thought it meant. Dee pointed out that the word for parrot, *wu*, was made up of Wu's own surname and the image of a bird. The parrot represented Wu herself, the great imperial phoenix that ruled China, while the two broken wings were her disenfranchised sons, Ruizong and Zhongzong.[4]

That, at least, is the poetic version of the story. In fact, Judge Dee had been stoically pressing for the reinstatement of Zhongzong for some time. With the setbacks in the north and the continued disappointments of her nephews and cousins, Wu finally relented, and ordered that her wayward son be secretly smuggled back into the palace. With Zhongzong hiding behind a screen, she then called Judge Dee in for an audience, and asked him what he would say if she brought Zhongzong out of exile. Judge Dee wept with happiness, allowing Wu the pleasure of dramatically sweeping back the curtain to reveal Zhongzong.

Judge Dee, however, immediately pressed Wu to be more open about her change of heart. Zhongzong, no doubt growing increasingly irritated at his treatment, was duly smuggled back out of the palace again, and then allowed to 'arrive' with pomp and ceremony with an entourage that had hastily been assembled out of town. Zhongzong's younger brother Ruizong was once more instructed to 'volunteer' his resignation as crown prince, and Zhongzong became the imperial heir for a second time.

Gaozong's oldest surviving son was now the heir apparent once more and was immediately dispatched north to deal with the Turks, with his second-in-command Judge Dee expected to do the actual work. A cynic might immediately suspect that Wu hoped they would both get killed, but her appointment of the pair as new leaders seems deliberately intended to rally the people of the north in support of respected public figures. The operation was a success. Although Qapagan escaped to fight another day (he would try again in 702), the invasion was thwarted, making heroes of both Dee and Zhongzong. But, in finally allowing herself to be drawn on the succession, Wu was forced to admit that her personal Zhou dynasty was over. Whether it had been her plan all along or not, it was plain to see that a Wu nephew would not now be taking over after her. Zhongzong would inherit the throne that Wu had dragged him from so many years ago and, even though he had taken the Wu surname as a gesture of loyalty, he was sure to reinstate his real clan name once his mother was in her grave. The Zhou dynasty with its goddess incarnate would become a forgotten footnote to history, and the Tang would be restored.

As her seventies approached, Wu was still in fine health, seeming to take after her long-lived mother. It would have been rude to discuss her impending demise openly – a standard term of address and honour to an incumbent Chinese sovereign was the exhortation: 'Live for Ten Thousand Years!' One could hardly proceed from such a greeting to discuss funeral arrangements, although it was assumed that Wu would be buried in the mausoleum that had been waiting for her for half a century, at the side of her late husband Gaozong.

Wu's first recorded acknowledgement of her old age came in spring 699, when she called a meeting in the Hall of Illumination, to be attended by the princes Zhongzong and Ruizong, their sister Taiping, and the surviving nobles of the Wu clan, largely comprising her grand-nephews and distant cousins. The assembled nobles were forced to swear a pact guaranteeing that they would live in harmony once Wu was gone. This assurance was so important to her that she had it carved into an iron tablet and deposited in the imperial archives. The likelihood of her offspring keeping their promise was, as even she must have known, remote indeed.[5]

But Wu would have to die first. Now in her seventies, she developed an interest common to Chinese rulers, and consulted with wise men over just how many of those ten thousand years she might expect to see. In 699, she announced the formation of a new department in her government – the Office of the Crane.

A crane was the chosen mount of Daoist immortals, who, in times of legend, were supposed to ride on the back of the bird to Heaven. Now, Wu's Office of the Crane was put to work searching for potions, elixirs, pills and diets that might help the Empress cling on to life. There was nothing particularly strange about the inauguration of such a department, and Empress Wu was certainly not the first to do so. What scandalised her courtiers was the allegation of Empress Wu's favourite method of rejuvenation.

Over time, courtiers began to develop suspicions about the Office of the Crane. Its chief officers were a pair of brothers, Zhang Yizhi and Zhang Changzong. They had been at the court since 697, when they had first been associated with Wu's daughter Taiping. Before long, they had made the acquaintance of the Empress herself, and were often to be found drinking, gambling and otherwise partying with the living goddess. For two pretty youths to be this close to an empress, even a widowed one, would usually require their castration. But, as with the case of Xue Huaiyi, this appears to have been waived. Although they were supposedly eunuchs, it was not lost on the court that they behaved more like gigolos. They were dressed in fine silks, bestowed with great gifts (Wu even let Changzong have her kingfisher cloak) and, according to palace gossips, regularly brought to the bed of the 72-year-old Empress for her sexual satisfaction.[6]

The Zhang brothers were just the first and most famous of a string of attractive young boys who formed Wu's entourage in her later years. Some complained that the Office of the Crane, far from being a legitimate department of medical enquiry, was merely a sinecure post designed to smuggle a series of beautiful young boys into the palace for Empress Wu's entertainment. Matters reached the point where officials began to recommend family members for appointment on new criteria, not of knowledge of the Confucian classics or mastery of the law, but of the pallor of the skin and the fine lines of their profiles. One minister was even heard to boast that he was far better endowed in both size and stamina than either the late Xue Huaiyi or the Zhang brothers, and that consequently he hoped the Empress would promote him to her inner circle.[7]

Empress Wu liked her boys to be beautiful. Her attendants, wearing make-up like girls and clad in sensuous silks, were regarded by Wu's ministers as subhuman, and deeply resented. But, even if the Zhang brothers were servicing Empress Wu on a nightly basis, the censorious attitude of the courtiers betrays a remarkable double standard. Nobody would have thought twice about a similar set-up for a male emperor in his seventies. In fact, old emperors were encouraged to spend their time with a variety of fresh young concubines, spiritually feeding on their *yin* essence in order to prolong their lives. Wu herself had begun her career as one of several hundred imperial concubines – it had been her duty to pleasure the Emperor in any way he required, in order to preserve the harmony of the palace. Since Wu was now the sovereign, it was only natural that she would seek to behave in a similar fashion, which would logically involve multiple exposures to male *yang* essence. In the absence of any other immortality treatments, Empress

Wu craved orgasms and semen, and the more she got, the longer she would stay alive. If the Office of the Crane was a smokescreen to hide dozens of male concubines from the public eye, the only real mystery was why Wu felt the need to hide them at all.

Meanwhile, the entertainments provided by the Office of the Crane became increasingly bizarre. In one courtly spectacle, the brothers kept geese and ducks in a cage with nothing to drink but condiments, roasting them alive in a slow process designed to strip them of their feathers and stuff them with tasty sauce. When this was found to be a success, they tried the same experiment on a larger scale, with a live donkey.[8]

Possibly, Wu's interest in her young boys was wholly innocent – an old, rich lady's wish to spend her time with handsome men, waiting on her every need, laughing at her jokes, bringing her fine foods and wines, and letting her win at games. But even in that regard, was she really any different from the many emperors of Chinese history? For a man in a position of supreme power, multiple sexual partners were a perk of the job. The Confucians may have begrudged Wu her attendants, but they also begrudged her very presence as ruler and empress.

Wu's ministers may also have feared the effect this was having on other women. For several generations now, Chinese women had been growing bolder and more aggressive, adopting fashions of the northern barbarians, laying aside their veils, enjoying the freedom of movement presented by barbarian breeches instead of long heavy Chinese gowns. During the reign of Wu, women had gained further ideas above their station – Wu's heartfelt grief for her late mother had even given women equal status in the afterlife, requiring that dutiful children mourn their mothers for the same time as they might mourn their fathers.

Wu's sexual liberation – one baulks at calling it promiscuity, when her behaviour was little different from that of uncountable male emperors before her – also appeared to be having an effect on other court ladies. Wu's daughter, Princess Taiping, was now in middle age, and enjoyed the attentions of several young men of her own – in fact it was rumoured that Taiping had first had sex with the younger of the Zhang brothers, and passed him on to her mother with a recommendation. Wu's daughter-in-law, the once and future Empress Wei, was conducting an affair with Wu's nephew Sansi. Meanwhile, Sansi was also secretly bedding Shangguan Wan'er, the granddaughter of the fallen minister Shangguan Yi, who had grown up in a state of slavery after her grandfather's demise.

Wan'er had inherited her grandfather's intelligence and had become something of a child prodigy. Demonstrating early aptitude for writing poetry and songs, often on demand, she had been Empress Wu's speechwriter for several years, and scandalised courtiers all on her own through the simple sin of being better at administration than most of the men. Miraculously, she also seems to have borne Empress Wu no ill will for killing her father – Wan'er had been thoroughly brainwashed by her palace upbringing and was one of Wu's most trusted servants. However, not even she was safe from the anger of the Empress. Wan'er wore her hair in a strange, lopsided fashion, half her forehead always covered by her curls, in order to hide a scar inflicted by Wu herself, who had lunged for the girl with a golden knife at a party when she appeared to be flirting with one of the Zhang brothers.[9]

As her eighties approached, Wu appeared to mellow somewhat. She became more open to criticism from her ministers, particularly the fearless Judge Dee, and ordered the reopening of many of the case files of the 'cruel clerks' from the Office of Prosecution. This led to the rehabilitation of some former enemies of the state, although many of them had been executed, so the restoration of titles and property benefited only their surviving relatives. With provincial administration in something of a mess, Wu was forced to confront the long-term effects of her policies in the capital. Wu had spent so long in the capital, be it Chang'an or Luoyang, that she had come to regard urban life and its luxuries as the pinnacle of existence. This attitude reflected on her treatment of her ministers, regarding provincial postings as a punishment or demotion, and ultimately stocking the outlying regions with incompetent or disillusioned officials who failed to improve conditions for their charges.

Wu even made some limited efforts to curb corruption in the Buddhist monasteries, many of which still retained sinecure positions and tax-dodging appointees. Despite her status of a living god, she began to lose interest in Buddhism, perhaps because of her own guilty conscience surrounding how she might be treated in the afterlife. Accordingly, she began to develop a greater interest in Daoism, with its emphasis not on reincarnation, but on immortality – Wu seems to have decided not to take her chances with reincarnation, not after all the deaths she had caused.

As evidence of this change of heart, we need look no further than one of the last recorded acts of Judge Dee, who knelt in front of Wu's carriage as she was attempting to leave for a Buddhist shrine.

'This Buddha', said Judge Dee, 'is a barbarian god.' He remonstrated with Wu for devoting her attentions to a non-Chinese deity, but also pointed out other follies inherent in her journey. He suspected that the temple had invited her only in order to promote itself as a place where Wu had prayed, and alluded to a more pressing concern, that the road to the temple had far too many places where an ambush party might be waiting. Wu took Judge Dee's advice, although it is unclear whether she was motivated by concerns for her personal safety or by the more controversial argument that Buddha was not worth her attention. Her waning interest in Buddhism was certainly enough to alarm some Chinese Buddhists, whose reports of Buddhist miracles and portents increased in the early 700s, possibly in an attempt to regain her attention or to warn her off an outright denunciation.[10]

When Judge Dee died in 700, of natural causes, Wu is said to have wept openly, and proclaimed: 'Now the court is empty.' In fact, it had been filled with Judge Dee's last legacy, a series of appointees whom he had personally recommended and with whom Wu was often at odds.

Wu remained blind or uncaring of corruption elsewhere in her government. The Zhang brothers found postings for their family members, and were even found to be selling court positions for gold. This sleaze was taken to ludicrous levels in the case of one

Xue, a graduate of the imperial examinations who had not yet been offered a court position. He approached Zhang Changyi, a sibling of the two more famous brothers, and offered him 50 ounces of gold if he could smooth the process of appointment. Changyi agreed, ordering the board of civil servants to give the man a job, but did so with such lack of care that he forgot who had bribed him. The vice-president of the board asked for clarification, but all the minister was able to offer him was the surname of the new appointee, which appeared sixty times on the list of new graduates. Unwilling to incur the wrath of the Zhangs, the vice-president appointed all sixty of the graduates.

Somebody had it in for the Zhang brothers. For as long as they kept the Empress happy, they were relatively safe, but as they came to enjoy their power over her, they made new enemies. Attempts by the Zhang brothers to cover up their corruption led to several wrongful deaths at court, causing one unknown graffiti artist to daub the words 'How long lasts the spider's web?' on the wall of Zhang Changyi's mansion. The words were scrubbed off on several occasions, only to reappear, until Changyi added a tart reply of his own: 'Even one day is enough.'[11]

Empress Wu's patronage of the Zhang brothers was to lead to the downfall of several of her own grandchildren. In its own ironic way, it even united the rival clans of Li and Wu. Deprived of any hope of inheriting the throne from Wu, the nephews and cousins fell back on family ties. While the imperial heir Zhongzong kept his head down, his long-suffering wife had begun an affair with Wu's nephew. Two of Zhongzong's daughters were married to grandnephews of the Empress, uniting the former rivals in their concerns over the growing influence of the Zhangs.

Meanwhile, all was not well among Zhongzong's children. Several of them had fallen out over an unspecified grievance – likely to have been the fact that Zhongzong's eldest, Chongfu, was merely the son of a concubine, and hence passed over in the line of succession in favour of his half-brother Prince Yide. Knowing that he would never get anywhere through standard means, the sidelined Chongfu became friendly with the Zhangs and informed them that his brother Prince Yide, sister Princess Yongtai and brother-in-law Wu Yanji had all been complaining bitterly among themselves about the growing power of Empress Wu's attractive young boys.

Either Chongfu came up with more damning evidence than such paltry gossip as was reported in the annals, or Wu's old age had left her with no patience. Even if one believes much of the negative material written about Wu by her enemies, her reaction seems strangely brutal. Not even out of their teens, Princess Yongtai and Prince Yide were killed. Inscriptions on their tombs maintained half-hearted lies about deaths through childbirth or disease, but in fact both were flogged to death, presumably with Wu's approval. Yongtai's husband was ordered to hang himself.

Power in the Tang court was addictive. As Wu had desired to hang onto her own status from year to year, and her sons and nephews and cousins had clung to luxury and sought to own it, the Zhangs began to wonder what would happen after the inevitable death of their patroness. A poster campaign in Luoyang accused them of conspiring against the throne. This anonymous attack was eventually backed by an official, who claimed to have heard that one of the Zhangs had developed ideas above his station. Supposedly, he had arranged a consultation with a fortune-teller, who had advised him that his face prophesied imperial status for him in the future, if only he would commission a Buddhist temple at a predetermined location. When the temple project was put into action, courtiers suspected the worse.

There were several attempts to undermine the authority of the Zhangs, but Empress Wu would not hear a bad word said about her boys. Some Confucians may have even seen the irony of it all. Just as Confucius had once warned against the unwelcome influences of female sexual partners of an emperor, so it would seem that male sexual partners of an empress could be similarly troublesome to the running of a government. The influence of the Zhangs was turning Wu into a laughing stock – although none dared laugh. A loyal minister made several attempts to call her attention to the damage being done in her name, only to find himself banished from the capital. When fellow courtiers met him to wish him well, an irate

Wu at first called for their execution. A courtier timidly pointed out that the minister had not been charged with anything and was simply leaving the capital on Wu's orders, and now Wu wanted to kill the people who wished to wave him off.

The Empress relented, but the damage was done. A second case against one of the Zhangs was successful, but the Empress quashed it after the fact by granting an amnesty to the youth after his conviction. The Zhangs were untouchable, at least by legal means.

TWELVE

The Palace of Dawn

In the autumn of 704, Empress Wu fell ill. Too poorly to attend any government meetings, she disappeared from public view for two months, attended only by her two favourite Zhang brothers. Not even her own sons were permitted to see her, leading many at court to suspect the worst.

The downfall of the Zhang brothers was engineered by Wu's newest chief minister, Zhang Jianzhi (no relation), one of the last recommendations made by Judge Dee before his death. Himself in his eighties, Jianzhi called in every possible favour, surrounding himself with sympathetic officers and soldiers. If something was to be done, it would need to be done swiftly, and with the cooperation of the imperial heir, since the faintest whiff of a revolution could cause provincial military garrisons – many of which were under the leadership of members of the Wu clan – to rise up in revolt.

Jianzhi did not even tell some of his associates what he was planning. In one case, he simply reminisced with an old associate about a conversation they had once had on a boat on the Yangtze

YOU – RAISE [YOUNG]
During Wu's reign, the word for 'raising young' was altered to comprise characters meaning 'hidden history with a tail'.

River, when they had been transferring offices. The boat trip had been the only moment when the two men could have been sure of not being overheard, and Jianzhi urged his associate to remember what they had discussed. The officer, unsure of what he was agreeing to, acquiesced nonetheless.

Another conspirator was interrogated about the source of his loyalty. He replied that his power and position derived from the late Emperor Gaozong. Jianzhi asked him how he would feel if unscrupulous individuals sought to harm the children of Gaozong. The man replied that his loyalty was to the state, and that he was Jianzhi's to command. At no point did anyone raise the idea of disloyalty to Empress Wu; the architects of the revolution saw themselves as maintaining the wishes of Gaozong, and perhaps Wu herself, by ensuring the next emperor on the throne would be Zhongzong. For all they knew, the Zhang brothers were plotting a coup of their own, a forged imperial will, a proclamation, perhaps, that one of Wu's nephews was her newly nominated successor, and they could not afford to risk it.

On the appointed evening, 20 February 705, the conspirators arrived at the house of Zhongzong, the imperial heir. They informed him that several hundred men were ready to move in on Wu's residence and deal with the Zhangs. Zhongzong immediately demonstrated the uselessness that had manifested itself throughout every other moment of his political career, by asking if they were doing the right thing. He had known that a plan was afoot, he had tacitly approved of it, but now it came to the crucial moment, with military men already moving in, and with no chance of recalling the agents, he asked if it was possible to put off the revolution to another day.

'Her Majesty is not well', he said gormlessly, 'and we should not alarm her.'

There was simply no way that the conspirators would be able to halt the attack; Zhongzong was effectively asking everyone who had yet to play their hand to forget about it and go home, leaving those already en route to the palace to suffer the consequences. Eventually, the impasse was broken by one Li Zhan, a minister who had inherited a silver-tongued charm from his father, the infamous Li 'Sword-in-a-Smile' Yifu. Lying through his teeth, Li Zhan informed Zhongzong that the only way to deal with it was for him personally to ride to the palace and order the coup to stop. This clearly appealed to Zhongzong, who probably saw it as the ideal chance to have his cake and eat it – he would be part of the revolt, but also would be seen to have attempted to stop it if any of his enemies survived. What Zhongzong did not know was that his mere presence was the signal for action – many conspirators had only agreed to involve themselves if they could be sure that they were acting for the imperial heir and not for just another conspiracy.

At the sight of Zhongzong arriving, the soldiers sprang into action, smashing in the gates of Wu's compound and rushing through. Empress Wu's guardian eunuchs were bound, and the two Zhangs were dragged out into the courtyard and beheaded. Wu herself emerged from her bedchamber, woozy from sleep and weak from her illness. She saw her eldest surviving son in the torchlight, and noted the faces of her ministers among the crowd.

'So it was you,' she said, as if finally having the answer to a long-standing question. 'The raiders have done their killing. Now you can get back to the Eastern Palace.'[1]

The words imply that she still thought she was in charge – despite having her favourites slain in front of her, she had not yet registered that Zhongzong would not be returning to the residence of the heir, since he was just about to proclaim her reign was over. The revolutionaries were thus in the bizarre position of having successfully carried out their mission, even though Wu had not yet realised she had been defeated. Eventually, a minister had to explain to her, and it seems, to Zhongzong, who had been just about to do as he was told and go back home. No, the minister said, Zhongzong was taking over, as Gaozong his late father had always intended, to continue the tradition of the imperial family, the Li family.

Wu answered with a few choice insults directed at long-standing associates, asking them what their fathers would have thought of their participation in such a brave military action, sending almost a thousand soldiers to cut down two defenceless boys in a palace courtyard. Leaving some red faces behind her, she then went back to bed. According to one folktale about the coup, the corpses of the Zhang brothers were then thrown into the street, where enterprising citizens roasted and ate them, claiming that they tasted like fine, succulent pigs.[2]

Two days later, Empress Wu formally abdicated. A day after that, Zhongzong was enthroned as the new emperor, and immediately offered a general amnesty to literally everyone except the surviving Zhang brothers. Notably, even Empress Wu's favourite, Princess Taiping, received new honours in the aftermath of the palace coup – apparently she had fallen out with the Zhang brothers herself over her latest lover, and consequently had sided with the conspirators.

Only four days after the murders in the palace, the former Empress Wu left her imperial residence for the relative seclusion of the Palace of Dawn, set on the western edge of Luoyang, where she could see the sun rise each morning over the capital that had once belonged to her. As the symbol of the end of more than five decades of her influence, it was a tense and moving day – even one of the former conspirators is supposed to have wept at the sight of her departure.

For the next ten months, as Wu slowly declined, her son the new emperor would come to visit her once a fortnight, for an audience that was unpleasant for both parties. He would tell her of his latest acts, and she would laugh at him, and tell him it was all going to go wrong. Wu may have been ousted by her own courtiers, but not even her many purges had removed all the antagonism from the ruling family.

As death approached, Wu put her house in order. She wrote a will in which she revoked her divine status, going so far as to reject the posthumous title of *huangdi*. She preferred, instead, to be buried with her beloved Gaozong, and to be remembered not as Wu the living goddess, not even as Wu the 'female emperor', but simply as Gaozong's loyal wife. Just in case it did her any good in the afterlife, she also pardoned some of those she had wronged – including several ministers and the two women she had had dismembered and drowned.

Wu's list of those she believed she had harmed was considerably shorter than one might have expected. Hoping to escape retribution in the afterlife, she limited her own list of victims to the two concubines and a handful of courtiers whose executions she now believed she had wrongly approved. There was no mention of the daughter she was accused of strangling. Nor did Wu attempt to seek forgiveness from the sister she may have poisoned, or the niece who had collapsed, choking, in front of her at a family dinner. There was little mention of the dozens of imperial relatives who had gone to their deaths in Wu's reign, accused of conspiracy, compelled to take their own lives or sentenced to a living death in inclement, disease-ridden outposts like Hanoi or Hainan.[3]

Does this mean that Wu was blameless for many of the crimes that later generations would pin on her? In her last days, presumably with nothing to lose, she does not seem to have believed that she was responsible. Others may have committed terrible crimes in her name, but her list of regrets was remarkably short.

Sometimes, when discussing Empress Wu, the historian is apt to worry that he is starting to sound like one who is denying the Holocaust. Wu herself believed that, while she may have been indirectly responsible for the deaths of many thousands in border conflicts and famines, these were the collateral damage of any political career. When faced with the opportunity to ask for forgiveness, she appears to have acknowledged responsibility in only a handful of cases – is this a sign of the self-delusion that appears to have confused her in advanced old age, or was that always her belief?

Wu undoubtedly made mistakes. Undeniably, she was ruthlessly ambitious; faced with a life of virtual imprisonment in an obscure convent, or the luxuries and diversions of life as the nominal ruler of the entire world, she made her choice and did what she thought she had to do. Life was cheap in the Tang court, and there is no reason not to suspect that Wu's own life was held in similarly low regard by her enemies. Was it kill or be killed? Sometimes, yes.

In that moment where we see her diving for Shangguan Wan'er with a knife, we also see an acknowledgement of something else.

The Tang dynasty may have been born in swords and fire, but the gentle life of the imperial palace was anything but safe. An environment of constant pressure, fragile protocols and icy conspiracy served to rear an imperial family that was as pitiless as she was. Nowhere is this more obvious than in the seven years after she passed away.

Far from returning to a state of harmony, life in the palace continued as before, complete with poisonings, murders and executions. Soon after Empress Wu's death, her inheritors had largely annihilated each other. Zhongzong's wife, Empress Wei, continued her affair with Wu's nephew Sansi, and arranged for his son to marry her daughter Princess Anle.[4] Inspired by the example of Empress Wu, Wei and her daughter hoped to orchestrate a female takeover, but did so by pushing their menfolk to act for them. The result was a stand-off in the palace between the armed supporters of Emperor Zhongzong and his son – the latter was eventually murdered by his men. Princess Anle took great pleasure in taking the head to their tomb to show the spirits of her husband and father-in-law, who had been killed during the troubles. She then rushed off to marry her late husband's cousin Yanxiu, with whom she had been having an affair for some time – he was the same man who had once been sent to the Turks as a bridegroom for Qapagan's daughter, and apparently kept Anle entertained with the exotic dancing and Turkish songs he had learned during his years in captivity.

In 710, five years after the death of Empress Wu, her daughter Princess Taiping planned another coup, working through Xuanzong, the third son of the former emperor Ruizong. Hoping to pre-empt her, Empress Wei and Princess Anle mounted a coup of their own, poisoning the hapless Zhongzong and putting his 15-year-old son Chongmao on the throne while they planned their *real* takeover – which was to be the installation of Princess Anle as China's second female sovereign, in imitation of Empress Wu.

Seeing though the plan, Princess Taiping went into action. In a repeat of the palace scuffle that had ushered in the reign of Taizong all those years before, two wings of the family fought in the grounds of the imperial residence. Princess Anle took her time fleeing, and was beheaded as she laboured over her eye make-up in front of her mirror. Shangguan Wan'er, the scar-faced prodigy who had been a powerful minister for both Empress Wu and Emperor Zhongzong, approached the rebels with a draft decree in their support, but was cut down by Ruizong's son Xuanzong before she could offer to change sides. It was Princess Taiping herself, in late July 710, who dragged the uncrowned emperor Chongmao from the throne, and arranged for the crown to be offered to Ruizong for a second time.

Ruizong accepted with extreme reluctance – now in his forties, he had spent his entire life as a puppet or prisoner of Empress Wu, and he had no wish to live out his days under the thumb of her daughter. He got his revenge by a new and innovative method – he abdicated, but not before firmly nominating his third son, Xuanzong, as his successor. When Taiping gathered fellow conspirators to depose him, Xuanzong and his men surprised them, killing several of the high-ranking soldiers involved. Taiping fled to a Buddhist monastery, but returned when she saw all was lost, and was permitted to take her own life.

Finally, a grandson of Gaozong sat on the throne, and, moreover, he seemed to have elements within his character of his great-grandfather Taizong. His own elder brothers had revoked their rights to succeed, citing Xuanzong's own active participation in the coup as proof of his desire and right to become the new emperor. The Tang dynasty would live on for another two hundred years, until the day that Chang'an, once the greatest city in the world, was dismantled, evacuated and abandoned in favour of a new capital far to the east.

How was Wu treated when her relatives buried her? Did they take her at her word, and inter her with scant ceremony and minimal grave-goods? Or did they act as loyal descendants had acted for a thousand years, defying the family matriarch in an act of good-natured hubris, burying her with great ceremony and untold riches?

Wu's tomb has yet to be opened – it would be something of an anticlimax if it were found to be as blank and bare as the wordless memorial that stands in front of it. But it seems more likely that the tomb contains treasures, both of Gaozong and of his infamous wife;

regardless of her family's feelings towards her, they were unlikely to risk angering her in the afterlife.

It was during Xuanzong's reign that the Tang chroniclers wrote up the reign of Empress Wu. They based their records on documentation and minutes of court meetings, but also on the recollections of those who had known her. Perhaps it is no surprise that the official record of Wu's reign should present her in such a bad light, compiled by men who remembered the errors and indulgences of her later years, still smarting at the undignified scuffle for power between lesser women after her death. But, if even they were unable to judge her, how can we? Dynastic records might record moments of historical moment, invasions, great ceremonies and carnivals, but they have little to say about the minutes and the hours – the pressures of month after month of courtly intrigues. For eighty years, Wu clawed her way from obscurity into a position of authority, dodging incredible reversals of fortune, bending the laws of a dynasty, bewitching two emperors, proclaiming herself a living god, all in a society that demanded women remain powerless and invisible.

She was probably responsible for the deaths of many others, although we cannot know what torments she endured as a Talent, a nun or a powerless pawn in the intrigues of a desperate empress. She proved herself to be as intelligent, calculating and, yes, merciless as the men who opposed her. There is evidence that she was an evil, callous despot, but is there any other kind? Was there really any difference between her behaviour and that of Taizong and Gaozong, both of whom are regarded as heroes? Empress Wu was a woman, and it remains tantalisingly possible that, in the eyes of her chroniclers, that was her one true offence.

Appendix I: Other Fictions of Wu

Empress Wu's fictional adventures began with the work of the fourteenth-century author Luo Guanzhong, world famous for *The Romance of the Three Kingdoms* and *The Water Margin*. Luo made Wu a major character in his lesser-known work, *Investigations of the Sui-Tang Era* (*Sui-Tang Yanyi*). This would later form the basis for a series of novels of the same name by the twentieth-century Japanese author Yoshiki Tanaka. Wu remains a popular subject in Japan, and one of the best-selling versions of her story, even back in her native China, is a multi-volume novel by a Japanese author, Momoyo Hara.

Judge Dee, the magistrate who gained Wu's trust and respect in the late 680s, became the subject of a series of Chinese detective stories in the Ming dynasty. Some of these were translated by Robert van Gulik, who also wrote his own 'Judge Dee mysteries' with Wu as a background character. Several of Dee's later cases are tied to the intrigues of the 'cruel clerks', and the jockeying for power between the Wu and Li clans, although other historical elements are less accurate – van Gulik deliberately preserved the anachronisms of the Ming dynasty originals, such as pigtails and tobacco. Several decades after van Gulik's death, Judge Dee has reappeared in mysteries by the French author Frédéric Lenormand. He also plays a major role in the novels of Eleanor Cooney and Daniel Altieri: *Iron Empress* (1991) and *Deception: A Novel of Mystery and Madness in Ancient China* (1994).

Fang Peilin's 1938 film *Wu Zetian: A Queen* chooses to begin with Wu's return to the palace from the Ganye convent. It presents Gaozong as a portly buffoon, besotted with Wu but easily manipulated by Empress Wang. In a movie made at a time when it would have been impossible to discuss Wu's sexual scandals or history openly, the movie presents her as something of an innocent, driven to extreme intrigues by the behaviour of others around her. She is abandoned by Gaozong at the naming ceremony of her own child, and the turning point comes when Wu stands over her new-born daughter's cradle, her arms lifting up as if to grab her, although the actual strangulation is not shown. Portents arise in the form of animated lightning, scratched directly onto film images of rolling clouds, and it is not long before Gaozong is stricken by his ailment and Wu is enthroned as his chief wife. This, it seems, suffices to stand in for her other intrigues, since the story then leaps ahead to Wu's latter days. Judge Dee, Xue Huaiyi and the Zhang brothers all briefly feature, until Wu sees ghosts glaring at her in the flames of the burning Hall of Illumination, and the coup finds her retiring unhappily to her bed, the maids drawing a curtain across the dais as if taking a final bow at a theatre.

The novel *She Was the Emperor* (1951) by Keith West (presumed to be a pseudonym for Kenneth Westmacott Lane) is a bold attempt to simplify the cast of characters in Wu's life to more manageable levels, although some sacrifices are made to historical accuracy in the process – such as the replacement of her half-brothers with a single sibling. West does not give his sources, but the romanisations he chooses for some names imply that he had access to materials that had been translated by a Cantonese speaker – an obscure Hong Kong publication, perhaps. This leads to some interesting off-hand comments not repeated elsewhere, such as his suggestion that Wu was not hijacking the Feng-Shan ceremony, but restoring it to the male–female split that had existed in ancient times, before a legendary emperor (coincidentally called Wu) had commandeered it for himself and excluded women thereafter. West's book is rich with poetic quotations, a fair evocation of upper-class conversations of the time, although the author persists in turning many such poems into rhyming doggerel. It also provocatively discards any elements of 'romance' between Gaozong and Wu – it begins with the death of Taizong and Wu's subsequent exile, and notes that the traditional 'three-year' (that is, twenty-five-month) mourning period has elapsed before Wu is recalled. Hoping to undermine her rival Xiao Liangdi, the Empress Wang bundles Wu back to the palace in a wig, and Gaozong proclaims his irritation at the transparent machinations of women, although this does not stop him ordering Wu to strip naked and get into bed anyway.

The book *Lady Wu: A True Story* (1957) by Lin Yutang is one of the most historically accurate accounts of her life – I believe it to be his translation of his own *Nühuang Wu Zetian*. Written at the height of the Cold War, and with an author's preface that likens Wu to Joseph Stalin, it is framed as a memoir of Wu, written after her death by her grandson or grand-nephew the Prince of Bin (672–741), son of the suicidal prince Xian. This device allows the author to deal in much greater depth with Wu's atrocities – there is no need to attempt to present her as a sympathetic character, and the author happily lets loose a string of recriminations, backed up with charts and tables. Nor are these idle suppositions – Lin was a professional historian, and quotes directly from genuine historical sources on almost every occasion, making his book seem less like a novel than a drama-documentary. He also introduces some unsupported but intriguing ideas, such as his suggestion that Huaiyi hit upon the idea that Wu was Maitreya while examining her naked, exclaiming that her pot-belly resembled that of the Laughing Buddha. However, since he generally relies so heavily on what was written by Wu's historians, he also inherits their negative attitude – the decade following the publication of his book would see the first attempts to rehabilitate Wu in the public eye.

The novel *I Am Heaven* (1973) by Jinsie Chun demonstrates the perils of presenting Wu as a Chinese Cinderella, with a heroine recommended for imperial service by a spiteful half-brother, idling away her days in the palace compound, forced to share a pokey, austere courtyard with a fair-weather friend, waiting for the moment when her Prince Charming will notice her. Chun's Chang'an is a place of contrasts, with lavish court entertainments staged for an uninterested Taizong, for which the palace ladies must rehearse with harsh and punitive directors. Chun's Wu is an innocent – she barely even meets Taizong, and there is no bedroom intrigue or assignation with Gaozong. Instead, she hears that Taizong is dead, is packed off to the nunnery, and thereby freed up from any unpleasant associations that might otherwise taint her romantic involvement with Gaozong. Empress Wang plays the role of the Ugly Stepsister, persecuting Wu for her beauty and, subsequently, her bearing of a male child. This is all very well, but it makes it hard to believe the sudden change in Wu's character brought about at the time of the deaths of Empress Wang and Xiao Liangdi. The author also introduces new scandals, claiming that Wu's nephew Minzhi was 'living in sin' with his own grandmother, and that Wu had a passionate affair with her doctor, to help prevent herself dwelling on the absence of her beloved Xue Huaiyi on a military campaign. On his return, Huaiyi burns the Hall of Illumination in a fit of pique because life back in Luoyang seems dull after all the fun he has had 'raping the Mongolian women'. The result is an unintentionally bipolar portrait of the Empress, like a Mills and Boon protagonist inexplicably prone to sporadic fits of murderous rage. Given the right treatment, this could have been an interesting fictional way to resolve the conflicts in the character of the historical Wu, but here it just seems silly.

Li Han-hsiang's 1960 film *Empress Wu* (*Wu Zetian*), starring Li Lihua, begins with the arrival of Empress Wang at the Ganye convent, and her scheme to bring Wu back to the palace in order to distract Gaozong's attentions from the Pure Concubine. As if Wu's life needed more scandal and confusion, it also introduces the novel idea that Gaozong and Wu had two male children while Taizong was still alive, and that the boys were passed off as Helan's offspring in order to save face. The film also suggests that Wu's name as a nun was Ming Kong, or 'Brilliant Void', and hence an inspiration to her in the creation of one of her new characters in later life. Other deviations from history, albeit minor and often plausible, include the Empress Wang's sorcery being blamed directly for Gaozong's dizzy spells, and the suicide of Helan after Wu discovers that she is seeing Gaozong in secret. Gaozong realises the errors of his ways shortly before his own death, when one of his sons reveals that he had helped Wu plant false evidence in Empress Wang's chambers as a child, not realising that a simple 'game' would lead to Empress Wang's death. The movie also introduces a folksong, sung all over China, taken by some to be an indication that Pei Yan was destined to inherit the throne, and contributing to Wu's suspicion of his involvement in the rebellion of Li Jingye. The film rockets through the events of the first forty years of Wu's life, slowing to a moderate pace only for the story of Wu and Shangguan Wan'er – obviously a preoccupation of the times, since it also forms a major aspect of a 1959 stage play by Guo Moruo.

By far the most entertaining incarnation is the 1984 ATV series *Wu Zetian*, starring Petrina Fung in the title role. It chooses to present its heroine first as a homespun country girl, enjoying one last party in the countryside before being called to Taizong's palace as a Talent. En route, she is waylaid by assassins sent by Taizong to kill her before she can bring her prophecy to bear. In this version, Taizong is fully aware that Wu is the one who can bring down his dynasty. She is saved by two dashing swordsmen, who escort her to the palace and swear undying loyalty, even if they must watch the doors of the palace close on her forlorn figure. Across its forty episodes, *Wu Zetian* never misses the opportunity for acrobatic kung-fu combat – the homosexual 'Turkish' prince is introduced in the midst of a combined martial-arts session and tryst with his boy-lover, into which the hapless Wu stumbles while chasing after her escaped pet rabbit. Meanwhile, Taizong is determined to get rid of her, packing her off to serve three years at a monastery chanting sutras for the late Empress Wende. After further intrigues with her brave swordsmen protectors, the story eventually grinds back onto a historical track. There is never a dull moment at the Tang court, which regularly halts the politics for scenes of dancing, acrobatics or martial-arts displays. Gaozong and his cronies are presented as a bunch of superhuman warriors, and so is Shangguan Wan'er, who ends up secretly married to one of Wu's warrior-protectors. Historical accuracy is obviously not a strong point of this version, but many dull moments are spiced up by the medieval Chinese equivalent of an attack by ninja. It is this version that was later screened on British television by the BBC.

Evelyn McCune's *Empress: A Novel* (1994) contains several unique interpretations of Wu's life. Herself a widow, McCune concentrates on Wu's affectionate relationship with Taizong, a disenchanted monarch who finds a new lease of life after falling for her. McCune dismisses any notion of impropriety between Wu and Gaozong, retaining the infamous 'rain and mist' flirtation, but presenting it as a joke in full view of Taizong. After Taizong's death, Wu embraces life in the Ganye convent, hoping to rise through the ranks to become its abbess, and returning to court only with extreme reluctance when ordered to do so by Empress Wang. Romance with Gaozong follows only long afterwards, after an extended and platonic friendship. McCune's text offers several other interesting ideas, keeping to the historical record, but embellishing with new possibilities. She offers the tempting explanation that Wu's short-lived baby daughter was born prematurely, which helps both in explaining her poor prospects for survival and the possibility that Wu may have had two children in the same calendar year. In the interests of humanising her subject, McCune also ensures that the blame for any and all atrocities is laid firmly at the feet of others.

The 1995 CCTV series *Wu Zetian* also pays close attention to historical accuracy. Featuring Liu Xiaoqing in the title role, it begins with Wu's arrival in Taizong's palace, where, after first enjoying the attention of dressers and bathers, she is brought trembling to the Emperor's chambers, where he sexually assaults her. Although she attempts to grin and bear it, he does not even remember who she is next time they meet, and much is made of the drudgery and competition of the palace life of the concubines at the palace, who are often portrayed more like cleaners than consorts. Some suspension of disbelief is required – whereas the earlier movies began with Wu in her twenties, this version requires its audience to forget that Wu would have been only in her early teens at the time of her first arrival. Wu is presented as a virtuous heroine (who would really want to watch thirty episodes of a scheming bitch?), heartbroken by Taizong's dismissive treatment of her as little more than a bed-warmer, but soon winning over the palace girls with her charm and wit. Early episodes present life in the palace almost as a modern workplace drama, with the uniformed palace ladies sweeping and dusting by day, getting into scrapes, and tucking themselves in for the evening in the hope that there will be a summons from their imperial master's bedroom. Meanwhile, the fresh-faced crown prince Gaozong, clad in impeccable white robes, soon develops a crush on Wu, which she dutifully attempts to dispel like a good Confucian concubine. It is only with the death of Taizong that Wu realises how she must fight her fate – the banishment to the convent is presented almost as a military attack, as Gaozong's household occupies the apartments of his father's regime, and Wu and her fellow low-ranking wives are dragged off by anonymous guards to be shaved and imprisoned in the convent. With a running time ten times that of the average movie, the TV series is able to concentrate in much greater depth on incidental details of Wu's life. Her time in the convent is presented as a baptism of fire, in which Wu endures torments and persecution (plus one attempted lesbian assault) from embittered, hateful nuns and fellow aspirants, until she realises that this will characterise the rest of her life unless she somehow attracts the attention of Gaozong and makes it back to the palace.

The 1998 TV series *Palace of Desire* (*Da Ming Gong Ci*), featuring Gui Yalei as Wu, chooses a different focus, moving away from standard portrayals of Wu's life to concentrate on her later years. It begins with Wu supernaturally pregnant for fourteen months, fretting that the child in her womb is the angry ghost of the daughter whom she strangled. When news arrives of the Tang dynasty's victory over Turkish invaders, Wu finally gives birth, and the rest of the series concentrates on her relationship with her favourite child, Taiping, the Princess of Peace – played first by Zhou Xun and then by Chen Hong. This version makes Taiping the centre of the intrigues, presenting her as a loyal daughter who protects her mother from numerous rebellions, until, with Wu dead, she herself is betrayed because of the thwarted incestuous yearnings of her own brother.

Wu was played by Alyssa Chia in *Lady Wu* (*Zhizun Hongyan Wu Meiniang*) in 2003, a GTV series that played up Wu's fish-out-of-water status among the nobles of China. This version has Taizong realising that Wu could be the prophesied *wu wang* who will destroy his legacy and murder his family. He plans to kill her, but eventually relents, realising that she will be taken to a nunnery on his death, and refusing to believe that a woman would ever achieve the necessary power anyway. The series follows Wu's life as found in the history books, but emphasises at all points her high standing with the common people, presenting those who opposed her as embittered and jealous adherents to the Li clan – an imperial family that refuses to admit she is a better ruler than anyone they can provide. Wu also returned to the Beijing opera in 2003, with Wu Rujun's opera *Wu Zetian*. Like many of the previous dramatisations, it presents her as an innocent tainted by the oppression of others. Once again, the pivotal scene is the smothering of the infant daughter, where Wu is torn between a mother's love and her hatred of the Empress Wang.

Empress (*Impératrice*, 2003) by Shan Sa is the most recent of the Empress Wu novels. It begins with Wu in her mother's womb and chronicles a childhood of persecution – her father is deeply disappointed that she is a girl, and, following his death, her half-brothers are callous and disrespectful towards Wu, her mother and her sisters. Shan Sa's text is notable for introducing overt elements of lesbianism, with Wu's early days in Taizong's palace perceived through a Sapphic relationship with another concubine. Shan's empress is a creature of sensual pleasure, delighting in the attentions of the Zhang brothers and simple 'miracles' like the growing of a new tooth. She is also a workaholic, finding that politics and administration are far better at holding off old age than the immortality drugs prescribed by her doctors. Fittingly enough for a story that begins before Wu is born, it continues after her death, with Wu first observing the intrigues surrounding the succession, and then haunting the places of her youth, now given over to factories and power stations. In her final summary, she observes: 'With passing time, the truth became unclear, and the lies took root.'

In 2006, as this book was being finished, yet another *Wu Zetian* TV series was announced, to be produced by the famous Tsui Hark, and starring the 55-year-old Liu Xiaoqing, returning to the role to play Wu in her later years.

There were also rumours that director Xu Jinglei would be returning to *Days in the Palace*, a movie project that she had previously abandoned, but that she now felt able to recommence with American backing. Meanwhile, Zhang Yimou, a director who had previously commissioned five Chinese authors to write separate Wu novels on the off chance one of them would be suitable for him to adapt, announced that he, too, was gearing up to make a Wu feature film, starring Gong Li and Chow Yun-fat. Shan Sa, author of *Empress*, let slip in a Korean interview that she had been to Japan for talks on a Wu project based on her novel, while a TV company based in London began development on a Wu TV series of its own, this time with an 'educational' angle. Remarkably, all the above came to light in the time this book took to go from manuscript to galleys. Some of them may never happen, or all of them, or none. Whatever the truth about Empress Wu, her life still tantalises storytellers all around the world, even thirteen hundred years after her death.

Appendix II: Notes on Names

Chinese names present difficulties for the lay reader, particularly with subjects such as this, in which a dozen people with the monosyllabic surname Li contest for power with a dozen members of the Wu family. Accordingly, I have followed the policy adopted by many historians of China's imperial era, and refer to emperors and empresses by the names by which they are known in the official chronicles of their dynasty, even though such titles were conferred upon them only posthumously. On occasion I have also attempted to differentiate characters by referring to their given names, such as in the case of Xue Huaiyi – I risk familiarity by calling him Huaiyi, but at least avoid mixing him up with several other Xues.

One notable exception is the subject of this book, Wu herself, to whom I have referred by her surname throughout. It was considered impolite to address a lady by her given name in traditional China, making it very rare that any are recorded at all. The daughter of Wu Shihou was thus likely to be known to most around her as Lady Wu. However, thanks to prohibitions on using the given names of emperors during their reigns, it is possible to work out what Wu's given name may have been through examining which characters people were forbidden from using. The prime candidate is Zhao, meaning 'Bright' or 'Shining', roughly equivalent to the Greek *Fotini* or the French *Claire*. The modern French novelist Shan Sa prefers to render Wu's given name as *Lumière* (*Heavenlight* in the English translation) in her book *Impératrice* (*Empress*).

In Wu's days as a servant at Taizong's palace, the Emperor conferred upon her the nickname *Mei* – a combination of the characters for 'woman' and 'eyebrow' in order to create the term literally translated as 'Flirty', hence Fair Flatterer Wu. Some fictional accounts have suggested that she used the name *Ming Kong* (Brilliant Void) during her brief sojourn at the Ganye convent. In later life, she would combine the characters *Ming* and *Kong* to create the new word *Zhao*, used to replace her given name after her elevation to empress. As empress, she was also often known as *Wu Zetian* (Wu Following Heaven), and reigned as *Shengshen*, Holy Goddess. Posthumously, she was also known as *Wuhou* (Empress Wu) or *Zetian Shunsheng* (Sage Following Heaven).

OTHER NAMES USED IN THIS BOOK

Anshi. In Chinese, *Anshi Cheng*; in Korean *Ansi Song*.

Baiyan. In Chinese, *Baiyan Cheng*; in Korean *Paekam Song*.

Black Piebald. *Qingzhui*. Qing is black here, but can also be blue and sometimes green. A *zhui* is a piebald horse. According to museum texts at the Temple of Confucius in Xi'an, this horse was wounded five times at Hulao Pass – but see Red Stripe.

Chang'an. Literally 'Long Peace', the city was often referred to as Daxingcheng, only officially being renamed Chang'an, in an echo of its ancient Han dynasty title, in 654. In modern times it is known as Xi'an.

Dappled Lion. *Shizicong*. The horse's name combines the characters *shizi* (lion) with *cong*, an obscure term for an equine colouring sometimes translated as 'blue roan'. This, however, is a rather modern definition hailing from America – since Wu herself specifies that the horse is actually grey, I have gone for the more traditional translation of 'dappled'.

(Judge) Dee. His given name was Di Renjie (Ti Jen-chie), although I have chosen to use the name and spelling by which he is better known in later fiction.

East Liao Fort. In Chinese, *Liaodong Cheng*; in Korean, *Ryotong-Song*.

Empress Wende. Her surname was Zhangsun (Ch'ang-sun), but she was better known by her title Wende (Wen-te), 'Cultured and Loyal'.

Gaozong. His given name was Prince Li Zhi. The name Gaozong, 'High Ancestor', was awarded to him only as emperor.

Helan. Strictly speaking 'Lady Helan' was the *married* name of Wu's sister. Her actual name is not known. Her maiden name was Wu, like her sister. Helan was also the surname of her children, named in this book as Minzhi and Guochu.

Purple Storm. *Saluzi*, combining the characters for 'sound of wind' and 'dew', perhaps a reference to whinnying, and the colour purple or amethyst. Possibly a reference to the horse coloration known as 'blue dun' or *grulla*. I have resisted the temptation to translate his name as Purple Snort, which might also be a possibility. The horse was wounded by an arrow in the chest at a battle in Henan in 620, but one of Taizong's generals pulled the arrow out, and the horse fought on regardless. Fitzgerald's *Son of Heaven*, pp. 76–7, prefers 'Rushing Wind' as a translation.

Qapagan. The Chinese called him Mo Chuo (Mo Ch'üeh).

Qianjin (Ch'ien Chin).

Red Stripe. *Shifachi*. Shifa means 'multiple slashes'; *chi* is a form of red, but can also mean bare or naked. Since he was supposedly wounded by five arrows at the battle of Hulao Pass (a claim suspiciously similar to that made for Black Piebald, above), this may refer to its scars, although other sources in China specify that the horse's hair was red (i.e. chestnut). Considering that arrow wounds in many Chinese texts seem to come in multiples of five, I am tempted to suggest that such numbers are poetic licence and not intended literally. See, for example, the wounding of Zhou Quanbin in my *Coxinga and the Fall of the Ming Dynasty*, p. 168, in which I faithfully report another fivefold salvo from a Chinese chronicle.

Ruizong. Ruizong's given name was Li Dan (Li Tan). He was later known as Ruizong, the 'Far-Sighted Ancestor'.

Taizong. His given name was Li Shimin; he was awarded the name Taizong ('Supreme Ancestor') only later.

Tan Fist. *Quanmogua*. Literally 'Fist-Hair-Tan'. A horse with black lips and yellow hair, it was shot out from under its rider during a battle in 622, where it received nine arrow wounds. The nature of 'fist hair' is difficult to comprehend – perhaps his name was actually something closer to Clumpy.

Tripitaka. His given name was Chen Yi or Chenhui, although as a monk he adopted the name Xuanzang. Sanzang, or 'Three Baskets', was a term of address given to a monk who had supposedly mastered the three canons of Buddhism. Xuanzang was also referred to sometimes by this honorific term, better known abroad in its Sanskrit form, Tripitaka. A fictionalised version of Xuanzang appears in the Chinese novel *Journey to the West*, source of most contemporary legends about his mythical travelling companion, the Monkey King. I have referred to him throughout under this title, partly to reflect his fictional fame, but largely to avoid confusion with the name of Wu's grandson Xuan*zong*.

Valiant. *Teqinbiao*. *Teqin* is an 'especially hard worker', while *biao* can mean a gallop, valiant, or yellow-white colouring, presumably what we would now call 'palomino'.

Whitefoot Raven. *Baitiwu*. Literally 'white hoof raven', named for his black hair and the white flashes on his fetlocks.

Xian, more properly Li Xian (Li Hsien). Some sources refer to him with the unorthodox spelling of Li Hsian, in an attempt to differentiate him from another prince with a similar name.

Xuanzong. Also known as Li Longji (Li Lung-chi) or Prince Xian. Xuanzong (Hsüan-tsung) or 'Profound Ancestor' was also known as Ming Huang ('Brilliant Emperor'). After the intrigues of the years immediately after Wu's death, he would rule until 756.

Xue Huaiyi (Hsüeh Huai-i) was born as Feng Xiaobao, but adopted the surname Xue from Princess Taiping's husband in the bizarre retroactive adoption used by Wu to make him seem more publicly acceptable. He was also sometimes referred to as the Abbot of *Baima-si* (White Horse Monastery).

Yide. Prince Yide's given name was Li Chongrun (Li Ch'ong-jun).

Zhangsun Wuji (Chang sun Wu chi).

Zhongzong (Chung Tsung). His given name was Li Zhe, and he was also known in his youth as the Prince of Ying. His imperial title, Zhongzong, means 'Moderate Ancestor'. During his time in exile, 684–98, he was referred to as the Prince of Lu Ling.

Appendix III: Chronology

618   Foundation of the Tang dynasty by a group of rebel dukes, ministers and commoners who have rebelled against the Sui dynasty.

620   Marriage of Wu Shihou and Lady Yang, the parents of Wu.

625   Birth of Wu.
(possibly 623)

626   A skirmish at the Gate of the Dark Warrior results in the death of the imperial heir and his brother. In the aftermath, the incumbent emperor is 'encouraged' to step down.

627   Enthronement of the Taizong Emperor. His father, the retired emperor, goes into seclusion.

628   Birth of the future Gaozong Emperor.

629   Tripitaka sneaks out of China on his journey to the west.

630   The Chinese general Li Jing scores an impressive victory against the eastern Turks, effectively bringing peace to the region and leading to an age of Chinese prosperity.

635	Death of the Taizong Emperor's father, the former Gaozu Emperor. Death of Wu's father, Wu Shihou.
636	Death of Empress Wende. Her son, Gaozong, is only 8 years old. The Emperor orders wall carvings of his six favourite horses to be added to the Gate of the Dark Warrior; years later these are moved to his tomb.
638 (perhaps 636)	Wu 'summoned to court' by the Taizong Emperor. She receives the nickname 'Fair Flatterer Wu'.
639	An embassy from Kashgar offers gifts to the Taizong Emperor, taken to be a sign of its new tributary status. Chinese, Korean and Japanese records all report an impressive 'sparkling star' in the sky.
642	In Koguryo (Korea), minister Yon Kaesomun assassinates the king and seizes control. He prepares to invade the two kingdoms in south Korea, imposing unwelcome taxes on his subjects in the process
643	Uncovering of two imperial conspiracies, and subsequent disgrace of Prince Li Cheng-qian, 'The Turk', and several of his associates.
644	Taizong declares war on Korea, leaving ministers in charge in Chang'an while he journeys to Luoyang and thence to join the campaign.

645   Taizong reaches the Korean front line, and spends the summer besieging towns in the Liaodong peninsula.

Return of Tripitaka from the west.

646   Tripitaka begins to compile his *Great Tang Chronicle of the West*.

647   Gaozong, the Crown Prince, commissions the restoration of a Chang'an temple in honour of his mother, the late Empress Wende. It is named the Temple of Great Maternal Grace.

648   The planet Venus appears in the sky for prolonged periods in daylight, leading to the prophecy that a woman is about to come to imperial power, and risks overthrowing the Tang dynasty within forty years.

An embassy arrives from the 'Jiegu' people from the west, with 'red hair and blue eyes'.[1]

649   Taizong dies after a prolonged illness. He is attended at his bedside by his dutiful son the Crown Prince, and his nurse, Wu. Gaozong becomes emperor, and is forced to suppress his feelings for his father's 'widow'.

Wang Xuande, a Chinese ambassador, is robbed by Alanashun, the king of Tinafuti, north India. He flees to Nepal, where he raises an army of 1,200 Tibetans and 7,000 Nepalese, before re-entering India and defeating Alanashun in modern Bihar in north India.

650   Wu is sent away to the Ganye convent, along with the other harem women of the late emperor.

651   Wu returns to the palace as Gaozong's concubine.

652   The Scripture Pagoda is added to the Temple of
             Maternal Grace, as a fireproof storage area for
             Tripitaka's sacred scrolls. It is originally five
             storeys high, although Wu would later add five
             more storeys towards the end of her reign.

653   Wu gives birth to Gaozong's son, Li Hong.
             Conspiracy of Princess Gaoyang and her husband,
             Fang Yi'ai – they are permitted to commit suicide
             when they are found out.

654   Wu gives birth to a daughter, whose tragic early
             death is blamed on Gaozong's lead wife.
             Tang diplomats send a message to the Japanese,
             ordering them to attack the kingdom of Paekche
             in what is now Korea. As allies of Paekche, the
             Japanese ignore it.

655   In the aftermath of a scandal over the death of her
             daughter and allegations of sorcery, Wu replaces
             the Empress as Gaozong's lead wife.
             Death of the Empress and the Pure Concubine.

656   Wu's eldest son Li Hong is elevated to the rank of
             crown prince. Wu orders her half-brothers to
             remote postings.
             Wu gives birth to the future Zhongzong Emperor,
             whom she had originally promised would become
             a monk. Tripitaka hopefully bestows religious
             birthday gifts on the infant.

657   Han Yuan and Lai Zhi are disgraced and banished
             to the distant south.

Imperial decree frees Buddhist and Daoist clergy
from their duties to their parents.
Court moves to Luoyang.

658   Death of Chu Suiliang, a major opponent of
Wu.
End of effective ministerial resistance for the next
twenty years.

659   Zhangsun Wuji is implicated in the librarian
scandal and banished to a far outpost.

660   Gaozong is struck down by an unknown illness,
possibly a stroke. Wu begins to 'help' him with
official business.

661   Chinese invasion of Korea.

662   Wu gives birth to the future Ruizong Emperor.

663   Chinese forces defeat Japanese reinforcements in
Korea.
A unicorn is supposedly sighted in the south –
an omen of the imminent rise of a great
ruler.[2]

664   Wu gives birth to the Princess of Peace (Taiping),
her youngest child. She is almost demoted
following her implication in a sorcery plot that is
supposedly targeting Gaozong. Perhaps
uncoincidentally, the former crown prince,
adopted son of the late Empress Wang, dies this
year in the far south.
In his last sermon, the famous pilgrim Tripitaka
tells his followers to pray to Maitreya.

665	Peace is declared in Korea.
	Wu's stepbrother insults her mother at a banquet, leading to Wu's purge against her half-brothers and their sons.
	Birth of Shangguan Wan'er in captivity.
666	The supreme Feng-Shan sacrifice is conducted at Mount Tai, signifying that the reign of Gaozong is a pinnacle in Chinese history.
	Wu's niece Helan Guochu dies in convulsions after eating what is presumed to be poison.
667	Gaozong suffers a second stroke, presumed to be significantly more damaging and permanent than the first.
669	Wu officiates at the suburban sacrifices – the first woman to do so.
670	Death of Wu's mother, the Lady Yang.
	Death of Xu Jingcong.
	A series of 'bad omens', including a terrible drought, leads Wu to offer her resignation.
671	Death of Li Zhi.
672	The first wife of Zhongzong, a daughter of Princess Changlo, dies of starvation in prison – presumed by later writers to have been confined there by Wu out of fear she would otherwise attract the amorous attentions of Gaozong.
	China is struck by a famine.
673	China is struck by a drought.

674	Wu presents a series of proposed reforms, including the extension of a mourning period for a mother to match that for a father.
675	Sudden death of Wu's oldest son, Crown Prince Li Hong, aged 23. Supposedly admitting that his health is fading, Gaozong attempts to gain ministerial approval for the appointment of Wu as regent, but meets strong opposition. Back from Korea, Li Rengui is appointed to a high court position. The first wife of Wu's son Zhongzong dies in prison, apparently by Wu's order.
676	Chroniclers all over the world report a massive comet in the sky in late summer.
677	War with Tibet. Strange lights lead Chinese farmers to the discovery of Buddhist relics at the future site of the Guangjai temple.
678	Chinese army defeated by the Tibetans at Ching hai.
679	The new crown prince, Prince Li Xian, arranges the murder of a fortune-teller who has told him he does not have the face of an emperor.
680	Crown Prince Xian (Wu's nephew, but listed in all documents as her son), is exiled to the provinces.
681	Wedding of Wu's daughter Taiping, the Princess of Peace. Famine in China.

682	Birth of Prince Li Chungrun (i.e. Prince Yide).
	Floods in Luoyang wash away the three bridges in front of Wu's palace. Several thousand deaths are reported in the region. Drought in the summer, followed by a plague of locusts and the outbreak of several epidemics. Earthquake in October.
683	Actual death of the Gaozong Emperor. Empress Wu is presumed to have been ruling in his name for some time. Plans are called off for a second Feng-Shan sacrifice.
684	Wu's son, the Zhongzong Emperor, rules for six weeks, but is deposed and replaced by his brother Ruizong. Rebellion of Li Jingye. Prince Xian commits suicide in the provinces.
685	Birth of the future Xuanzong Emperor – Wu's grandson.
686	Xue Huaiyi begins to gain prominence at court.
	Di Renjie (Judge Dee) is a magistrate in Gansu.
687	Persecution of Tang loyalists reaches its height.
	A farmer reports that one of his hens has turned into a rooster.
688	Revolt of the Tang princes.
	Construction of the Hall of Illumination in Luoyang.
	Taiping's first husband dies in jail.
	Judge Dee is dismissed, but soon appointed mayor of Fuzhou.
	A stone carved with a 'prophecy' of a Sage Mother of Mankind is supposedly uncovered in the Luo River.

689   Execution of the Tang princes.
               Wu creates twelve new characters.

690   Wu deposes her son Ruizong and proclaims herself
                  to be the sovereign ruler of China.
               Taiping marries for a second time, to her distant
                  cousin Wu Yuji.

691   Persecutions of Lai Chunchen.
               Flowers bloom in Shanglin park in late January –
                  later said to be by royal decree.

692   Acquittal of Di Renjie (aka Judge Dee).
(possibly 693)

693   Ruizong's consorts are killed on a charge of
                  witchcraft. An 'unseasonal snowfall' is reported
                  in Tang annals.

695   Destruction of the Hall of Illumination by fire –
                  presumed arson by Xue Huaiyi. Death of Xue
                  Huaiyi.
               Wu forbids 'superstitious practices' a second
                  time.
               Wu performs a variant of the Feng-Shan sacrifice at
                  Mount Song in Henan.
               The empire is granted a year free of tax.

696   Ming Tang rebuilt. A second monument, an iron
                  pillar 105 feet high and topped by a fire
                  orb, is designed and built for Wu by
                  Mao Polo.
               Judge Dee is appointed mayor of Weizhou.
               The slave-girl Shangguan Wan'er becomes a
                  speechwriter for Empress Wu.

698	Zhongzong returns from exile to become crown prince a second time. He is appointed head of two armies to repel foreign invaders. His vice commander is Judge Dee.
699	Formation of the Office of the Crane.
700	Death of Judge Dee.
701	Deaths of Prince Yide and Princess Yongtai. The court returns to Chang'an for the first time in years.
705	After the lynching and murder of the Zhang brothers, Wu is deposed by Zhang Jianzhi (no relation – a former appointee of Judge Dee). She retires to the Palace of Dawn, and dies some months later. Wu's son, the Zhongzong Emperor, returns to power.
710	Emperor Zhongzong is poisoned by his wife, Empress Wei, who dies shortly afterwards. A putative successor is swiftly ousted by supporters of Taiping, the Princess of Peace, who persuades her brother Ruizong to return to the throne.
712	Facing increased pressure from Princess Taiping, Ruizong defeats her in the only way available to him, by abdicating a second time, but firmly nominating his son Xuanzong as his successor before doing so.

Notes

Introduction

1. Chen, *Tang Shiba Ling*, pp. 50–2. The twin hills are called *Naitou Shan* by the locals – literally, the Nipple Mountains. Eckfeld, *Imperial Tombs in Tang China*, p. 23, claims that the ostriches replace phoenixes in traditional tomb layout, in order to demonstrate Wu's far-reaching power.
2. Guisso, *Wu Tse-T'ien and the Politics of Legitimation*, p. 2; a nice thing for Zhongzong to say about his mother, who had killed his first wife, charged him with treason and ordered the deaths of two of his children.
3. Wechsler, *Offerings of Jade and Silk*, p. 158, claims that the second memorial was intended as a silent testament to Gaozong, and left blank at Wu's insistence. Considering other gestures of false modesty by Tang rulers, it is more likely that Wu had expected her grieving relatives to override her 'orders' and dedicate it to her with suitable words of praise. Centuries after the death of Wu, tactless visitors have added their own carvings to the once-blank memorial tablet.
4. Guisso, *Wu Tse-T'ien*, p. 9.
5. van Gulik, *Sexual Life in Ancient China*, pp. 201–2.
6. Clements, *Confucius: A Biography*, p. 84.
7. Legge, *The Sacred Books of Confucianism*, pp. 302–3.
8. Yan, *Family Instructions for the Yen Clan*, p. 19, from the introduction by Deng Siyu.
9. Stone, *The Fountainhead of Chinese Erotica*; Wu, *Female Rule in Chinese and English Literary Utopias*, p. 85.
10. Lin, *Lady Wu*, p. 170.

11. Giles, *A Glossary of Reference*, p. 278.
12. Guisso, *Wu Tse-T'ien*, p. 6. Notably, the biography *Wu Zetian*, by Li Tang, written at the height of the Communist era, is so busy praising Wu for her political achievements that it barely mentions any of the scandals at all.

Chapter One

1. In fact, when I visited in early 2006, it was so understated that there was not even any electricity, and, having been relieved of my entrance fee, I was left to poke around with a torch. Taizong's tomb seems so modest today, at least in part, because it utilised natural features of the terrain – instead of a conspicuous earth mound, his tomb was set into a pre-existing mountain. By the time one arrives to visit it, one has already spent an hour or so motoring up its slopes.
2. See, e.g., Wechsler, *Offerings of Jade and Silk*, p. 60, in which Taizong laughs off the supposed good fortune signified by the nesting of albino magpies in the palace grounds.
3. Folklore is particularly difficult to extricate from history here. Wu Cheng-en's novel *Journey to the West*, vol. 1, pp. 176–210, includes an extensive account that, if it has any basis in fact at all, could be an allegorical description of an ageing Taizong, troubled by nightmares and hallucinations, lapsing into a coma and only barely recovering.
4. The most famous modern example is probably Bruce Lee, named Little Phoenix as a child, and sent to a girl's school with a pierced ear, supposedly to protect him from the attentions of an evil spirit that preyed upon the first-born boys of the Lee family.
5. Fitzgerald, *Empress Wu*, p. 214.
6. Guisso, *Wu Tse-T'ien*, p. 43.
7. There is some debate over this date. Kegasawa's *Sokuten Bukô*, p. 10, compares evidence from the story of the cradle-side prophecy with that of a stone tablet unearthed in Sichuan in 1954, and also straightforward common sense, over whether Wu's mother would have been able to give birth to her at the

age of 48, and to her younger sister at the age of 50. To confuse matters, the *Old Book of Tang* favours a birth date in 623, whereas the *New Book of Tang* favours 625. A three-year ballpark does not make a whole lot of difference with Empress Wu, since, whichever way we count, she still dies in her early eighties. The only place where it has a significant impact is in the discussion of her entry to the palace and her alleged associations with the Taizong Emperor, since it is difficult, but not impossible, to imagine the Taizong Emperor being sexually active with an 11-year-old girl. However, Wu had a decade at the palace to catch his eye, so perhaps not even this makes much difference. Nor is it all that necessary for us to expect that Wu had sex with the Taizong Emperor at all – in fact, if her marriage to him was unconsummated, it presents all the more reason for her and Gaozong to fly in the face of tradition, since their 'incestuous' act would have been in name only.

8. *XTS* 204, quoted in Kegasawa, *Sokuten Bukô*, p. 17.

9. Benn, *China's Golden Age*, p. 81. The resort would find greater fame in the days of Taizong's great grandson, Emperor Xuanzong, where it would become the setting for his tragic romance with Yang Guifei.

10. They did not remain there. After his death, they were placed inside his tomb, and subsequently recovered by modern archaeologists. They are still extant, although two of them were smashed into fragments to aid their removal to America by unscrupulous treasure seekers.

11. Kegasawa, *Sokuten Bukô*, p. 99, although Fitzgerald, *Empress Wu*, p. 13, claims that there are nine, not six, ladies of the second grade. Note that the set-up I have described here matches only that of the Taizong Emperor's era. Other Chinese rulers had their own systems and titles, so that any one dynasty's organisation rarely matched that of another.

12. *ZT* 178, quoted in Kegasawa, *Sokuten Bukô*, p. 100.

13. Fitzgerald, *Son of Heaven*, p. 174.

14. *Ibid.*, p. 184.

Chapter Two

1. Kegasawa, *Sokuten Bukô*, pp. 124–8.
2. Graff, *Medieval Chinese Warfare*, pp. 195–6.
3. Fitzgerald, *Son of Heaven*, p. 191.
4. ZT 198, quoted in *ibid.*, p. 196.
5. *Ibid.*
6. Stone, *The Fountainhead of Chinese Erotica*, p. 204, n. 34. Xiong, *Emperor Yang of the Sui Dynasty*, pp. 29–30, 139. The wide age-gaps between older and younger wives of rich men, making the latter often closer in age to the formers' sons, made such incestuous attractions (or *nei-luan*) a rare but recurring feature of Chinese history; see, e.g., Clements, *Coxinga and the Fall of the Ming Dynasty*, pp. 11, 233–4.
7. Fitzgerald, *Empress Wu*, p. 17, with his Chinese source reprinted in full on p. 248; Kegasawa, *Sokuten Bukô*, pp. 106–7. The longer variant comes from *The Lord of Perfect Satisfaction (Ruyijun Zhuan)*, in Stone, *The Fountainhead of Chinese Erotica*, p. 134 (Chinese text, p. 162).
8. See Fitzgerald, *Empress Wu*, p. 17, in which a later accusation is recounted that she seduced the Crown Prince while he was 'changing his clothes', generally understood as a euphemism like 'visiting the restroom'.
9. Stone, *The Fountainhead of Chinese Erotica*, pp. 134–5 (Chinese text, p. 163).

Chapter Three

1. Chang and Saussy, *Women Writers of Traditional China*, p. 47. For the Chinese, see Stone, *The Fountainhead of Chinese Erotica*, p. 172.
2. Kegasawa, *Sokuten Bukô*, p. 110, depicts Gaozong sneaking out of the palace to visit Wu at Ganye, implying that he made multiple trips to see her. Fitzgerald, *Empress Wu*, pp. 18–19, clearly states that the Gaozong Emperor visited the Ganye temple 'on the anniversary' of the Taizong Emperor's death, implying that the late emperor's spirit was somehow associated

with the temple and, perhaps, that Wu had been assigned to it to care for him in death as she had in life.

3. Wu's son Li Hong was born in 653. Exact dates were not given for the children of concubines, only of the Emperor's actual wives.

4. Kegasawa, *Sokuten Bukô*, pp. 109–10.

5. One should, however, remain mindful that the histories of the Tang are written by men, and that it seems rather convenient that a decision of such catastrophic consequences should be accredited to a woman. The chance remains that it may have been Gaozong's own decision, later pinned on Empress Wang in order to absolve him of the blame for causing such disaster.

6. Kegasawa, *Sokuten Bukô*, p. 118, suggests that Wu was already pregnant when she returned to the palace; Fitzgerald, *Empress Wu*, p. 20, instead submits that she became pregnant at the palace on her return. Either way, her identity was known officially from the time of the birth of her son.

7. Zhao-yi was an established name for one of the second-grade positions, but may have seemed particularly apposite for Wu since Zhao (Bright/Luminous) was also probably her given name.

8. Kegasawa, *Sokuten Bukô*, p. 118.

9. *ZT* 178, quoted in *ibid.*, p. 120.

10. Fitzgerald, *Empress Wu*, p. 22.

11. *ZT* 178.

12. Kegasawa, *Sokuten Bukô*, p. 134.

13. *JTS* 69, *ibid.*, p. 135.

14. *XTS* 76, *ZT* 178.

15. *ZT* 178, quoted in Fitzgerald, *Empress Wu*, p. 26.

16. *XTS* 89, quoted in Kegasawa, *Sokuten Bukô*, p. 140.

17. *Ibid.*, p. 103.

18. *Ibid.*, p. 143.

19. *ZT* 178.

20. The meaning of 'family' is taken here to mean their parents, siblings and cousins, not their children. Xiao Liangdi had two daughters by Gaozong who were exempt from the order, and

kept under virtual house arrest for several years, before Wu got rid of them by arranging marriages for them to minor officials.

21. ZT 178, quoted in Fitzgerald, *Empress Wu*, p. 29. Fitzgerald's translation is a readable simplification of the original decree, which is written in a language so flowery, and with allusions so obscure, that it is almost meaningless without line-by-line annotations. For a variant from ZT 200, see also Chen, *Yidai Nüwang*, p. 37.

Chapter Four

1. Fitzgerald, *Empress Wu*, p. 30.
2. Guisso, *Wu Tse-T'ien*, p. 21.
3. *JTS* 51, quoted in Hu, *Wu Zetian*, p. 31; Kegasawa, *Sokuten Bukô*, p. 148. Fitzgerald, *Empress Wu*, p. 31, quotes similar material from *XTS* 76, which contains a biography of Empress Wang. Of the non-Chinese sources, Kegasawa and Fitzgerald, the former translates Wu's insult as 'old woman', the latter as 'witches'. 'Old woman' is actually a slightly more literal translation of the original Chinese insult *yu*. Dien, *Empress Wu Zetian in Fiction and in History*, p. 35, prefers 'hags'.

   Fitzgerald has the former empress referring to her persecutor as 'Wu Zhao', breaking protocol by using the given name of an imperial wife. Although such a lapse is quite understandable from a woman about to be executed, the original text reads 'Wu Zhaoyi' – i.e. Wu of Bright Virtue, using Wu's official title, which coincidentally also contained the same character as her real name. The deaths have been subject to many authorial embellishments in books on the subject. The precise nature of their confinement, and the manner in which the punishments reach them, is a topic of some debate, particularly since their final fate is suspiciously similar to that visited on two rivals of the historical Empress Lü in the Han dynasty. Regarding their mutilation, some authors have suggested that their hands and feet were broken, but not cut off. Some authors present the place of their confinement as a mere cell, others a free-standing pavilion. But

Chinese slang retains the term 'Cold Palace', presumed to have originated in the abode for a concubine who has fallen out of favour – compare to the English term 'sent to Coventry'. In requesting that their prison be renamed the *Court* of Reconsideration (*Huixin Yuan*), the ladies imply a relatively large prison – probably a walled courtyard with one or more buildings within it, with the blocked 'door' being at the gate, not the front door. They were probably not, as some non-Chinese writers have suggested, confined to a single room.

4. Lin, *Lady Wu*, p. 41.
5. *Ibid.*, p. 171, suggests Cobra and Vulture as alternate translations of the two posthumous surnames, and also notes that the women's surviving relatives, exiled to the south, were forced to use the surnames themselves.
6. Li Zhong survived in obscurity, until the purge of Zhangsun Wuji in 659. Accused of being set up for restoration by Zhangsun's faction, the former crown prince began to fear for his life, believing every new arrival from Chang'an to be a death squad sent to deal with him. Under unbearable stress, he took to wearing his wife's clothes to foil assassins. Empress Wu's supporters later used this behaviour as an excuse to strip him of all noble titles, reducing him to the status of a commoner and exiling him to the far south, to the same residence where Prince Cheng-qian 'the Turk' had died some years earlier. The former heir eventually committed suicide in the aftermath of the 'conspiracy' of Shangguan Yi in 664.
7. *ZT* 178, quoted in Fitzgerald, *Empress Wu*, p. 38. Wu's complicity in the forgery is argued in Kegasawa, *Sokuten Bukô*, p. 151.
8. Kegasawa, *Sokuten Bukô*, p. 153.
9. Lin, *Lady Wu*, p. 164, observes that the method of transportation for prisoners was often in an open carriage, and that a report of an 'accidental' death en route could often be attributed to exposure.
10. Kegasawa, *Sokuten Bukô*, p. 154, has 'dug up his grave'. Fitzgerald, *Empress Wu*, p. 41, has 'opened his coffin', although

the latter usually implies the former, unless Han Yuan's family hoped to be allowed to bury him closer to civilisation.

11. Kegasawa, *Sokuten Bukô*, p. 154.
12. In fact, Wu's purge of the old guard was so complete that, upon a visit to old Chang'an, Gaozong was scandalised to discover that only Xu Jingcong was able to function as a tour guide to places of historical interest. Nobody else, apparently, knew much about it. *JTS* 86, quoted in Fitzgerald, *Empress Wu*, p. 43.

Chapter Five

1. Sadly, I was not permitted to photograph them, hence the detailed descriptions given here.
2. Imperial annals record only the births of boys, making the birthday of Taiping, the Princess of Peace, a matter of guesswork.
3. *XTS* 20, *ZT* 200.
4. van Gulik, *Sexual Life in Ancient China*, p. 208.
5. *ZT* 178, *XTS* 76, *XTS* 105, quoted in Fitzgerald, *Empress Wu*, p. 44.
6. van Gulik, *Sexual Life in Ancient China*, p. 201. However, others have speculated that the couple in the picture are not Wu and Gaozong at all, but their grandson Xuanzong and his legendary lover Yang Guifei.
7. *Ibid.*, p. 194. The quote is from *Fangnei Buyi*, which he translates as *Healthy Sex Life*, although more literally it is *Bedroom Benefits*.
8. *Ibid.*, p. 190.
9. Fitzgerald, *Empress Wu*, p. 46. Shangguan's granddaughter, born into palace slavery in 665, was the child prodigy and imperial adviser Shangguan Wan'er. Fitzgerald quotes the *New Book of Tang*, although the *Old Book of Tang* has a similar passage; see Hu, *Wu Zetian*, p. 33.
10. *JTS* 5, quoted in Hu, *Wu Zetian*, p. 33.
11. Previous Feng-Shan sacrifices had been conducted twice during the Han dynasty, and on one infamous occasion before that in the Qin dynasty, when the First Emperor tried to cut corners

and ended up hiding from a thunderstorm under a pine tree. See Clements, *First Emperor of China*, pp. 113–15.

12. Wechsler, *Offerings of Jade and Silk*, p. 181; Kronk, *Cometography*, pp. 103–4.

13. Guisso, *Wu Tse-T'ien*, p. 217.

14. Wechsler, *Offerings of Jade and Silk*, p. 187.

15. ZT 201, quoted in Lin, *Lady Wu*, pp. 74–5.

16. There would only be two more Feng-Shan sacrifices after Wu. One was conducted by her grandson, the Xuanzong Emperor. The other was not until 1008. In 725, the scholar Zhang Yue would argue that Wu's participation in the Feng-Shan was the moment at which the Tang dynasty was halted in its tracks, and the first flourishing of Wu's short-lived Zhou interregnum. See Guisso, *Wu Tse-T'ien*, p. 29.

Chapter Six

1. Eckfeld, *Imperial Tombs in Tang China*, p. 25.

2. Graff, *Medieval Chinese Warfare*, p. 205. Within two generations, the Tang military would slide towards professional soldiery, recruiting men with lifetime commissions, rotating through border postings in three-year tours of duty. By the time of Wu's grandson, the Tang military was using foreign officers on the borders – a policy that would play a part in the An Lushan rebellion in 755.

3. XTS 206, quoted in Kegasawa, *Sokuten Bukô*, p. 187.

4. Guisso, *Wu Tse-T'ien*, p. 21.

5. Lin, *Lady Wu*, p. 58, is prepared to suggest that Helan was also poisoned by Wu, although his claim seems based on Gaozong's *suspicion*, as reported here, rather than on any earlier evidence.

6. Kegasawa, *Sokuten Bukô*, p. 185. Here, for those who wish to speculate, is another possible course of perversion for Gaozong – was Guochu Gaozong's own secret daughter by Helan and, if so, was he hoping to rear a *third* incestuous generation? Furthermore, if breast-milk was an obsession of Gaozong's, he may have developed renewed interest in Wu when she gave birth to Princess Taiping around 664, which would have been tailing

off again by 666, leading him to seek a new source. For the alleged effects of consuming human milk, see Benn, *China's Golden Age*, p. 236.

7. Chang and Saussy, *Women Writers of Traditional China*, p. 48.

8. Guisso, *Wu Tse-T'ien*, pp. 21, 215. For the charges against Minzhi, see Benn, *China's Golden Age*, p. 23.

9. Hu, *Wu Zetian*, p. 45.

10. Fitzgerald, *Empress Wu*, p. 79.

11. Hu, *Wu Zetian*, p. 53.

12. Lin, *Lady Wu*, p. 97. The girl's parents would eventually be executed after they were (understandably) implicated in the 'Revolt of the Tang Princes' in 688; see Fitzgerald, *Empress Wu*, p. 123.

13. Guisso, *Wu Tse-T'ien*, p. 215; Eckfeld, *Imperial Tombs in Tang China*, p. 59, notes that Li Hong's death came suspiciously soon after he suggested that Wu should find husbands for the children of the Pure Concubine Xiao Liangdi. But see Fitzgerald, *Empress Wu*, p. 84, for the point about natural causes.

14. Lin, *Lady Wu*, p. 100.

15. Guisso, *Wu Tse-T'ien*, p. 23; Fitzgerald, *Empress Wu*, p. 87.

16. *JTS* 191, quoted in Hu, *Wu Zetian*, p. 59. The original Chinese, in terse five-character phrases, simply has *qin* for the objects of the Prince's plot – literally meaning 'dear ones' or family members. They would plainly not be 'dear' if he were going to kill them, hence my embellishment of 'those who should'.

17. Lin, *Lady Wu*, p. 108, dates this event precisely as January 683.

18. *XTS* 81, in Fitzgerald, *Empress Wu*, p. 88. It was an old trick, most famously employed by Li Si and Zhao Gao, the wily ministers of the First Emperor, who kept their sovereign's death secret until a suitably malleable replacement had been manoeuvred into position. See Clements, *First Emperor of China*, pp. 139–44.

Chapter Seven

1. Guisso, *Wu Tse-T'ien*, p. 51.

2. *XTS* 76, quoted in Hu, *Wu Zetian*, pp. 62–3.

3. *JTS* 87, quoted in Hu, *Wu Zetian*, p. 64

4. Guisso, *Wu Tse-T'ien*, p. 52; for their uniforms, see Schafer, *Golden Peaches of Samarkand*, p. 96.

5. Hu, *Wu Zetian*, p. 64. Hu's Chinese text plainly uses 'thou' (Chn: *Ru*), hence my retention of it here. Other writers, such as Kegasawa, *Sokuten Bukô*, p. 207, drop the arcane language.

6. Kronk, *Cometography*, pp. 109–10. This is the last cometary observation recorded in Tang annals until 707, even though Japanese and Korean records mention several in the period. For the three-legged chicken, see Guisso, *Wu Tse-T'ien*, p. 218.

7. Lin, *Lady Wu*, p. 60.

8. Guisso, *Wu Tse-T'ien*, pp. 55–7. I repeat here, because I largely agree with it, Guisso's provocative suggestion that, far from making 'preparatory steps on the road to usurpation . . . [Wu] perceived a dynastic crisis with which legitimate succession could not cope, a challenge from the new Emperor's consort family and from powerful ministers like [Pei Yan], and she took extreme steps to meet it'.

9. Fitzgerald, *Empress Wu*, p. 94.

10. *Ibid.*, p. 95.

11. Lin, *Lady Wu*, p. 116.

12. See Kegasawa, *Sokuten Bukô*, p. 224, for a more in-depth study of the rebel campaigns and the Tang retaliation.

13. *JTS* 67, quoted in Hu, *Wu Zetian*, p. 68. I have exercised my own judgement regarding punctuation marks, which are absent in the original. Lacunae represent several lists of obscure classical parallels. See also *JTS* 71.

14. Guisso, *Wu Tse-T'ien*, p. 59.

15. *JTS* 67, quoted in Hu, *Wu Zetian*, p. 68.

16. Guisso, *Wu Tse-T'ien*, p. 60.

17. *Ibid.*, p. 233.

18. Schafer, *Golden Peaches of Samarkand*, p. 176.

19. Benn, *China's Golden Age*, p. 204.

20. *XTS* 209, quoted in Hu, *Wu Zetian*, p. 88.

21. Guisso, *Wu Tse-T'ien*, p. 61.

Chapter Eight

1. Waley, *The Real Tripitaka*, p. 93.
2. For details of what this entailed, see Clements, *First Emperor of China*, pp. 15–17.
3. Lin, *Lady Wu*, p. 156. Two other farmers would report transsexual chickens in 689, the year that Wu put a stop to discussions of such weird phenomena.
4. Fitzgerald, *Empress Wu*, p. 119.
5. Waley, *The Real Tripitaka*, p. 115.
6. *Ibid.*, p. 119.
7. Paludan, *Chronicle of the Chinese Emperors*, p. 78.
8. Walcy, *The Real Tripitaka*, p. 129.
9. Benn, *China's Golden Age*, p. 107. See also Schafer, *Golden Peaches of Samarkand*, particularly chapters X, XI and XIII.
10. Benn, *China's Golden Age*, pp. 107, 114.
11. Guisso, *Wu Tse-T'ien*, p. 36. Qianjin's recommendation was literally that Huaiyi was *feichang caiyong*, which could be interpreted as praising his intelligence and scientific knowledge, but has been read by some as a reference to his ability in bed. See also Kegasawa, *Sokuten Bukô*, p. 244.
12. Fitzgerald, *Empress Wu*, p. 131.
13. Wechsler, *Offerings of Jade and Silk*, pp. 196–7. It is possible that some earlier reports of imperial strangeness may have been garbled observations of attempts to set up something like a Hall of Illumination. See, e.g., Clements, *First Emperor of China*, p. 132.
14. Schafer, *Golden Peaches of Samarkand*, pp. 238–9. The date I give is Schafer's; Fitzgerald, *Empress Wu*, p. 132, prefers 24 December 688.
15. See, e.g., Clements, *First Emperor of China*, p. 39.
16. Hu, *Wu Zetian*, p. 79; also Chen, *Yidai Nühuang*, pp. 99–101.
17. Hopkins, *Buddhist Advice for Living & Liberation*, pp. 20–2.
18. Guisso, *Wu Tse-T'ien*, p. 37.
19. *Ibid.*, p. 41.
20. *Ibid.*

Chapter Nine

1. Fitzgerald, *Empress Wu*, p. 120.
2. *Ibid.*, p. 117. Fitzgerald notes that the oppressions miraculously ceased after Wu's accession, implying that their purpose was served.
3. Benn, *China's Golden Age*, pp. 202–4. Note that Benn places the Gate of Beautiful Scenery in the 'south-west' of Luoyang itself, whereas it appears to have been in the south-west of the 'north city', i.e. at the south-west of the imperial compound, near the Bridge of Heaven's Ford (*Tianjin-qiao*), and just north of the central Luo waterway that split the city in two on a horizontal axis. See the map in Kegasawa, *Sokuten Bukô*, p. 234.
4. Lin, *Lady Wu*, p. 144. The details of the torture equipment became widely known to non-victims only in 692, during a court case against the members of the Office of Prosecution. Years after Wu's death, the Prince of Bin, son of Prince Xian, impressed the court with his ability to predict the weather, and then embarrassed the court by revealing that his supposedly magical power derived from the aches and pains he felt in the sites of wounds inflicted by the Office of Prosecution.
5. Fitzgerald, *Empress Wu*, p. 120. Lin, *Lady Wu*, p. 150, claims that the secrets *were* disclosed, and that they concerned Wu's relationship with Xue Huaiyi.
6. Hu, *Wu Zetian*, p. 82. Lin, *Lady Wu*, p. 160, claims that the false subject of Huang's letter was his 'old wife', and not himself.
7. Guisso, *Wu Tse-T'ien*, p. 65; Fitzgerald, *Empress Wu*, p. 123.
8. Lin, *Lady Wu*, p. 172.
9. Guisso, *Wu Tse-T'ien*, p. 62.
10. Fitzgerald, *Empress Wu*, p. 125.
11. Kegasawa, *Sokuten Bukô*, p. 297, notes that since Dee's death in 700 at the age of 71-*sui* (i.e. 70) is a matter of public record, it is reasonable to date his birth as 630.
12. Kegasawa, *Sokuten Bukô*, p. 299. Dee's route was not actually so direct. To save face, he was first sent to a provincial posting, but then recalled to the capital.
13. Lin, *Lady Wu*, p. 178.

Chapter Ten

1. Lin, *Lady Wu*, p. 155.
2. Kronk, *Cometography*, p. 112.
3. Chang and Saussy, *Women Writers of Traditional China*, pp. 48–9. The authors date this event as 691, but surely the 'twelfth lunar month' of 691 would actually be shortly before the Chinese New Year, in other words, the early days of January 692.
4. Schafer, *Golden Peaches of Samarkand*, p. 114; for the tooth, which I presume to be nothing more exciting than a wisdom tooth arriving late, see Guisso, *Wu Tse-T'ien*, p. 285.
5. For the cat, see Fitzgerald, *Empress Wu*, p. 139; for the dog, Schafer, *Golden Peaches of Samarkand*, p. 77.
6. Fitzgerald, *Empress Wu*, p. 136; Schafer, *Golden Peaches of Samarkand*, p. 238.
7. ZT 178, in Fitzgerald, *Empress Wu*, p. 133.
8. Lin, *Lady Wu*, p. 153, presents an entertaining attempt to marshal the contradictory reports of this incident from the Tang annals, suggesting that Huaiyi was seen to be cutting his own flesh in public, in order to convince the audience that an image of Buddha daubed in bull's blood actually used Huaiyi's own.
9. Fitzgerald, *Empress Wu*, p. 135.
10. *Ibid.*
11. *Ibid.*, pp. 135–6.
12. Lin, *Lady Wu*, p. 169.
13. XTS 209, quoted in Kegasawa, *Sokuten Bukô*, p. 301. See also, Fitzgerald, *Empress Wu*, p. 139, who relates the similar story of Dee's fellow captive Wei Yuanzhong, who said to his captors: 'If you want my head, why not cut it off? Why bother about confessions?'
14. Two of Dee's fellow captives made the grave error of making a counter-claim, accusing their former captors of sedition. Before long, the investigators arranged a *counter*-counter-claim, and the luckless officials were executed on a new charge of conspiracy. See Fitzgerald, *Empress Wu*, p. 141.

15. ZT 204, quoted in Guisso, *Wu Tse-T'ien*, p. 131, and Fitzgerald, *Empress Wu*, p. 141.

16. Lin, *Lady Wu*, p. 195, claims that the two women simply 'disappeared', and that Ruizong was called to dinner with his mother. By not mentioning the suspicious absence of his women, he was permitted to live. After Wu's death, Ruizong buried two sets of empty robes – the bodies were never found.

17. Guisso, *Wu Tse-T'ien*, p. 132. Lin, *Lady Wu*, p. 197, suggests instead that the man sliced open his own belly, and notes the marvels of Tang doctors in their ability to save his life. It would seem that, along with architecture, fashions and sports, *seppuku* may have been another Tang dynasty invention that flourished in distant Japan.

18. This argument is taken from Guisso, *Wu Tse-T'ien*, pp. 133–4.

19. The flow of money from the west would rise even further in the following century, particularly after the opening of the Benjahir silver mine in Afghanistan, a mother lode of precious metal that would vastly improve the fortunes of the Abbasid caliphate, generating massive demand for both Chinese silk and foreign slaves. The result did not merely pour money east into China, but west into Europe. See Clements, *A Brief History of the Vikings*, p. 105. The expansion of Islam would also curtail Chinese influence in Central Asia by 750, effectively reducing the length of the Silk Road under Chinese control.

20. Gernet, *History of Chinese Civilization*, pp. 257–8, strongly disagrees, calling the Tang era an 'epoch of waste' in which 'the small peasantry . . . was crushed under the weight of taxes and dues. The number of tenant farmers multiplied.' However, it should be noted that a 'tenant farmer' who had officially signed his land over to a tax-free Buddhist monastery would have shown up on government records as poverty-stricken, whereas he might have really been a wily tax dodger.

21. Fitzgerald, *Empress Wu*, p. 144; Guisso, *Wu Tse-T'ien*, p. 134, quoting *JTS* 6.

22. Fitzgerald, *Empress Wu*, p. 161. Fitzgerald places his account of the dream after many events that I have kept until the following

chapter, but if this dramatic encounter took place, it would surely have to do so *before* the reinstatement of Zhongzong. A chess man is a *qizi*, literally a 'chess son'.

Chapter Eleven

1. Guisso, *Wu Tse-T'ien*, p. 137.
2. Fitzgerald, *Empress Wu*, p. 157.
3. ZT 176. Note that Fitzgerald, *Empress Wu*, p. 158, frames the same story so as to imply that Dee's warning came after the letter had arrived.
4. Stone, *Fountainhead of Chinese Erotica*, p. 89.
5. Fitzgerald, *Empress Wu*, p. 162.
6. See, e.g., Fitzgerald, *Empress Wu*, p. 163, which interprets the annals' suggestion that Wu 'granted them her favour' as evidence that she was having sex with them.
7. Guisso, *Wu Tse-T'ien*, p. 148. The boast was made in 700, by which time the name of the Office of the Crane had been changed to the Office of Imperial Attendants. Note that some sources, e.g. Stone, *Fountainhead of Chinese Erotica*, p. 139, refer to the Zhangs as 'fraternal cousins' not brothers. The erotic novel *The Lord of Perfect Satisfaction*, based in equal parts on Tang annals and idle speculation, suggests that the brothers took turns pleasuring the princess, with Changzong and his 'large meaty implement' dealing with her on one night, and Yizhi on the next. However, the brothers came to regard sex with the aged Wu as something of an ordeal, leading her eventually to bestow her attentions on Xue Aocao, a (probably) fictional character whose penis was so massive that only the living goddess Wu could cope with it. See Stone, *Fountainhead of Chinese Erotica*, pp. 142–60, much of which comprises descriptions of their varied sexual acts.
8. Benn, *China's Golden Age*, p. 130. The question, one feels obliged to ask, is how *noisy* such a spectacle would be, and how it would be fun for any of the spectators?
9. Lin, *Lady Wu*, p. 223.

10. See, e.g., Guisso, *Wu Tse-T'ien*, p. 218, with its tale of the discovery of 'Buddha's footprint' somewhere in China.
11. *ZT* 178, quoted in Fitzgerald, *Empress Wu*, p. 168.

Chapter Twelve

1. *ZT* 178, quoted in Kegasawa, *Sokuten Bukô*, p. 332.
2. Benn, *China's Golden Age*, p. 130.
3. See Lin, *Lady Wu*, pp. 171–5, for a five-page list of Wu's alleged victims, in small print and not even exhaustive!
4. Anle was in fact the only surviving child of Empress Wei. While Zhongzong may have hoped to put one of his other children by concubines on the throne, Empress Wei had sworn revenge on them for the deaths of Yongtai and Yide.

Appendix III

1. Fitzgerald, *Son of Heaven*, p. 200, suggests these are proto-Vikings from the Urals, but this seems unlikely.
2. Wechsler, *Offerings of Jade and Silk*, p. 75. Wu and Gaozong attempted to seize the omen for themselves by renaming his reign 'Unicorn Virtue'. Others, however, may have regarded the alleged sighting as a call to revolution.

Bibliography

Primary Sources

References to dynastic histories, the *Old Book of Tang* (*Jiu Tang Shu – JTS*) and the *New Book of Tang* (*Xin Tang Shu – XTS*) are to the online versions at www.hoolulu.com/zh/. These valuable records of Wu's time include chronicles of reigns and biographies of many figures. The most relevant sections are:

JTS 1	Gaozu (Father of Taizong, founder of the Tang dynasty)
JTS 2–3	Taizong
JTS 4–5	Gaozong
JTS 6	Empress Wu
JTS 7	Zhongzong and Ruizong
JTS 55–6	Empresses and Concubines
JTS 67	Li Jingye
JTS 69	Zhangsun Wuji
JTS 80	Lesser Sons of Taizong
JTS 86	Xu Jingcong (among others)
JTS 90	Lesser Sons of Gaozong and Zhongzong
JTS 91	Pei Yan (among others)
JTS 93	Judge Dee (among others)
XTS 1	Gaozu
XTS 2	Taizong
XTS 3	Gaozong
XTS 4	Empress Wu and Zhongzong
XTS 5	Ruizong and Xuanzong
XTS 89–90	Empresses and Concubines
XTS 92	Lesser Sons of Gaozu
XTS 93	Sons of Taizong

XTS 94   Sons of Gaozong
XTS 96   Lives of Minor Princesses
XTS 204   Yuan Tian-gang (among others)
XTS 209   'The Cruel Clerks'

Another useful source for Wu is Sima Guang's *Comprehensive Mirror to Aid in Government* (*Zizhi Tongjian* – ZT), written in the eleventh century and available online at: www.chinakyl.com/rbbook/big5/sjcy/ztj.htm. Wu's life is contained in ZT 174–201, her reign as *huangdi* in ZT 202–8.

Secondary Sources

Adshead, S., *T'ang China: The Rise of the East in World History*, Basingstoke, Palgrave Macmillan, 2004

Benn, C., *China's Golden Age: Everyday Life in the Tang Dynasty*, Oxford, Oxford University Press, 2002

Bingham, W., *The Founding of the T'ang Dynasty: The Fall of Sui and Rise of T'ang: A Preliminary Survey*, New York, Octagon Books, 1970

Bullough, V., *Sexual Variance in Society and History*, Chicago, University of Chicago Press, 1976

Chang, K., and Haun Saussy, *Women Writers of Traditional China: An Anthology of Poetry and Criticism*, Stanford, Stanford University Press, 1999

Chen, A., *Tang Shiba Ling* (*The Eighteen Tang Tombs*), Beijing, China Youth Press, 2001

Chen, H., *Yidai Nühuang* (*Life of an Empress*), Shenyang, Liaoning People's Press, 2004

Chun, J., *I Am Heaven*, Philadelphia, Macrae Smith, 1973

Clements, J., *Confucius: A Biography*, Stroud, Sutton Publishing, 2004

_____, *Coxinga and the Fall of the Ming Dynasty*, paperback edn, Stroud, Sutton Publishing, 2005

_____, *A Brief History of the Vikings*, London, Robinson, 2005

_____, *The First Emperor of China*, Stroud, Sutton Publishing, 2006

Devahuti, D., *The Unknown Hsüan-tsang*, Oxford, Oxford University Press, 2001

Dien, D., *Empress Wu Zetian in Fiction and in History: Female Defiance in Confucian China*, New York, Nova Science Publishers, 2003

Eckfeld, T., *Imperial Tombs in Tang China 618–907: The Politics of Paradise*, Abingdon, Routledge Curzon, 2005

Fitzgerald, C., *Son of Heaven: A Biography of Li Shih-Min, Founder of the T'ang Dynasty*, Cambridge, Cambridge University Press, 1933

_____, *The T'ang Dynasty in Communist Historiography*, Ditchley Manor, Conference on Chinese Communist Historiography, 1964

_____, *The Empress Wu*, Vancouver, University of British Columbia, 1968

Garnaut, A., 'Hui Legends of the Companions of the Prophet', *China Heritage Newsletter*, No. 5, 2005

Ge, X., *Wu Zetian Dadi (Great 'Emperor' Wu Zetian)*, 2 vols, Beijing, Beijing Library Press, 2001

Gernet, J., *A History of Chinese Civilization*, Cambridge, Cambridge University Press, 2nd edn, 1982

Giles, H., *A Glossary of Reference on Subjects Connected with the Far East*, London, Curzon, 3rd edn, 1900

Graff, D., *Medieval Chinese Warfare: 300–900*, London, Routledge, 2002

Guisso, R., *Wu Tse-T'ien and the Politics of Legitimation in T'ang China*, Bellingham, Western Washington University, 1978

Guo, M., *Selected Works of Guo Moruo: Five Historical Plays*, Beijing, Foreign Languages Press, 1984

Hayashi, R., *The Silk Road and the Shosoin*, New York, Weatherhill, 1975

He, J., *et al.*, *Hair Fashions of Tang Dynasty Women*, Hong Kong, Hair and Beauty Co. Ltd, 1987

Hopkins, J., *Buddhist Advice for Living & Liberation: Nagarjuna's Precious Garland*, Ithaca, NY, Snow Lion Publications, 1998

Hu, J., *Wu Zetian Benzhuan (Biography of Wu Zetian)*, Xi'an, Sanqin Publishing, 1986

Kegasawa, Y., *Sokuten Bukô (The Empress Wu)*, Tokyo, Hakuteisha, 1995

Kronk, G., *Cometography: A Catalog of Comets, vol. 1, Ancient–1799*, Cambridge, Cambridge University Press, 1999

Legge, J., *The Sacred Books of Confucianism: The Texts of Confucianism, Part 1. The Shu King, the Religious Portions of the Shih King, the Hsiao King*, Oxford, Clarendon Press, 1879

Levy, H., *Harem Favorites of an Illustrious Celestial*, Taichung, Chung T'ai Printing Company, 1958

Li, R., *Flowers in the Mirror*, trans. Lin Tai-yi, London, Arena, 1985

Li, T., *Wu Zetian*, Hong Kong, Won Yit Book Co., 1963

Lin, Y., *Lady Wu: A True Story*, London, William Heinemann, 1957

Matsumoto, N., *The Glory of the Court: Tang Dynasty Empress Wu and her Times*, Tokyo, Tokyo National Museum, 1999

Mooney, P., Maudsley, C., and Hatherly, G., *Xi'an, Shaanxi and the Terracotta Army*, Hong Kong, Odyssey Books and Guides, 2005

Paludan, A., *Chronicle of the Chinese Emperors: The Reign-by-Reign Record of the Rulers of Imperial China*, London, Thames & Hudson, 1998

Peng, S., *Wu Zetian Waizhuan* (*Legends of Empress Wu*), Hong Kong, Boyi Publishing, 1983

Reed, C., *A Tang Miscellany: An Introduction to Youyang Zazu*, New York, Peter Lang, 2003

Schafer, E., *The Golden Peaches of Samarkand: A Study of T'ang Exotics*, Berkeley and Los Angeles, University of California Press, 1963

Shan, S., *Empress: A Novel*, New York, Regan Books, 2006

Shi, M., and Liang Fen, *Huosui, Suihuo: Baigong Wu Zetian Xilarui* (*Troubled Water: Hillary R. Clinton – Empress Wu in the White House*), Hong Kong, Ming Jing, 1996

Stone, C., *The Fountainhead of Chinese Erotica: The Lord of Perfect Satisfaction* (*Ruyijun zhuan*), Honolulu, University of Hawaii Press, 2003

van Gulik, R., *Sexual Life in Ancient China: A Preliminary Survey of Chinese Sex and Society from ca. 1500 BC till 1644 AD*, Leiden, E.J. Brill, 1974

_____, *Murder in Canton: A Judge Dee Mystery*, 1966; reprinted Chicago, University of Chicago Press, 1993

Waley, A., *The Real Tripitaka and Other Pieces*, London, George Allen & Unwin, 1952; Routledge reprint, 2005

Wang, Z., *Ambassadors from the Isles of the Immortals: China–Japan Relations in the Han-Tang Period*, Honolulu, Association for Asian Studies and University of Hawai'i Press, 2005

Wechsler, H. *Offerings of Jade and Silk: Ritual and Symbol in the Legitimation of the T'ang Dynasty*, New Haven, Yale University Press, 1985

Wright, A., and Denis Twitchett (eds), *Perspectives on the T'ang*, New Haven, Yale University Press, 1973

Wu, C., *Journey to the West*, trans. W.J.F. Jenner, 3 vols, Beijing, Foreign Languages Press, 1986

Wu, Q., *Female Rule in Chinese and English Literary Utopias*, Liverpool, Liverpool University Press, 1995

Xiong, V., *Sui-Tang Chang'an: A Study in the Urban History of Medieval China*, Ann Arbor, Center for Chinese Studies, University of Michigan, 2000

——, *Emperor Yang of the Sui Dynasty: His Life, Times and Legacy*, Albany, NY, State University of New York Press, 2006

Yan, Z., *Family Instructions for the Yen Clan*, Leiden, E.J. Brill, 1968

Zhang, Y., and Hu Ji, *Wu Zetian yu Qianling* (*Wu Zetian and the Qianling Tomb*), Xi'an, Sanqin Publishing, and the Empress Wu Research Society (Wu Zetian Yanjiu Hui), 1986

Zhao, K., *Tang Taizong Zhuan* (*Biography of Tang Taizong*), Beijing, People's Press, 1984

Index

Act of Grace, 108–9
Afghanistan, 1, 226
Alanashun, 204
Altieri, Daniel, 188
An Lushan, 220
Anding, *see* Princess Anding
Anshi, 34–5
ATV, 192

BBC, 192
Beijing, 33
Benjahir, 226
Bihar, 204
Biographies of the Goddesses, 74
Blackhorse Mountain, 19
Book of History (Shu Jing), 7
Book of Later Han (Hou Han Shu), 99
Book of Rites (Li Jing), 36, 82
Book of Tang, New (Xin Tang Shu), 4, 51, 90, 97, 107
Book of Tang, Old (Jin Tang Shu), 4, 51
Bridge of Heaven's Ford (Tianjin-qiao), 224
Buddhism, 6–7, 42, 71–2, 92–3, 108, 120–7, 123–7, 129, 133–4, 152, 154–6, 166, 176, 178, 186

Canton, 153, 159
CCTV, 193

Celestial Pillar, 155
Chang'an (now Xi'an), 8, 23, 26, 32, 42, 63–4, 68–9, 71, 98, 100, 102, 112, 120, 175, 186
Chen Hong, 194
Chia, Alyssa, 194
Chongfu, *see* Prince Chongfu
Chongmao, *see* Prince Chongmao
Chow Yun-fat, 196
Chu Suiliang, 53–5, 57, 65
Chun, Jinsie, 190
Classic of Entrapment, The, 119, 140, 158
Clinton, Hillary, 11
concubine ranks, 21–2, 27, 51
Confucianism, 6–7, 14, 17, 36, 41, 58, 79, 92–4, 98, 105, 107, 108, 122–4, 126, 131, 174, 178
Confucius, 7, 14, 36, 104, 122–3, 151, 154–5
Constantinople, 3
Cooney, Eleanor, 188
cosmetics, 127–8
Court of Reconsideration, 62, 218
cruel clerks, 118–19, 140–1, 144–5, 157, 160

Da Ming Gong Ci, 194
Daoism, 42, 77, 94, 107, 130, 172, 176
Days in the Palace, 196

Deception, 188
Di Renjie, *see* Judge Dee
Dien, Dora, 10
Dingzhou, 33
Dragon Inauguration, 109
Duke Huang, 142–3
Dunhuang, 135

East Liao fort (Liaodong), 33
Empress Dowager Cixi, 9
Empress (Impératrice), 195
Empress Lü, 9, 112
Empress Wang, 29, 41–8, 51–2,
    54–5, 57, 61–3, 116, 217–18
Empress Wei, 104–6, 170, 175,
    185
Empress Wende, 20, 23, 29, 40, 41,
    47, 58, 125
Empress Wu, *see* Wu Zetian
Empress Wu (1960), 191
Empress: A Novel, 193

Famen temple, 71–2, 166
Fang Yi'ai, 49–50
Feng-Shan, 81–5, 86, 101, 122–3,
    131, 133, 220
First Emperor (Qin Shi Huangdi), 9,
    122, 165
Fitzgerald, C.P., 10, 199
Flowers in the Mirror, 9
Fung, Petrina, 192

Gandhara, 125
Gansu, 146, 167
Ganye convent/temple, 39–40,
    42–3, 61, 96
Gaozong Emperor
  as prince, 29–30
  as heir, 33, 34–8
  as Emperor, 1, 39–43, 46–8,
    51–3, 56, 59–62, 64, 66–7,
    69, 76–80, 83, 94, 126
    illness of, 70, 72, 74–75, 88–92,
      96–103
    death of, 102
    legacy of, 104, 105, 107, 109,
      110–11, 116–17, 142, 151,
      162–3, 166, 169, 172, 181–2,
      186–7
Gaozu Emperor, 72, 82
Gate of Beautiful Scenery (Lijing-
    men), 140, 147, 159, 224
Gate of the Dark Warrior (Xuanwu-
    men), 14, 25, 67
Genghis Khan, 9
Gobi desert, 168
Gong Li, 196
Grand Canal, 113
Great Cloud Sutra, 135–6, 148,
    152
Great Goose Pagoda (Scripture
    Pagoda), 120, 125
Great Tang Chronicle of the West,
    204
GTV, 194
Guangjai temple, 208
Guisso, Richard, 10
Guo Moruo, 192
Guochu, 79–80, 88, 220

Hainan, 184
hairstyles, 42–3, 127–8
Hall of Illumination, 131–6, 143–4,
    147, 152, 154, 156, 164, 172
Halley's Comet, 107
Han dynasty, 9, 81, 112, 152
Han Yuan, 55, 60, 65, 68
Hanoi, 184
Hao Chujun, 96, 142
Hara, Momoyo, 188
Heart Sutra, 126
Helan, 18, 20, 45–6, 79, 89, 98–9,
    116
Hulao Pass, 199

I Am Heaven, 190
India, 125
Investigations of the Sui-Tang Era, 188
Iron Empress, 188

Japan, 69, 107, 152
Jiang Qing (Madame Mao), 10
Jiegu people, 204
Judge Dee, 146–7, 157, 159–60, 164–5, 168, 170–1, 175–6, 180, 188

Kaemosong, 33
Kashgar, 203
Kashmir, 69
Kegasawa, Yasunori, 10
Khitans, 122, 167–8
Koguryo, 30–3, 73, 86–7
Korean peninsula, 29–35, 66, 69, 73–4, 82, 86–7, 112, 152, 167
Kum River, 73–4

Lady Yang, 17–8, 80, 87, 89, 91–3, 116, 121
Lai Chunchen, 119, 145, 157–60
Lai Ji, 60, 65, 68
Lao Zi, 94, 151
Legalism, 122
Lenormand, Frédéric, 188
Li Han-hsiang, 191
Li Hong, *see* Prince Li Hong
Li Jing, 202
Li Jingye, 113–17, 141, 144
Li Shiji, 33, 87
Li Shimin, *see* Taizong Emperor
Li Yifu, 52–3, 64–5, 76, 182
Li Zhan, 181–2
Li Zhaode, 161–2
Li Zhi, 55–6, 113
Li Zhong, *see* Prince Li Zhong
Liao River, 30, 32–3, 87

Liaodong peninsula, 33, 87
Lin Yutang, 10, 190
Liu Rengui, 73–7, 86, 110, 112–14
Liu Xiaoqing, 193, 196
Lizhou, 18
Longmen, 116, 154
Lord of Perfect Satisfaction, The, 9
Luo Binwang, 115
Luo Guanzhong, 188
Luo River, 148
Luoyang, 32–3, 65, 69–70, 83, 99, 101–2, 108, 111, 118, 127, 130, 136, 138, 140, 142–3, 147, 152, 154–5, 157, 165, 168, 175, 178, 183

McCune, Evelyn, 193
Maitreya, 127, 135–6, 154
Mao Polo, 155
Mao Zedong, 9–10, 71
Marshal Hao, 141–2
Ming dynasty, 71
Ming Tang, *see* Hall of Illumination
Minzhi, 88–92, 113, 191
Mount Song, 101
Mount Tai, 81, 83–5, 87, 101

Nalanda, 125
Nanjing, 114
Nepal, 69
Nine Tripods, 133
Nühuang Wu Zetian, 190
Nuremberg Chronicles, 107

Office of the Crane, 172–4
Office of Prosecution, 117, 140, 159, 224
omens, 101, 107, 109, 123–4, 143, 148, 152, 153, 155, 176

Paekche, 30, 73–4
Palace of Dawn, 183

Palace of Desire, 194
Pei Yan, 102, 105–6, 108, 116–17, 192
Peshawar, 125
Prince Cheng-qian 'The Turk', 19–20, 23–7
Prince Chongfu, 177
Prince Chongmao, 185–6
Prince Han, 25, 27
Prince of Langya, 143, 145, 146
Prince Li Hong, 44, 60, 63, 90, 96–8, 126
Prince Li Zhong, 40, 218
Prince Xian, 3, 46, 98–102, 104, 113–14
Prince Yide, 177–8
Prince Zhi, 25–6
Princess Anding, 46–7
Princess Anle, 185
Princess Gaoyang, 49
Princess Qianjin, 129, 154, 159
Princess Taiping, 77, 90, 130, 144, 157, 172, 174–5, 183, 185–6
Princess Yongtai, 3–4, 178
Pyongyang, 30, 34, 73–4, 87

Qapagan, 167–70, 185
Qianjin, *see* Princess Qianjin
Qianling tomb, 1–4
Qin dynasty, 152
Qin Qiong, 15
Qing dynasty, 9

Ruizong Emperor
  as prince, 101
  as Emperor, 106–9, 117, 123–4, 129, 133, 139–41, 143–4, 147–8
  abdication of, 150, 151, 161–3, 169, 170–2, 226
  restoration of, 186

Sabi, 73
Samarakand, 125
Shan Sa, 195–6
Shandong, 25, 28, 73, 143
Shangguan Wan'er, 175, 184, 186
Shangguan Yi, 78–9, 175
Shaolin temple, 89
She Was the Emperor, 189
Shengdu, 112
Sichuan, 18
Silk Road, 64, 69, 71, 121, 124, 165, 167
Silla, 30, 73–4
Song of the Cucumber Plant, 113–14
Stalin, Joseph, 9
Stonehenge, 132
Su Dingfang, 73 4
Sui dynasty, 8, 30, 32–3, 50–1, 163
Sui-Tang Yanyi, 188
Sun Wei, 74

Taedong, 73
Taiping, *see* Princess Taiping
Taizong Emperor, 5, 13–17, 18–20, 24–30, 39, 40, 42, 43, 45, 49, 51, 58, 60, 66–7, 69, 82, 86, 87, 95, 110, 111, 114, 121, 125, 135, 137, 147, 163–4, 168–9, 187
  horses of, 19–20, 22, 198–200
  and Korea, 32–6, 73
  illness and death of, 36–42
Taklamakan desert, 168
Tanaka, Yoshiki, 188
Temple of Maternal Grace, 120, 125
Thanh Hoa, 65
Tibet, 122, 167, 169
Tinafuti, 204
Tripitaka, 121–3, 125–7

Tsui Hark, 195
Turkestan, 153
Turks, 19, 23, 35, 68–9, 122, 125, 154, 167–9, 185

Unicorn Virtue, 109

van Gulik, Robert, 188
Vietnam, 65

Wan Guojun, 159
Wang Xuande, 204
Wei dynasty, 47, 50
Wei Jifeng, 65–6
Wei Xuanjen, 105–6
Wei Yuanzhong, 225
Wei Zheng, 82, 98
Weichi Jingde, 15
Weizhou, 210
West, Keith, 189
Westmacott Lane, Kenneth, 189
White Horse Monastery, 129, 155–7
witchcraft, 42, 50, 77–8, 99
Wu Chengsi, 112, 138, 141, 154, 159, 161
Wu Huaiyun, 87–8
Wu Niang, 15
Wu Rujun, 195
Wu Sansi, 164, 175, 185
Wu Shihou, 17–8, 60, 147–8
Wu Weiliang, 87–8
Wu Yanji, 178
Wu Yanxiu, 168, 185
Wu Yuning, 164
Wu Zetian (1984), 192
Wu Zetian (2003), 195
Wu Zetian (Empress Wu)
  memorials, 3–4
  physical appearance, 5, 20, 36, 42
  intelligence, 5

sexuality of, 6, 36–7, 74–6, 77, 83, 130, 173–4, 194, 214, 227
as murderer, 9, 47, 114, 158
as Chinese 'Cinderella', 10–11, 44, 190–1
prophecies concerning, 15, 17, 62, 108, 127, 133, 135–7, 151, 165, 170
names/titles of, 17, 21, 62, 79, 134, 136, 138, 149, 151, 191, 197–8
as nun, 39–40, 42
poems of, 40, 90, 153
as mistress, 41–6
pregnancies of, 44, 77, 126
intrigues of, 48–9, 62, 65, 76, 78, 84, 88, 90, 99, 106, 114
as Imperial Concubine, 51
as Empress (wife), 59, 66, 68–70, 72, 74, 82–3
and cats, 62, 63, 153
as regent, 91–3, 96, 101–2, 107–19, 133–4, 146
reforms of, 93–6, 108–11, 118, 148–9
as Empress Dowager, 104–6
and religion, 108, 121–3, 135–6;
as Empress (ruler), 134, 149–50, 151–82
as living god, 137, 150, 151, 162, 166, 168, 170
last days of, 183–4
fictional accounts of, 188–96
Wu Zetian (in production), 195
Wu Zetian, A Queen (1938), 188

Xi'an, 1, 71, 120
Xian, *see* Prince Xian
Xiao Liangdi, 29–30, 40–5, 52, 57, 61–3, 96, 116, 121, 153, 217–18
Xu Jingcong, 57, 65–8, 78, 82, 95

Xu Jinglei, 196
Xu Yugong, 145–7, 157
Xuanzang, *see* Tripitaka
Xuanzong Emperor, 140, 162,
    185–7, 219, 220
Xue Aocao, 227
Xue Huaiyi, 127–37, 144, 154–7,
    165, 167, 173

Yalu River, 30
Yang Guifei, 219
Yangdi Emperor (Sui), 33, 37
Yangtze River, 113–14, 180
Yellow River, 168
Yellow Sea, 30, 73
Yon Kaesomun, 87
Yongtai, *see* Princess Yongtai
Yuan Tian-gang, 18

Zhang Changyi, 177
Zhang Changzong, 172–83, 227

Zhang Jianzhi, 180–1
Zhang Yimou, 196
Zhang Yizhi, 172–83, 227
Zhang Yue, 220
Zhangsun family, 8, 20, 163
Zhangsun Wuji, 29, 33, 47–50, 52,
    54, 56, 66–8
Zhizun Hongyan Wu Meiniang,
    194
Zhongzong Emperor
    as prince, 97–8, 126
    as heir, 101
    as Emperor, 103–6
    overthrow and exile of, 108, 113,
        117, 139, 152
    recall and restoration of, 169–72,
        177, 181–5
Zhou dynasty, 151, 159, 170
Zhou Quanbin, 199
Zhou Xing, 119, 157–8
Zhou Xun, 194

The First Emperor of China

Jonathan Clements

The first emperor has been demonised for centuries. Here is the first biography charting the life of this imposing figure and the world he lived in.

The First Emperor is the true story of Ying Zheng – the man who unified China, built the Great Wall, and whose tomb is guarded by the famous Terracotta Army. The leader of a brutal regime, he was the product of a family, community and state run by 'Legalists', Machiavellian manipulators who would rather be feared than loved. His ruthless reforms laid the foundations for China as it is today.

This new book is not just a 'life and times' of this phenomenal ruler. As well as documenting Ying Zheng's extraordinary life, Jonathan Clements demonstrates what it was like to live in his world, in a land constantly under surveillance. The author describes the laws that defined the emperor and the legends that have engulfed him – there were rumours that he was not the son of the king, but the child of a secret affair between a royal concubine and an ambitious minister.

This is the first biography outside Asia to deal with Ying Zheng's life in such intimate detail and gives the reader a terrifying glimpse into a land under absolute rule, and an unprecedented insight into the birth of China.

Coxinga and the Fall of the Ming Dynasty

Jonathan Clements

His mother was a samurai. His father was the richest pirate in the world. He was taught by Japanese swordsman and Chinese philosophers, and raised in luxury. Besieged by invaders and betrayed by his family, he stayed fiercely loyal to a dying dynasty. The decline of the Ming Dynasty altered Coxinga's life, transforming him from a wealthy child of privilege to a renegade with a price on his head. After his death, his sworn enemies worshipped him as a god. This is the incredible true story of the infamous pirate king, Coxinga. Filled with a host of extraordinary characters – the sword-wielding priest Adam Schall, the trader and conman Captain China and Coxinga's African bodyguards – this is a book that will appeal to everyone with a taste for adventure.

Jonathan Clements is the author, co-author or translator of over thirty books, including *The Moon in the Pines* and *Confucius: A Biography*.